EARLY AMERICAN ROOMS

THE PINE CEILED ROOM AT THE CONCORD ANTIQUARIAN SOCIETY
WALL C (SEE PAGE 23)

LOOKING-GLASS
WILLIAM-AND-MARY STYLE
WALNUT VENEER. *c.* 1700

DESK BOX
CARVED PINE. *c.* 1700

CHEST WITH DRAWER
OAK AND PINE
Last quarter 17th Century

SLAT-BACK CHAIR
MAPLE
1st half 18th Century

"PILGRIM SLAT-BACK" CHAIR
MAPLE. *c.* 1700

Early American Rooms

A Consideration of the Changes in Style between the Arrival of the *Mayflower* and the Civil War in the Regions Originally Settled by the English and the Dutch

With articles by

FREDERICK LEWIS ALLEN

ELLIOT W. BISBEE

JOSEPH EVERETT CHANDLER

KENNETH JOHN CONANT

GEORGE FRANCIS DOW

JOSEPH DOWNS

ALLEN FRENCH

HOLLIS FRENCH

TALBOT FAULKNER HAMLIN

EDWIN J. HIPKISS

ROLAND MATHER HOOKER

J. FREDERICK KELLY

RUSSELL HAWES KETTELL

BERNHARD KNOLLENBERG

CHARLES NAGEL, JR.

FREDERICK A. SWEET

THOMAS TILESTON WATERMAN

SAMUEL W. WOODHOUSE, JR.

EDWIN B. WORTHEN

PHILIP N. YOUTZ

RUSSELL HAWES KETTELL, *Editor*

DOVER PUBLICATIONS, INC.
NEW YORK

Published in Canada by General Publishing Company, Ltd., 30 Lesmill Road, Don Mills, Toronto, Ontario.

Published in the United Kingdom by Constable and Company, Ltd., 10 Orange Street, London WC 2.

This Dover edition, first published in 1967, is an unabridged republication of the work originally published by The Southworth-Anthoensen Press in 1936.

Standard Book Number: 486-21633-0
Library of Congress Catalog Card Number: 67-14251

Manufactured in the United States of America
Dover Publications, Inc.
180 Varick Street
New York, N.Y. 10014

PREFACE

THIS rather radically made-up book has grown out of an interest in the broader meaning of what is now known as the "Period Room." The editor has felt that there was far more to be seen in an eighteenth-century Salem interior — to use a single illustration — than the refinement of the McIntire carving and the splendor of the plate. One should be reading between the lines — about sailing vessels plowing the waters of the Seven Seas, about Thomas Chippendale and the Brothers Adam at work abroad, about rum and deacons and dancing school and the exciting fullness of a life that probably seemed as wonderfully mad in those days as does life to us to-day.

It is the purpose of this book, therefore, to help people to look at the artistic efforts of the more important periods of American history in the broadest possible way. With such a start as he may get from these pages the reader may be inclined to follow up some of the many leads with reading of a more detailed kind.

There are twelve chapters, each considered with reference to a particular room, permanently available for public study. All twelve of the rooms may be visited on a motor trip between Philadelphia and Boston; and by their original locations and dates they bring into the discussion the colonies between Massachusetts Bay and Virginia during the seventeenth, eighteenth, and the first half of the nineteenth centuries.

Rooms that were the social centers rather than bedrooms have been chosen, since they were more completely decorated and more elaborately furnished. We start with a seventeenth-century New England hall and end with the parlor of a brown sandstone residence in New York City, built just before the Civil War.

The drawings are all of them done in direct orthographic projection so that measurements may be taken wherever they are desired. To give scale and a feeling of life to the elevations we have shown the rooms completely furnished, even to an occasional figure in costume of the proper date. One plate reproduces the color scheme of each room,* while at the front of the book will be found a list of the major color areas according to the system followed on Ridgway's well-known charts. Such minor illustrations as tailpieces and decorated initials have been drawn from objects or details found in the room itself.

In addition to the drawings, each chapter has four sections of reading matter. First, an historical background discussing everyday life as well as the vital social and economic forces that combined to produce such an architectural flowering as we are showing in our illustrations. Second, a general exposition of the contemporary conventions and styles to be seen in a typical interior of the date. Third, an authentic document selected to throw light on the period as a whole or on some particularly colorful aspect of it. And, finally, two pages of newspaper items that once appeared within the dates given at the head of each

---

*In the present edition, only 10 of the 12 rooms are represented by color plates, which appear on the covers.

[vii]

Preface

page and are now reprinted in such form as will carry out the spirit of their original typography and arrangement.

Perhaps a word of explanation should be made in regard to these Contemporary Documents and Newspaper sections. During the editor's researches he came across so many old manuscripts, quotations, and diaries that gave a keen, quick feeling of reality—an unobserved peek through the fast closing door of Time—that he decided to incorporate a complete series of them. But they should be read slowly. The spelling is unusually, shall we say, independent; and the grammar often is quite different from what it would be to-day. There is a reward for the reader who will take the time and trouble to understand them.

As for the newspapers, are they not in the long run the most revealing witnesses that we can summon? When any one says of the morning paper that there is "nothing in it"—realize that he speaks only for the day. The time soon comes when even the humblest paper begins to take on value, little by little, but steadily, as in the process of silver plating; for there is no source of information about the past more human or more alive than its newspapers. No one item in them may, perhaps, be accurate or even true; yet viewed at the distance of, say, two hundred years, the picture is accuracy itself. Pirates, frigates, slaves, stagecoaches, Indians, appear before us and live their lives again, not self-consciously, as if they knew that they were making history, but naturally, busily carrying on civilization as it was handed to them and cheerfully making the best of things before it is their turn to give way to younger actors in fresh scenery.

Certainly one of the major pleasures of working on a complicated enterprise of this kind lies in the acquaintances that it develops. The editor has many persons to thank for their assistance, and he wishes to acknowledge the amount that their friendships have added to his enjoyment.

First of all, he thanks the nineteen men who have so kindly written the articles that form the bulk of the reading matter of the book. As these men have collaborated because they believed the idea of the book was sound, the editor feels an especial responsibility about the final result.

He would like to express his gratitude also for the generous permissions and assistance that he has received from the several museums and public houses whose rooms he has thus been able to use as illustrations. The capable artists are given credit for their drawings in the table of contents, but the work of Mr. and Mrs. William B. Allen, Mr. Linton Wilson, and Mr. Prescott Kettell in connection with the newspapers and early documents should not be overlooked; of Mrs. George H. Eberlein in reading the unusually fussy pages of proof; and of Miss Louella D. Everett in doing countless hours of her highly experienced secretarial work.

Preface

The following men have contributed a much appreciated mixture of encouragement and guidance: Professor Charles M. Andrews, Mr. William Sumner Appleton, Mr. Laurence V. Coleman, Mr. Henry W. Erving, Mr. Frederick P. Keppel, Mr. Alexander F. Law, Professor Paul J. Sachs, and Professor Theodore Sizer. We are indebted to Mr. T. I. Hare Powel for the privilege of showing the portrait of Mrs. Margaret Willing Hare in its appropriate position over the mantel in the drawing of the Powel House.

Now follows a book which (in the skillful phraseology of Samuel McChord Crothers) is "to help us reset the stage, to recall the actors, to turn on the lights...."

TABLE OF CONTENTS

Table of Contents

LIST OF ILLUSTRATIONS

[The illustrations preceded by an asterisk are also reproduced in color on the covers of this edition.]

List of Illustrations

List of Illustrations

A Schedule of Rooms Illustrated, their Dates, and their Districts

	Mass.	Conn.	N.Y. & N.J.	Penn.	Va.
1650					
	Paul Revere House Living Room 1650-80				
1675					
1700					
	Pine Ceiled Room 1700-25	Rose House Living Room c. 1710			
	Green Dining Room 1720-50				
1725		Newington Parlor 1725-50			
1750	Wayside Inn Barroom Typical late 17th and 18th Century		Schenck House Living Room c. 1760	Powel House Drawing Room 1768	
1775					Gadsby Tavern Assembly Room 1793
1800	"Oak Hill" Dining Room 1801		Irvington Parlor c. 1820		
1825					
1850			Roosevelt House Parlor c. 1858		
1875					

COLOR SCHEDULE

Following is a schedule of the principal colors appearing in the twelve rooms illustrated in this book, designated according to the system used in Robert Ridgway's *Color Standards and Color Nomenclature*, published in 1912 in Washington, District of Columbia, by its author. This book, though not easily found for sale, is nevertheless available for reference in most public libraries.

PAUL REVERE HOUSE LIVING ROOM

Wood beams and sheathing, aged to	13′	n
Plaster wall originally white but now covered with wall paper.		
Cradle, painted	19′	i

PINE CEILED ROOM, AT THE CONCORD ANTIQUARIAN SOCIETY

Doors, window sash, and boxed frame	43′	d
Sheathing, aged to	16″	i
Corner cupboard	4	j
Blanket chest	5″	m

GREEN DINING ROOM, AT THE CONCORD ANTIQUARIAN SOCIETY

Woodwork	29′′′′′	a
Plaster wall, painted	23′′′′′	f
Cement facing of fireplace, painted	Black	
Brick sides, back, and hearth of fireplace	12′′′′′	i

ROSE HOUSE LIVING ROOM

Wall panelling	31′′′′′	i
Stone sides, back, and hearth of fireplace, unpainted	5′′′′′	i
Rosettes, key block, and inside of cupboard	5	i

WAYSIDE INN BARROOM

Woodwork	25′′′′′	b
Ceiling beams, aged to	13′	m
Plaster wall, unpainted	White	

PARLOR FROM NEWINGTON, IN THE METROPOLITAN MUSEUM OF ART

Woodwork, aged to	10″	k
Bricks in fireplace	13′′′′′	b

SCHENCK HOUSE LIVING ROOM

Plaster walls and panelled woodwork, painted	Flat white	
Ceiling boards and beams	Whitewash	
Fireplace trim, painted	Flat black	
Sides and back of fireplace, gray cement	15′′′′′	b
Slat back arm chair, painted	5′	i

POWEL HOUSE DRAWING ROOM

Wall panelling	20″	d
Doors, mahogany, finished	9′	k
Marble facing of fireplace	21′′′′′	g
Back and sides of fireplace cement	21′′′′′	j

GADSBY TAVERN ASSEMBLY ROOM

Woodwork	24′′′′′	b
Plaster wall, painted	18″	d
Fireplace marble	35′′′′′	m
Bricks of fireplace	q′′′′′	

DINING ROOM FROM "OAK HILL," PEABODY, IN THE BOSTON MUSEUM OF FINE ARTS

Woodwork	23′′′	d
Plaster wall, painted	23′′′	f
Soapstone back and sides of fireplace	15′′′′′	i
Marble trim of fireplace opening	Black	

PARLOR FROM IRVINGTON, IN THE BROOKLYN MUSEUM

Mantel and other woodwork	21′′′	g
Plaster wall, painted	17	f
Window curtains	70	h

ROOSEVELT HOUSE PARLOR

Wood trim	23′′′′′	f
Plaster cornice and ceiling	White	
Marble mantel	Ivory	
Satin chair covering	43′′′′′	b

THE MEDIAEVAL CHARACTER OF
SEVENTEENTH-CENTURY NEW ENGLAND HOUSES

As illustrated by the LIVING ROOM OF THE PAUL REVERE HOUSE

in Boston, Massachusetts

WALL A

WALL B

WALL C

WALL D

Plan
Scale of feet
6 1 2 3 4 5

Historical Note

WHEN the English Puritans determined upon an emigration to New England they knew but little of the hardships that the sea and the land had in store for them. By far the greater number came from inland parishes and only vaguely could they know of the confinement and privations of a long sea voyage. The physical dangers from red Indians and wild beasts they must have sensed and also the terrors of the unknown. The New England climate —the heat of summer and the cold of winter—they experienced after arrival, and soon they also discovered that much of the soil of the land they were greedy to possess was unfriendly to the labors of English husbandmen. It therefore is surprising that so few gave up the struggle and returned to England or removed to the West India Islands. The settlements in the New England country were made and successfully continued because of a dogmatic determination on the part of the Puritans to create a religious and political haven for themselves; and no discomforts or dangers by sea or land were allowed to thwart the intended purpose.

The emigrating families were "strongly instructed what things were fittest to bring . . . for a comfortable passage at sea and for their husbandry occasions" on reaching land. Higginson, the minister at Salem, provided a catalogue of needful things—a meagre list of food necessary per person for the first year: meal, peas, oatmeal, butter, cheese, bacon, and spices; and a scanty equipment of household implements: a pot, a fry pan, a gridiron, skillets, a spit, spoons, and wooden trenchers. Others repeated the list with small additions. Each person must provide an ample store of clothing, including four pairs of shoes; also a coarse rug, a pair of blankets, and seven ells of canvas with which to make a bed and bolster. A long piece, a sword, ammunition, and tools for cultivating the soil and for working wood, completed the scanty equipment of these founders of a new nation.

A passage across the Atlantic usually cost £5, which also included ship's provisions: salted meats, haberdine (salted cod), hard bread, pease pottage, and six-shilling beer. A private stock of delicacies, however, was recommended, such as prunes, raisins, spices, conserves, rice, juice of lemons, etc. Conserve of wormwood was considered very proper to drive away seasickness.

The space between decks was seldom over six feet, six inches, and this was lighted from open hatches which were battened down whenever a storm arose. Light, air, and also salt water were admitted through the shuttered gunports. In this deck space families disposed themselves as best they could, sometimes scantily partitioned off from neighbors by a curtain. To be sure, there were cabins—small cubicles partitioned off in the open space below deck—but these cost £1.10.0 additional.

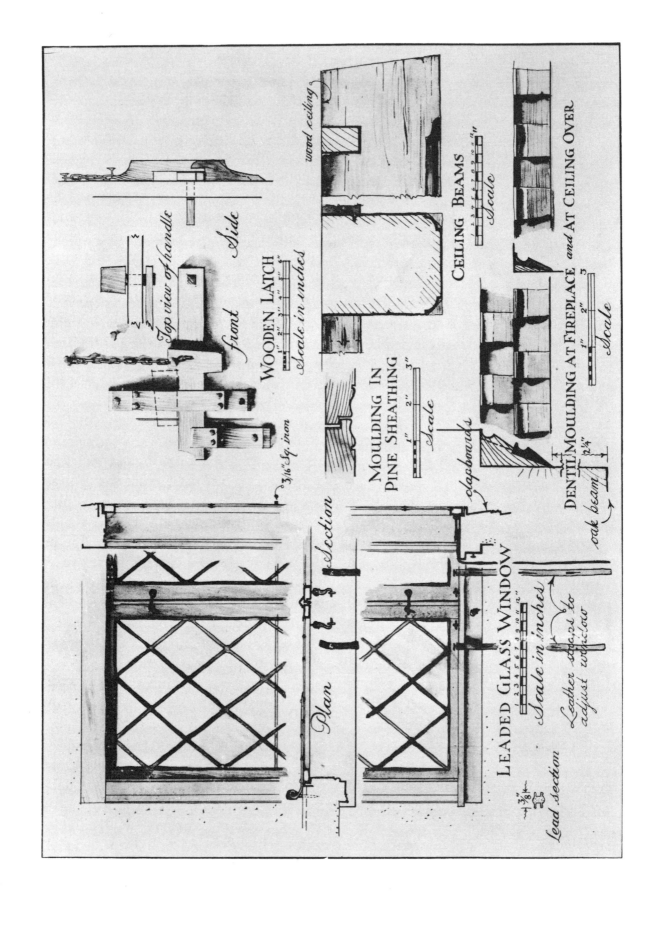

Hammocks, or "Brazil beds," were supplied the sailors and presumably some of the passengers, but much the greater number preferred a canvas bed stuffed with straw placed in rows on the deck at night. When the weather permitted food was cooked or warmed at a common hearth. The ship's officers and favored passengers were served by stewards from the ship's galley.

The stern business of life in the new country began when the ship anchored off-shore at its intended destination. At the outset only temporary shelters could be provided until houses were built. During the first winter in Charlestown, Boston, and elsewhere, many families lived in tents, and it was a cold New England winter that year. Some men dug caves in banks or hillsides, and palisading the front and sides, covered the structures with small logs which in turn were well covered with turf. Others constructed wigwams, patterned after those in which the Indians lived. Meanwhile the carpenters were at work building houses for the richer and more fortunate settlers, and in time all those who survived were properly housed. Wigwams, when provided with stone fireplaces and called "English wigwams," were occupied for some years and found to be dry and comfortable. Cabins built of notched logs in the later frontier fashion were unknown at the time of the settlement and for many years after.

The first framed houses built in New England were built by men who had learned their housewright trade in England through years of apprenticeship and who constructed after the matter and pattern with which they were familiar. A house with one room and an entryway, and with a chimney on the ground floor, was common at first. Later, another room was built on the other side of the chimney and, as the owner became more prosperous or his family increased, a lean-to would be added along the back side of the house. One of the first-floor rooms would be the kitchen or living room (at first called "hall," in the English manner) and the other the parlor. The kitchen fireplace was large, and inside, in a back corner, would be the opening of the brick oven. From a wooden lug pole bisecting the flue of the chimney, hung the pot chains and trammels. During the early years of the colony, lime was scarce and chimneys were laid up in clay until the ridge pole was reached. At the outset, because of a scarcity of bricks, many chimneys were built of wood—small limbs laid cob-house fashion and then daubed with clay. Governor Winthrop recorded in his diary that several English wigwams and also framed houses were destroyed by fire that caught from wooden chimneys where the daubing had fallen out. Many roofs were covered with thatch in the traditional English manner, and in the dry New England climate these, too, became a fire menace and in time led to repressive legislation by the Great and General Court.

The interiors of these houses were full of household goods and children. The kitchen not only was supplied with table and stools and the usual household utensils, but a wash bench (for sinks were unknown), powdering tubs for the salted meats, meal chests, a cheese press, spinning wheels, perhaps a loom, and, in a corner, a pallet bed on which father or grandfather slept. The parlor almost universally had its bedstead and the best of the family furniture, including chests for storage of clothing or bedding. The same was true of the chambers, sometimes with more than one bedstead in a room, with a trundle bed for a child sticking out at the end of each. Here, too, would be chests, barrels, and "other lumber," as one inventory has it, meaning a variety of objects of no great importance. The older children slept in the garret, which also was used for storage.

Much of the food of the average New Englander, until comparatively recent times, consisted of corn meal, boiled meats, vegetables, and stews. Every well-equipped household had its spits for roasting and many had gridirons, but the usual diet of the average family was "hasty pudding"—corn-meal mush and milk—varied by boiled meat or fish served in the center of a large pewter platter and surrounded by boiled vegetables. Baked beans and stewed beans appeared on the table several times every week in the year. Indian bannock, made by mixing corn meal with water and spreading it an inch thick on a small board placed at an incline before the fire and so baked, was a common kind of bread. When mixed with rye meal it became brown bread and was baked in the brick oven with the beans and peas. Much of this food was raised on the farm and nearly every family had its garden. Such articles of food as were imported usually were obtained at the shops in the larger towns by bartering the products of the farm.

In 1630 there were differences in dress even more than at the present time. The simple, coarse clothing of the yeoman and the worker in the various trades was far removed from the dress of the merchant and the magistrate. Leather clothing was very generally worn by laborers and servants. Deerskins were cheap and leather had been in common use in old England for jerkins and breeches, so, naturally, it was worn here. Stockings were made of a great variety of materials and most shoes had wooden heels. Higher in the social scale, men wore doublets and full breeches and clothed themselves as well as their estates permitted—sometimes even better than they could comfortably afford. Sleeves were slashed, falling bands at the neck were common, and a deep linen collar appears in portraits of the period. A beaver or felt hat with steeple crown was worn, and gloves, sometimes elegantly embroidered, were essential. Our accepted idea of Puritan dress should be revised and our Victorian standard of sentimental simplicity be discarded.

Fine clothing surrounded itself with fine furnishings, according to the standards of the period, and as the wealth of the colony increased with the successful exportation of fish, lumber, beaver, and peltry, it supplied the colonists with all kinds of luxuries and refinements. The ships were crossing frequently and the colony kept pace with the mother country much as the country follows the city at the present time.

Historical Note

The New England Puritans only allowed themselves one full holiday in the course of the year and that was Thanksgiving Day, a time for feasting. To be sure, there was Fast Day, in the spring, which gave freedom from work; but that was a day for a sermon at the meetinghouse, for long faces, and a supposed bit of self-denial—somewhere. The celebration of Christmas was not observed by the true New England Puritans until the middle of the nineteenth century. There were few amusements or intellectual diversions and they could only dwell on the gossip and small doings of their immediate neighborhoods. But all the while there was underlying respect for law, religion, and the rights of others. The fundamental principles of human life were much the same as at the present day, and men and women lived together then as now and as they always will—with respect and love.

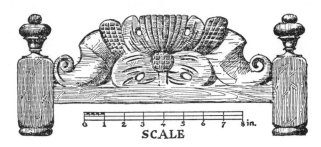

SCALE

The Mediaeval Character of Seventeenth-Century New England Houses

Y way of introducing the New England seventeenth-century house with proper respect and authenticity, we quote a few vivid sentences written by John Stockwell describing his capture by the Indians at Deerfield, Massachusetts:

About Sun-set, [September 19, 1677] I and another Man being together, the *Indians* with great shouting and shooting came upon us, and some other of the *English* hard by, at which we ran to a Swamp for refuge; . . . the Swamp being mirie, I slipt in, and fell down; whereupon an *Indian* stept to me, with his Hatchet lifted up to knock me on the head, supposing I was wounded, and unfit for Travel: . . . whereupon I yealded myself, and fell into the Enemies Hands, and by three of them was led away to the place whence I first fled; . . . I was now near my own House, which the *Indians* burnt last year, and I was about to build up again.*

What was this house probably like before the Indians destroyed it? What can we say of it, assuming that John Stockwell built and furnished it according to the custom of the locality and of the times?

In the first place, although it had not proved safe from Indian attack, we may be sure that its location had been decided upon after due consideration of such danger. The frame of mind of all who built out upon the frontier may be comprehended from the petition submitted by a group of men in the town of Lancaster, Massachusetts, in 1706, regarding the site of their proposed rebuilding of the meetinghouse:

Now so it is, may it please the governor and general assembly, that those of the inhabitants who dwell on this [that is, the east] side of the river, . . . use all their endeavor to have the meeting-house built on this side; whereas . . . should the meeting-house be built on this [east] side, the enemy might come, when the inhabitants are at meeting, and destroy the whole western part, and seize the bridge so that nobody should be able to resist them, or deliver their friends. But the meeting-house being built on the exposed side, (as it used to be,) the inhabitants on that side are a guard to the others on this side, as well as to themselves.†

We may be pretty sure, too, that the house was faced to the cheerful southern sun, which brought a maximum of light into the dark interiors all the year around, and helped to warm the rooms in winter. Is it not likely that even then the custom had been established of letting shade trees, as a protection from the heat of summer, cast their shadows over the clapboards and casement windows on either side of the

* From Richard Blome's *The Present State of His Majestie's Isles and Territories in America* (1687).
† From *The History of the Town of Lancaster, Massachusetts*, by A. P. Marvin.

[8]

WALL A

DESK-ON-FRAME
MAPLE AND PINE
Early 18th Century

THREE-LEGGED CHAIR
STAINED RED
17th Century

OVAL TOP GATE-LEG TABLE
CURLY MAPLE
c. 1700

12 IN.   0   1   2 FT.

heavy front door? Close by ran the road, such as it was; for the New England winter has always dictated short paths and driveways, as well as compact houses, for all who do their own chores. It was, undoubtedly, some distance to John Stockwell's nearest neighbor, for apparently he did not live in town. A man was forced to live near the center of his work and take his chances, however great they may have been. In reporting to England in 1665 concerning "Kenebeck," George Carr, Commissioner to His Majesty, Charles II, mentions "3 small Plantations belonging to his Royall highnesse the biggest of which hath not above 30 houses in it, and those very mean ones too. and spread over 8 miles of ground at least."*

John Stockwell's home, like the Paul Revere House, was surely of frame construction—that is, a structure consisting of a skeleton of heavy oak beams, posts, and rafters supporting the much less massive fabric of walls, floors, and roof. From the outside the character of such a house came chiefly from four elements: the central stack or chimney, the steep-pitched gables of the roof, the frequently overhanging second floor, and the small leaded-glass casement windows—all of them mediaeval elements. These appeared quite naturally when the early colonists built in the New World houses that should continue the spirit of their old homesteads and the conservative security that most of us associate with the places and people with whom we spent our earlier days.

Thus far we have been talking of country houses, using the Stockwell home as an example. But what of the little seventeenth-century town houses like the one built in 1658 that was to distinguish itself a hundred years later by sheltering the great American patriot and craftsman, Paul Revere?

It is a pity there is no 1650 view of the city of Boston. Whatever picture we may be able to form must come from such early references, usually quite indirect, as we may dig up from the old records. In 1665, for example, the Royal Commissioners speak of its houses as being "generally wooden," and the streets "crooked, with little decency and no uniformity." Probably the *Harvard Lampoon* was right when, three hundred years later, it offered: "'One good turn deserves another,' said the cow as she laid out the streets of Boston."

On this crooked pattern, nevertheless, there steadily grew up a town that ordered, before 1657, "That no person whatsoever, shall after the publication hereof, gallop any Horse within any [of] the streets of said Town, upon penalty of forfeiting three shillings and four pence for every such offence . . . unless it appear on extreme necessity"; and that distributed broadsides declaring and ordering (1678) "That all or any Person or Persons of what age or Condition soever, that shall from henceforth presume to shoot off any Gun or Guns, charged with Bullet

---

* From the original document in the Public Records Office, London. (See *Calendar of State Papers*, Colonial Series, Volume II, page 348.)

or Bullets, Swan, Goose, or other shot towards any Mark or place that the Militia in such Town or Towns have not appointed . . . whereby any person or persons shall or may be killed, wounded or otherwise damaged . . . shall be liable to answer for it." (There had been at least one lawyer in the colonies by this time!) And the city was developing a proper regard for its morals, as well as for its safety, since it was concerned over the "games of Shuffle-board and Bowling, in and about Houses of Common-entertainment, whereby much precious time is spent unprofitably, and much waste of Wine and Beer occasioned"; and ordered (1646) that no one "at any time Play or Game for any Money or Money worth, upon penalty of forfeiting treble the value thereof, one half to the party informing and the other half to the Treasury." Nor can we resist mentioning the order that all persons convicted of "Exorbitancy of the Tongue, in Railing and Scolding . . . shall be Gagged, or set in a Ducking-stool, and dipt over Head and Ears three times in some convenient place of fresh or salt-water, as the Court or Magistrate shall Judge meet."

There is no printed and published view of early Boston from which we can check up on the impressions that we form from these seventeenth-century manuscripts, until Captain John Bonner drew his map in 1722. It is a lively sheet, with sailboats in the harbor, and churches, "gramar" schools, "Writing Schools," and other public buildings shown in elevation, and a little fringe of gables indicating the uninterrupted run of quaint houses that to-day, but for the Paul Revere House and some of the later brick residences, are completely vanished. We can almost put the point of a pencil upon a doorway and say, "There is the Paul Revere House, half a century old at the time this map was published."

Stretching away from Dock Square in a southwesterly direction is the present Washington Street, then called, in true London fashion, Cornhill, Marlb[o]rough Street, Newbury Street, and Orange Street successively, as one drove out of the center of the town and the houses thinned. Under the scale of miles Captain Bonner gives us an interesting summary of what he has indicated on the map: "Streets 42   Lanes 36   Alleys 22   Houses near 3000.   1000 Brick   rest Timber.   Near 12000 People," and a list of eight dates of Great Fires ranging from 1653 to 1711, and of six General Small Pox epidemics between 1640 and 1721 —apparently the great unsolved problems that correspond to the combustible ocean liners and the automobile accidents of to-day.

There are plenty of out-of-the-way corners of England that possess to-day much of the flavor that must have existed in a New England town in the first century of its colonization. A double row of seventeenth-century houses separated by cobblestones and livened by the even sound-pattern of many hard-soled shoes strolling up and down of an evening just for sociability's sake; occasionally, the irregular rattle of

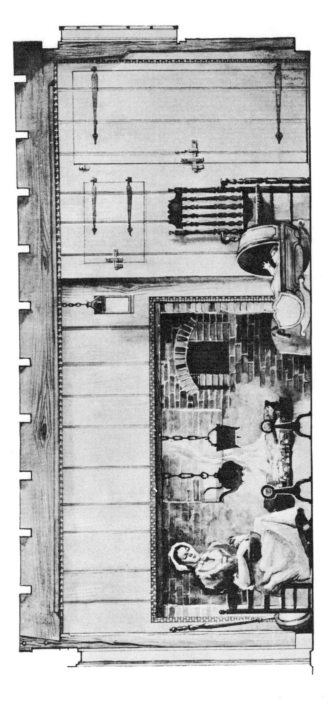

WALL B

SLAT-BACK CHAIR
MAPLE. *Early 18th Century*

BANISTER-BACK ARMCHAIR
WITH SCALLOPED CRESTING
PAINTED BLACK
1st quarter 18th Century

MAPLE AND PINE CRADLE
PAINTED YELLOW
17th Century

a cart wheel; and a Yorkshire, or Devonshire, or Irish accent—something that you can just recognize as being English but which you cannot possibly understand. That is perhaps how early Boston would appear to us if we could call it back.

We will walk up to the Paul Revere House and step inside. The plan is typical of the smaller sort of house, consisting of an entry with stairs to the second-floor bedroom; a "hall" at one side of the entry; and an extra room at the rear, which in connection with the earliest houses appears as a later addition, whereas in the buildings of the latter part of the century it might be included in the plans of the original house.

Among the records of the town of Plymouth of the year 1663, a lean-to for the minister's house is proposed in the following words: "The addition agreed on is to bee 14 or 15 foot in unto the building already erected to be in equall breath and heigth unto the same. . . ."

A larger house of the times would have a second room opening from the other side of the entry, its fireplace being back to back with that of the room at the other end.

Such was the general plan almost universally followed. The subsequent development from these three rooms with a single central stack, to four rooms with two inside stacks, and finally to four rooms with four stacks in the end walls, was the inevitable way of expressing the ever-rising standard of living throughout the colonies.

Every early house had its kitchen that served the combined purposes of cooking, dining, living, and frequently even sleeping. This general utility room was really the descendant of the old English Hall, and often was spoken of by that name. We would consider it dark, low-ceilinged, massively constructed, and distinctly mediaeval in its character. Wherever we look, the solid frame of the house is evident —in the ceiling beams, in the corner and intermediate posts, even in the sill that projects into the room at the floor level. As for texture, everywhere is hand surfacing to be seen. Interiors were never painted in that century (although a whitewash was usually applied to the plastered outer walls), and the marks left by the adze, or the hand plane, gave to the wood much the same honest character as that given to the plaster work by its own crude tools. Such wainscot as appeared was made up of wide boards of soft pine, rebated edge to edge with the joint camouflaged by a beautiful small-scale "shadow" moulding, planed along the grain on either side of the inevitable crack.

The room, of course, was dominated by the great and spacious fireplace, sometimes as wide as eight feet or more, with an oven built into the brickwork in a corner, and a green stick safely high above the flames yet directly over them, so that the pots and kettles could be hung from their pot chains and adjustable trammels into the heat of the fire.

The second most important feature of the room must have been the windows. Leaded-glass sashes, some of them fixed, some casements opening out, represented in the seventeenth century not merely the homely tradition, but at the same time not far from the most improved type and the largest glass areas obtainable. These held sway roughly until the beginning of the eighteenth century, when the improvement of the double-hung sash cut American architecture free from what was about its last mediaeval detail.

If we were to get back to genesis as far as American furniture is concerned, we should have to know just what came over on the "Mayflower"; and that, unfortunately, is an impossibility. There is not a single object, chairs and books included, that we can assuredly claim was on the original voyage. We can, however, work out a fairly reliable list of the sort of furnishings that were used by the early colonists if we peruse the oldest inventories of the Plymouth Colony and take note also of those articles mentioned by such contemporary recorders as Governors Bradford and Winslow.

The most valued piece of furniture was invariably the bedstead, which, with its fixings, ran up into an appraisal of several pounds. Curtains and valences, sheets, rugs and other bed covering, bolsters, pillows and mattresses (stuffed with feathers, wool, cotton, or straw)—all were necessary parts of relief from a very long and taxing day's work. In addition to beds, we find chests, and chests of drawers; cupboards, buffets, and cabinets; tables, table chairs, trestles and table boards; forms (i. e. benches), stools, chairs, and cradles; cushions and carpets and looking glasses. These were the things in common use at that time. If they had been imported they were probably substantial pieces worthy of the precious space they occupied on the adventurous voyage. If they were products of the new land the chance is they were simpler in design, for time was at a great premium, and men as a rule were their own furniture makers, as well as their own blacksmiths, farmers, apothecaries, and constables.

The center of every Pilgrim kitchen would be occupied, during mealtimes, by some form of folding or trestle table, with stools about it. The position of head of the table was a time-honored one, rating a good chair, if there was one, and all the rest of the household was related to it. In fact, so firmly did this order of things become established that it continued in the country homesteads well into the nineteenth century. Joseph Alonzo Warren, who was born in 1815, writes the following graphic recollections of his boyhood in Grafton, Massachusetts:

I will take you back when we (four brothers and all the sisters) were living at home in the large kitchen with the large fireplace, so high and wide that I could stand at the end of the fire in the fireplace and look out of the top of the chimney, and sometimes it would rain in my face. The oven was on one side and the ash-pit under it, shut up with a board and a block of timber to hold it up. Said block was the favored seat of the two small boys. The kitchen

WALL D

FLEMISH SCROLL SIDE CHAIR
WITH CANE SEAT
MAPLE, PAINTED BLACK
1690-1700

PANELLED BALL FOOT CHEST
OAK AND PINE PAINTED
BLACK AND RED
c. 1690

BANISTER-BACK SIDE CHAIR
WITH RUSH SEAT
1700-1710

contained a cupboard, sink, and a long table without leaves. At morning and at noon our father sat on one end, Mother at his left, the hired girl next, oldest daughter next, and so on down. On the right of Father was the hired man, then the oldest son, and so on to the last of the males; the older ones having chairs, the smaller ones standing at the table, or sitting on the block; the small boys using wooden plates, Mother dealing the food out to us.

Since the Warren homestead was obviously an old house, we can picture generation after generation going through the days, the seasons, the years, with the Pilgrim influence still strong, until finally the machine age revolutionized life even upon the farm.

But to return to the seventeenth-century kitchen. Space was much too small to allow the dining set-up to remain, once the meal was over. Chairs and benches were pulled away against the walls, dishes removed, and the table collapsed in one way or another so that it should take up as little room as possible. Perhaps the family had been eating from a table that had folding or drop leaves, or that may have consisted of a pair of trestles and a great wide pine top, all of which easily came apart and were stood against the wall in a corner. Then the room became the living room, with furniture arranged in reference either to the fireplace or to the light. Here the housewife could occupy herself by spinning yarn, be near enough to the fire to watch the cooking, and, at the same time, be within reach of the cradle, to rock it (when teeth were coming through).

In another part of the room an armchair, perhaps of the heavy-posted sort associated with Governors Carver and Brewster, would be backed up to one of the diamond-paned windows, while a little table stood conveniently near by with a carpet on it, a candlestick, and a book of brimstone sermons by Cotton Mather. Across the way might be a little joined stool before a "desk-on-frame," at which the family accounts were laboriously inscribed with the flowing lines from a quill pen. A chest or two of the "six-board" variety, decorated with moulded grooves across the front, or possibly of panelled construction in oak, served the purpose of present-day linen and clothes closets. Frequently, in those days of large families, a bed would occupy one of the corners opposite the entry. The room was indeed the direct descendant of the mediaeval Hall.

After sundown, for such time as then might be left, they lighted their little grease lamps, their dipped candles, or their rushes, and made the most of a darkness that was more picturesque than serviceable. Every effort that an ingenious people could devise had developed adjustments to the light holders, to bring each little flame close to the work that it was supposed to assist, but the light itself was no better and no worse than it had been for some two thousand years. The seventeenth-century world, knowing nothing of wax candles bought at the neighborhood store, flat wicks, glass chimneys, and kerosene, continued to "mind its lights" every few minutes or so, listened to the sputter of imperfect fuel, and inhaled the smell of burning grease and pitch with the patience of ignorance. Possibly that happy law of compensation recompensed them by getting them to bed early, thus keeping them fit to derive pleasure out of the hard fight they had to keep up for a none-too-comfortable existence.

The inventory of Joshuway Benjamin, of Charlestown, Massachusetts, taken in the year 1684, will give, in addition to a picture of the type and relative value of the things of these times, the quite correct impression of there being a distinct limit to the number of them. Benjamin's inventory is a typical one; yet we find among his furnishings but two tables, three chairs, two beds, four chests, two footstools, and a sideboard. The contrast with to-day's steady flow of cheap purchases and quick discard into the attic is a vivid one.

An Inventory of the Esteat of Joshuway Benjamin Deceased:

to one cloak	1— 5—0		to pillows and tine	1—14—0
to one camlet cotta [camel's hair coat]	0—15—0		to earthenware	0— 6—0
to one coat	0— 4—0		to one pair of andirons, tongs and	
to one coat and breeches	1— 8—0		fire basket	0—10—0
to one pair of breeches	0— 4—0		Iron kettle	0— 4—0
to one leather suit	0—10—0		Grid iron	0— 1—0
to stockings and shoes	1— 0—0		flash hook chafing dish	0— 2—0
to one coat	0— 3—0		frying pan: bottles	0— 5—0
to three hats	0—18—0		to one table	0— 4—0
to seven pairs of gloves	0— 4—0		to one brass kettle: skillets and pot	1— 5—0
to shirts and drawers	1—13—0		to one screen	0— 6—0
to handkerchiefs and neckerchiefs	0—10—0		to skins and small furs	0—15—0
to his arms and ammunition	3— 5—0		to small rings and wedges	0— 4—0
to five pairs of shirts	2—10—0		to books	0—12—0
to a sideboard	1— 6—0		to glasses	0— 5—0
to one dozen of linen napkins	0— 8—0		to forge	1— 0—0
to one dozen of napkins	0— 5—0		to tubs and barrels in the cellar	0—17—0
to towels	0— 1—6		to one grate	0—10—0
to table linen	0—10—0			£41—15—6
to a bed and bedstead and furniture	4—10—0			
to one table and carpet	0—12—0		to one cloth stole	0—15—0
to one chest and two trunks	1— 4—0		to shawls and waists	0—18—0
to linen and woolen yarn	2— 2—0		to six brushes one fox skin	0— 2—0
to flax	0— 4—0		to one dozen and half of [illegible]	1—16—0
to combed worsted	0— 1—0		to two seal skin jackets	2— 0—0
to brushes	0— 1—0		to four jackets	3— 0—0
to three chairs	0— 5—0		to one jacket	1— 0—0
to corn and meal	0— 7—0		to five jackets	3— 0—0
to one old trunk and books	0— 2—0		to brass buckles—two dozen	0— 8—0
to a parcel of hops	0— 5—0		to small buckles	0—12—0
to a razor and a hone	0— 4—0		to two dozen of buckles	0— 2—0
to one bed and furniture	4—10—0		to seven dozen pair of bosses	0— 8—8
to one case and glasses	0— 9—0		to bosses—several dozen	0— 3—0
to one warming pan	0—10—0		to three pair and two dozen of bosses	0—10—0
to one shawl and footstool	0— 3—0		to several bosses	0— 1—6
to shawl	0— 7—0		to half a pound of bosses	0— 2—6

to a pound and half of small bosses	0— 2—6		to one hammer	0— 2—6
to two dozen buckles	0— 2—0		to baskets	0— 2—6
to stoppers and rings	0— 6—0		to hothouse and herbs	0— 4—0
to three pounds of small nails	0— 6—0		to 19 pair of skins	0— 6—4
[Illegible]	0—18—0		to firewood	0— 5—0
to seven hogsheads	0—10—0		to furs	0—16—0
to three boxes of glass and a [illegible]	0— 8—0		to one weather vane	0— 1—0
to small shovels	0— 2—0		to cash: 0—14—4 0—6—0:	1— 0—4
to several augurs and bits	0— 4—0		to one gold ring	0—10—0
[Illegible]	0— 4—0		to lumber within doors and without	0— 5—0
to six dozen of glasses	0— 3—0		to one dwelling house and grounds	
to glasses	0— 3—0		that belong to it	110— 0—0
to one bear skin, one hog skin	0— 8—0			£113—12—8
to skins	1— 2—0		113—12—8	
to one pallet, bedspread and willie	0—10—0		021—13—2	
in gold	1— 6—0		041—15—6	
	£21—13—2		177— 1—4*	

The early settlers of New England were not people who expected either luxury or leisure. To them, as it was a privilege to be members of the colonizing adventure, they bravely took the chaff and were grateful for the wheat. When the "Mayflower" finally turned back sixteen weeks after her landing at Plymouth, of the one hundred and two Pilgrim passengers who had sailed from England, approximately one half had been buried at sea or in New England soil, yet so keen was their religious zeal that not a single passenger returned in her, although according to tradition the captain offered them such passage. Ten years later, the spirit of this New World adventure had so taken hold of the English imagination that men were filling out blanks printed in London binding themselves into five, six, and even seven years of servitude in the New World, in consideration for which a master did "promise and grant to and with the said *Edward Hurd* . . . to pay for his passing, [i. e. passage] and to find and to allow him meate, drink, apparrell and lodging, with other necessaries during the said terme, and at the end of the said tearm to give him one whole year's provision and lands according to the custome of the Countrey."†

Luxury, therefore, was not expected; leisure was as much out of the question as it is on our frontiers to-day; yet gradually, through a sifting in of styles and ideas from across the water, these ardent pioneers lost much of the jealous desire that induced them to criticize the neighbor that built too comfortable or magnificent a house, or to rule, for instance, in 1651, that "no person within this Jurisdiction, nor any of their relations depending upon them, whose visible estates real and personal, shall not exceed the true and indifferent value of two hundred pounds, shall wear any Gold or Silver lace, or Gold and Silver Buttons, or any bone lace above two

* This inventory is in the possession of the writer.
† From a 1637 indenture in the possession of the writer.

shillings per yard."* By the close of the century ships were bringing a steady flow of the latest European fashions in looking-glasses, silverware, fabrics, chests, tables, china, wearing apparel, etc., to an eager colony, glad enough to accept as many of the niceties of life as its individual purses could afford.

* From *The General Laws and Liberties of the Massachusetts Colony*, Revised and Reprinted, 1672.

CONTEMPORARY DOCUMENTS

English Visitors to Massachusetts write their Impressions.

1616 *Captain John Smith proposes:*

"And of all the four parts of the world that I have yet feen, not inhabited, could I have but means to tranfport a colony, I would rather live here than any where. And if it did not maintain itfelf, were we but once indifferently well fitted, let us ftarve."*

1632 *Captain Thomas Wiggin enthuses:*

". . . whereof this Kingdom will foon find the benifitt, if the plantation proceeds awhile without difcouragement as hitherto it hath done.

For the plantation in the Maffachufetts the Englifh there being about 2000 people, yonge and old, are generally moft induftrious and fitt for fuch a worke having in three years done more in buyldinge and plantinge than others have done in feaven tymes that fpace, and with at leaft ten tymes lefs expenfe."†

1665 *His Majestie's Commission complains:*

"The Colony of ye Maffachufets was the laft, and hardyeft perfuaded to ufe his Maties Name in their forms of Juftice.

The Comiff^{rs} vifited all other Colonies before this, hopeing both, that ye fubmiffion & condefcention of ye other Colonies to his Maties defires would have abated the refractorinefs of this Colony, which they much feared, And that ye Affiftance of Colonell Nicholls (whom they expected) would have prevailed much ; But neither Examples, nor Reafons could prevaile with them to let ye Comiff^{rs} hear & determine fo much as thofe particular Caufes (Mr. Deane's, & ye Indian Sachims) which ye King had Comanded them to take care of, & to do Juftice in ; . . .

They will not admit any who is not a Member of their Church to ye Comunion ; . . . Thofe whom they will not admit to ye Comunion, they compell to come to their Sermons, by forcing from them five fhillings for every neglect, yet their men thought their own paying of one fhilling for not coming to prayers in England was an infupportable Tyranny.

They have put many Quakers to death, of other Provinces (for which alfo they are petition'd againft.) firft, they banifh't them as Quakers upon pain of Death, & then Executed them for returning ; They have beaten fome to Jelly, & been (other wayes) exceeding crull to others ; & they fay, the King allowes it in his Letters to them.‡

*From *A Description of New England*, by Captain John Smith, in *Collections of the Massachusetts Historical Society*, Vol. VI, 3d Series, 1837.

†From the original report in H. M. Public Records Office, London.

‡This probably refers to the following passage in a letter of Charles II of June 28, 1662: "And fince the principle and foundation of that charter was and is the freedom of liberty of confcience, Wee do hereby charge and require you that that freedom and liberty be duely admitted and allowed, fo that they that defire to ufe the booke of common prayer and performe their devotion in that manner that is eftablifhed here be not denyed the exercife thereof, or undergoe any prejudice or difadvantage thereby, they ufing theire liberty peaceably without any difturbance to others; and that all perfons of good and honeft lives and converfations be admitted to the facrament of the Lords fupper, according to the faid booke of common prayer, and their children to baptifme. Wee cannot be underftood hereby to direct or wifh that any indulgence fhould be graunted to thofe perfons commonly called Quakers, whofe principles being inconfiftent with any kind of government, Wee have found it neceffary, with the advife of our parliament here, to make a fharp law againft them, and are well content you doe the like there."

[17]

Indeed they have mifconftrued all the Kings Letters to their own fence. They yet pray conftantly for their Perfecuted Brethren in England.

They have many things in their Laws derogatory to his Maties honour; . . . Amongft others, who ever keeps Chriftmas day is to pay five pounds.

They caufed at length a Mapp of their Territories to be made, but it was made in a chamber by direction and guefs; In it they claime Fort Albany, and beyond it all the Lands to the South Sea. By their South Line they intrench upon the Colonies of New Plymouth, Rode Ifland, & Conecticot; And on the Eaft they have ufurped Captain Mafon's & St Ferdinando Gorges Patents, . . .

They hope, by Writing to tire the King, the Lo: Chancellor, & ye Secretaries too, Seven years they can eafily fpin out by writing; & before that time a change may come. Nay, fome have dared to fay, who knows what ye event of this Dutch Warr may be. . . .

They did folicit Cromwell by one Mr Wenfloe to be declared a Free-State, and many times in their Lawes flile themfelves this State, this Comon-wealth, & now beleive themfelves to be fo. . . .

They convert Indians by hiring them to come & heare Sermons; by teaching them not to obey their Heathen Sachims, & by appointing Rulers amongft them over tenns, twenties, fifties etc. The lives, Manners, & habits of thofe, whom they fay are converted, cannot be diftinguifhed from thofe who are not, except it be by being hyred to heare Sermons, which the more generous Natives fcorne. . . .

Bofton is ye cheif Towne in it, feated upon a Peninfule, in the bottom of a Bay, which is a good Harbour, and full of fifh; it was fortified this yeare 1665 with two Block-houfes; They had before a Caftle upon an Ifland in the roade, where fhipps muft pafs, about five or fix miles from the Towne; Their houfes are generally Woodden, their ftreets crooked, with little decency & no uniformity, & there neither dayes, months, feafons of the yeare, Churches, nor Inns are known by their Englifh Names. At Cambridg they have a Wooden Colledg; & in ye Yard a Brick Pile of two Bayes for the Indians, where ye Comiff^{rs} faw but one; They faid, they had three or fower more at fchole; it may be feared that this Colledge may afford as many Schifmaticks to ye Church, & ye Corporation as many Rebells to the King, as formerly they have done, if not timely prevented. . . .

In this Colony too the King hath many loyall Subjects, . . . They are forry, that fo few (for there are fcarce above eight of the moft factions) fhould carry on fo ftrong a faction, yet they are fo over-awed that they can do nothing to remedy it. They only fay, that it is now with them, as it was with the King's Party in Cromwell's time. . . ."*

* From the report of His Majeftie's Commiffioners concerning the Massachusetts in H. M. Public Records Office.

The London Gazette.

Published by Authority.

Selections from Issues Between January and November, 1675.

Deale, Nov. 17.

THis morning arrived here the *John Adventure* from *New-England*, by which we have advice, That the diforder occafioned by the rifing of the *Indians*, hath put a great ftop to the Trade and Commerce there; That the *Indians* are very numerous, notwithstanding the *English* have killed and taken many of them; That a little before the departure of this ship from *Boston*, they had advice, That the *Indians*, by means of an ambush, had cut off 60 *Boftoners*, with a Captain and Lieutenant that commanded them : they appear not in any confiderable Bodies, by which means the *English* are not able to do fo much execution upon them, as otherwife they might.

Falmouth, Nov. 11. The 10 inftant came in here two *Dutch* Men of War, the one called the *Samaritan*, mounted with 30 Guns, and the other the *Brunfwick*, mounted with 16; having with them a *French* Prize, a Veffel of 80 Tuns, laden with Fish from *Canada*. By a fmall Veffel arrived from *Bourdeaux*, we have advice, That they have had a good Vintage there this year, and that feveral ships will be ready to come from thence with the next fair wind.

Tangier, Jan. 10. The Moors having laid an Ambush of about 30 Men without our Line, and our difcoverers going out, the fifth inftant early in the morning, they rofe, and killed one of our Men; at the fame time the Moors who lay in feveral Ambufhes, without the Line near our Forts, difcovered themfelves, but were fo warmly received by our Men, who were in the faid Forts, that the skirmifh lafted but a very fhort time, and they retired, with the lofs of feveral of their Men killed and wounded ; among the latter as we fince underftand from *Tituan*, was the Governor of *Alcazar*, who had his hand fhot off; and that *Buliffe* the Captain of thefe Fields, a great Enemy to the Englifh was killed.

London, Auag. 12. By a Veffel arrived from *New-England*, we have an account of the rifing of fome of the *Indians*, with defign to fall upon the Englifh ; that they had already killed feveral, and burnt and plundered their Houfes and Plantations ; upon which the *Boftoners*, and they of *Plymouth*, had fet out feveral hundred armed Men to purfue the *Indians*, who skulked here and there, but durft not appear in any confiderable Bodies.

Dantzick, Nov. 6. We have now the confirmation from all hands of the precipitated retreat of the *Turks* and *Tartars*, with thefe particulars ; That the *Turks* and *Tartars* having, upon the news they had that the King of *Poland* marched towards them, raifed the feige of *Bouchage*, they marched with all their Force to *Trembowla*, and fet down before it ; *Ibrahim Baffa*, General of the *Turks*, fending immediately to fummon the Governor of the place to furrender it ; who anfwered, That if they came to the Siege, with hopes of meeting with any purchafe in the place,

they were very much deceived ; for that there were only Soldiers and Peafants who defended it, and had nothing to lofe but their lives, which they were refolved to fell very dear. This anfwer ferved only the more to irritate the *Turks*, and to confirm them in their refolution to make themfelves Mafters of the place ; which they attacked with fo much vigor, that during 14 dayes they continued the Siege, they fhot above 2000 Cannon Bullets into the Town, and 500 Fire-balls: They fprung four Mines, though without any effect ; and made feveral affaults, in which they loft a great many Men : and notwithstanding all thefe ill fucceffes, they continued refolved to go on with the Siege; but a Peafant being taken Prifoner, who was charged with a Letter from the King to the Governor, in which his Majefty affured him, That he was coming in perfon with his whole Army to relieve him ; and that in order thereunto, he had already paffed a fmall River that was between him and the Enemies Camp, and that he marched directly towards them. Upon this news, *Ibrahim Baffa* gave immediate orders for the Artillery to be taken from the Batteries, which confifted in 100 pieces, and to march towards *Caminiec*, whither he followed the next day with his whole Army, marching above fifteen Leagues in fo much confufion and confternation, that he commanded the *Tartars* to keep near him, to cover his march.

Advertifements.

At A COUNCIL
Held at Boston the 9th. of April, 1677

THE COUNCIL being informed, that among other Evils that are prevailing among us, in this day of our Calamity, there is practised by some that vanity of Horse racing, for mony, or monyes worth, thereby occasioning much misspence of pretious time, and the drawing of many persons from the duty of their particular Callings, with the hazard of their Limbs and Lives.

It is hereby Ordered that henceforth it shall not be Lawful for any persons to do or practise in that kind, within *four miles* of any Town, or in any *Highway* or *Common Rode*, on penalty of forfieting *twenty Shillings* apiece, nor shall any Game or run in that kind for any mony, or monyes worth upon penalty of forfieting Treble the value thereof, one half to the *party informing*, and the other half to the *Treasury*, nor shall any accompany or abbett any in that practice on the like penalty, and this to continue til the General Courtt take further Order.

And all *Constables* respectively are hereby injoyned to present the Names of all such as shall be found transgressing, contrary to this Order to the *Magistrate*.

Dated the *ninth of April*, 1677.

By the Council
Edward Rawson Sec.

RURAL NEW ENGLAND IN THE EARLY SEVENTEEN HUNDREDS

As illustrated by the PINE CEILED ROOM AT THE CONCORD ANTIQUARIAN SOCIETY *in Concord, Massachusetts*

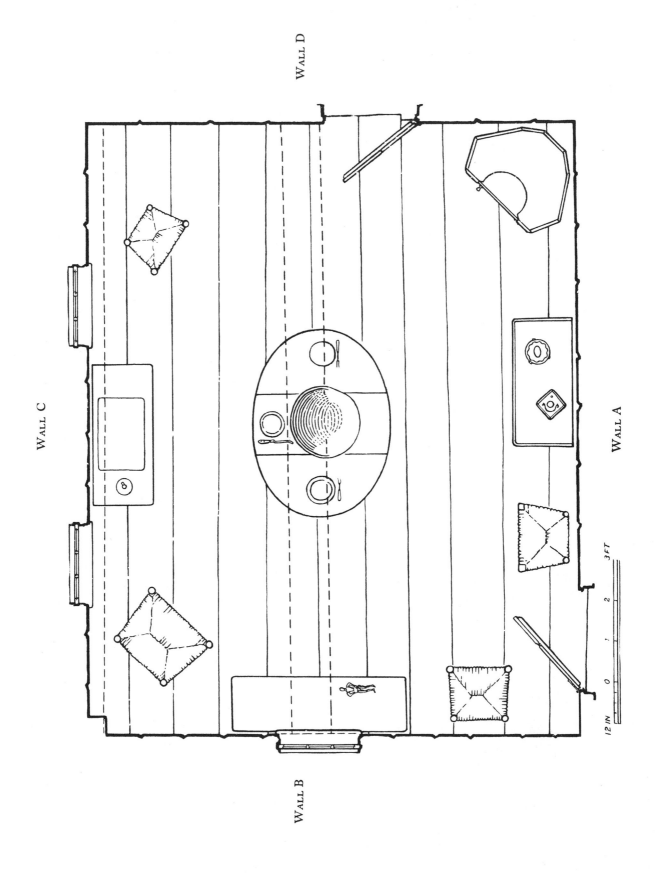

WALL C

WALL A

WALL B

12 IN   0   1   2   3 FT

Historical Note

NEW England history concerns itself chiefly with the larger towns and the more important people; for its background the country districts, though widely populated, form but an uncertain vista. Town records, local letters, and the dry facts of wills and inventories, have been comparatively little studied. Away from the larger towns, industries were few, for each household supplied its own needs of whatever kind; craftsmen scarcely existed, except as one farmer was a better carpenter, or his wife a better weaver, than another; almost alone the smith was a specialist; but he was farmer too, and his neighbor's own crude ironwork sufficed for many farm needs. But after the beginning of the century there began to appear, even in the smaller towns, a reaching toward better things.

Whether he knew it or not, the New Englander was under the influence of Europe, and to satisfy the ambitions of King Louis, or of the councillors of Queen Anne, he might at any time have to leave his farm and fight the French or Indians. There was scarcely a time, up to the year 1763, when raids might not threaten the New England frontiers, or governors might not appeal to farmer or seaman to strike in defence or reprisal. The attempts on Quebec, Crown Point, and Port Royal, were all a part of the struggle for a peaceful life in New England; and the taking of Louisburg in 1745 was an achievement in which the plans of Shirley, the leadership of Pepperell, and even the assistance of the British fleet, would have failed without the hardy and almost reckless courage of men who until then had scarcely crossed the limits of their townships. Because of the prevalence of war, the merchantman might at almost any time become a privateer, and the farmer's boy risk the campaign in the wilderness.

At the same time, ready as he might be to fight for the Empire, the New Englander was always resisting the authority of king and Parliament. In 1689 the men of the country towns marched down to Boston and deposed the governor, Andros, who was exercising in Massachusetts too much of Stuart rapacity and absolutism. Yet the charter of William, which followed, greatly extended the powers of the governor; and for many years the royal representative, whoever he might be, was in strife with the Assembly over his salary, and other appropriations for the use of the government. In this he was stubbornly opposed by the delegates from the country towns who, niggardly though they often were, stuck to the principle of levying their own taxes and spending their own money. They might quarrel among themselves over problems local or general; but when there arose the question of the right of the king to pry open their purse, they stood together to resist him.

This solidarity of opinion, and unity of action, existed in New England in spite of many obstacles. Newspapers at first were few, and circulated mostly locally.

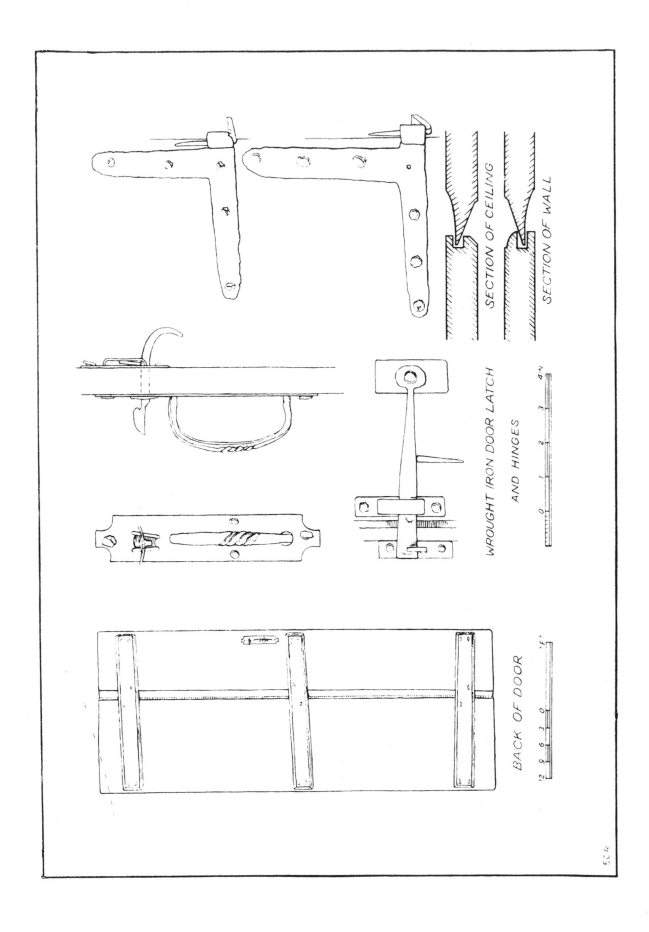

SECTION OF CEILING

SECTION OF WALL

WROUGHT IRON DOOR LATCH

AND HINGES

BACK OF DOOR

Travel was not general, and the means of it were defective. For the roads were poor, and the farther one went from the large towns, the rougher became the ways. The journey of Madam Knight in 1704-5, from Boston to New York and back, shows the inconveniences, almost the perils, of crossing the many streams by the crudest of ferries and the frailest of bridges. Over many stretches the roads were not wide enough for wheeled vehicles, and perforce the riding horse for the traveller, and the pack horse for his goods, long remained the chief means of transit. Madam Knight's frequent terrors for her life were not justified. At the same time she often found among the people great lack of culture, and a crudity of manners exciting the proper disgust of one who had lived in the great towns. Decent accommodation for travellers, and even cleanliness of living, must long have remained lacking in the country districts.

This has been called the dark age of New England. The first and second generations of settlers had gone, and with them had disappeared the close social connection with the old country which had maintained the culture of the new country at a fairly high level. In later times there was, for another few generations, a plain falling off from the former modest excellence. There were, in the first place, no such leaders as those who had directed the exodus from England. In the second place, as the struggle with the wilderness proved very hard, in too many cases the leaders of the newer generations lowered their standards before increasing difficulties. This was most apparent in schooling. Though the larger towns still maintained their schools, public or private, education disappeared almost entirely from many of the smaller. Not only the daughter of the well-to-do farmer, but often the farmer himself, could not sign a document, and marks in place of signatures were common. There can be no greater proof of the low level of culture of a community than the fact that the greater part of its members cannot read or write; and for a time it is true that sections of New England bore this unenviable stigma, with which naturally went backwardness of other kinds.

At the same time, self-improvement lay in the nature of the people. Their very inquisitiveness, mentioned by every traveller, showed them alive to the doings of the outside world. Their undeniable industry procured them not only a good living, but a small surplus to use in local barter. Massachusetts towns without schools were fined by the legislature. And an ingenuity and inventiveness, natural to the race, steadily brought about betterment of conditions on the farm and in industry. By the middle of the century, though the worst of all the wars with the French was impending, the people were ready for a desperate struggle, which was but the prelude to the Revolution, in which New England supplied a proportion of the armies much greater than its comparative area.

All this is but a sketch. And if one tries, in the scantiness of old records, to single out such a town as Concord, and make it appear individual, the task is difficult.

Here was a people not merely led by its minister, but willingly measuring all things (as did their fathers) by a religious standard, and strictly limiting themselves to the thoughts and occupations which showed the way to Heaven. Terrorized, indeed, by fears of hell which occupied even the minds of the children, these people yet met the conditions of a harsh existence with courage. In the demands of daily life they worked themselves and each other hard. Concord was, indeed, not out of reach of Boston; the newspapers came with frequency; the courts met here, and on those occasions men of provincial importance gathered in its streets. This pointed to the time when the Provincial Congress should meet in Concord church, and when the British troops should march to the town hoping to prevent the outbreak of a revolution. Yet even before such a time, in the earlier part of the century, the position of Concord gave it some prominence beyond its neighbors, and its slightly greater size gave promise of at least temporary importance. The life on the average of its farms (and all, even the minister, were farmers), was rigid and unyielding. The rumor of war meant the summoning of a son or a neighbor to service; but the struggle for the comforts and respectabilities of life went on unendingly.

But as in such a house as that of the Concord Antiquarian Society we study the domestic arrangements which speak to us, in a way different from document or newspaper, of the mental processes of our progenitors, we see how in each department they were determined to master conditions. Rushlight and candle gave way to the lamp; the shape of the fireplace was altered to throw more heat; the heavy furniture of the immigrant generation was improved in lightness and eventually in grace. Similarly the interior finish of a house was altered for both warmth and beauty. In the large towns the rooms became imposing, until some were panelled on all four walls. The beauty of some of these remains to impress us to-day. But equally significant are the mere beginnings of such luxuries as they have scantily survived in country towns. What the rich man of the seaport did from his superfluity, employing the best artisans at hand, the country farmer determined to have for his wife, though it might be but the work of his own tools. The illustrations which follow show how strongly the resolution to have some of the better things of life, even if in but a single room of his house, prevailed in an unnamed New England farmer about two centuries ago.

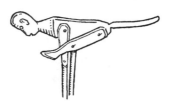

WALL A

CORNER CUPBOARD
PINE
PAINTED RED
Early 18th Century

LOOKING-GLASS
PINE
CARVED AND PAINTED
c. 1700

LANTERN
PINE, PIERCED IN
GOTHIC TRACERY
*17th or early
18th Century*

BLANKET CHEST
PINE, PAINTED RED. *c. 1710*

SPOON RACK
PINE, CARVED
Dated 1768

BANISTER-BACK
SIDE CHAIR
MAPLE AND ASH
PAINTED BLACK
1st quarter 18th Century

Rural New England in the Early Seventeen Hundreds

THE room and its furnishings that have been made the subject of this discussion represent an attempt to show the sort of home surroundings that existed during the beginning of the eighteenth century in rural New England. They do not illustrate the very latest styles of 1700-1725, but rather a combination of the new and the old of that date, just as we find them side by side in the average house of to-day. It is difficult for us to form a true picture unless we think also of the dangers, the obstacles, and the isolation against which the colonists were still contending. We read in *Public Occurrences*, a Boston paper of 1690, of the disappearance of two children from Chelmsford—just north of Concord—and find it assumed that they strayed too far from home and fell into hands of the "barbarous Indians" —"those miserable Salvages," as they are described in this paper. Scenes like this were taking place hardly out of sight of the windows of this pine-sheathed room! It must have taken a peculiar sort of fortitude to build fine chests and carve beautiful boxes when the threat of quick disturbance was never more than just beyond the edge of the clearing.

The spirit of this room would seem to come from the fact that there is practically nothing in it that has not been fashioned from the timber that grew right on the spot. From the boxed-in frame of the house down to the little doll on the carved pine chest, nearly everything is wood, locally grown, cut with much labor, and used to the last little stick.

Oak was generally given the heavier assignments. It was often selected for the frames of houses, customarily used in the frames of the grander chests, like the one between the windows on Wall "C," and in rare instances used for floors. Other hard woods, especially maple, were turned into table and chair legs. Soft pine was most commonly used for panels, chest lids, shelving of all kinds, wall sheathing and flooring, because it was wide and plentiful. Occasionally such woods as chestnut, butternut, walnut, cherry, apple, ash, birch, and whitewood were available and of course were put to use. Though the beauty of mahogany was recognized at this time, furniture made of it was rare and only for the very well-to-do.

It was a long time before the days of white paint, and wood was usually left in its natural color. The "India" red on the chest and corner cupboard, typical of early painting, is an application that outside of the cities can hardly have been made earlier than the middle of the century; the blue boxing of the beams, although it has not been touched in modern times, probably was not put on before late in the century, for here again we must recognize that we are dealing with a country rather than a city house.

By 1700 those early architectural traditions which we may speak of as "American mediaeval" had only just left the scene. Casement leaded-glass windows, shadow-moulded wainscot, exposed posts, sills, and beams of the frame had given place to double-hung windows, feather-edged sheathing, and, usually, a neat boxing about the heavy timbers, which were nevertheless still in evidence. The Renaissance, with its columns and its multiplicity of classic mouldings, had hardly reached across the Atlantic to the more pretentious houses, and it exerted no influence whatever on such a country room as this. Everything was still done informally, in as natural a way as possible. One of the doors here has never had anything more permanent than two squares of leather for its hinges!

The most distinguished feature of this room is its pine-sheathed ceiling, which unfortunately hardly shows in the illustrations. Panelled ceilings are extremely rare, while a sheathed ceiling such as this one stands perhaps alone in our architectural history. The boards, like those on the side walls, have never had paint applied to them during the many changes in public taste through which they have lived. The detail of the edge-to-edge joining here is unique, for the feather edge, instead of being held in place by the traditional quarter round, simply runs into a rebate whose extreme corner is delicately bevelled at forty-five degrees, as is shown in the plate of details.

The floor still bears evidence about its outer limits of the yellow ochre paint that it was at one time given. It was not a time when rugs were very commonly used. Floors were left in the natural wood, or were covered with a thin layer of sand in which patterns might be swept with a broom. Later in the century, as painting became gradually the custom, floors might also be colored, either evenly or spattered.

Let us consider the inventory,* taken in 1698, of the estate of Roger Sumner of Milton, and see the relative values of the main classifications. Of the total valuation of £460/12/0, three-quarters were in lands or houses of one sort or another. Less than a fifteenth of the total was furnishings, including four beds, a cupboard, three chests, two tables, "chairs," pewter, brass, ironware, and books to the value of 2/–/–. Wearing apparel amounted to 12/–/–; livestock—two steers, two cows, four calves, a horse, and some swine—17/10/0; growing crops 12/–/–; tools and such necessities (including "a cider mill and rope belonging to it") 12/13/0.

At this date (i.e., at the turn of the century) we are fifty years before the great cabinetmakers made their appearance. There were as yet no "styles"—a chair was called a chair, as in this inventory, unless it was further defined by such expressions as old, leather, matted bottom, carved back, or a similar natural description. The central feature of the room was usually a folding table of some kind—in this instance a well-turned gate-leg (which shows only in the plan of the room). One or two comfortable and several uncomfortable chairs, together with an array of chests and cupboards against the walls, completed the major pieces of furniture.

* In the possession of the writer.

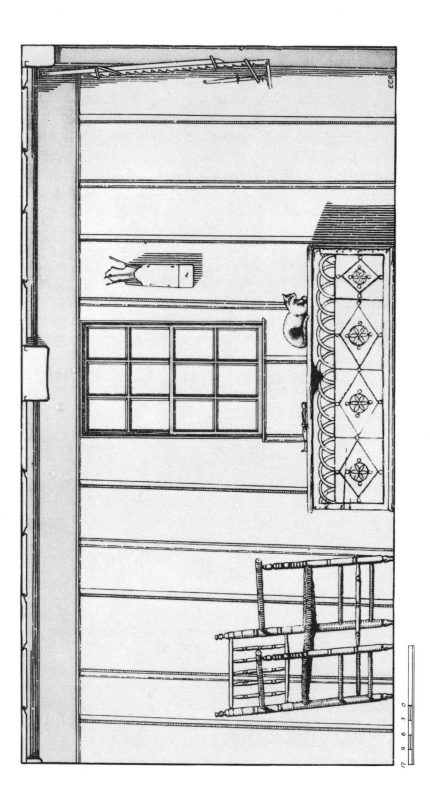

WALL B

HANGING RATCHET
LIGHT HOLDER
PINE
18th Century

PIPE BOX
PINE
18th Century

CHEST. PINE, WITH LINE CARVING
Late 17th Century

ARMCHAIR. CARVER TYPE
Late 17th or early 18th Century

The list of minor pieces was almost as varied as to-day. Looking-glasses, pipe boxes, spoon racks, candle-holders, stools, dishes, and even toys filled up all available places. Closets, as we think of them to-day, were unknown, and the only hope of keeping a well-to-do establishment in orderly arrangement lay in the use of chests and boxes, of which there were numbers in proportion to the prosperity of the owner.

At this date, the first hundred years of American furniture, so well pictured by Mr. Nutting as the Pilgrim Century, were drawing to a close, and much of the strong, homemade character was gradually giving place to a new and lighter treatment that the eighteenth-century designers were soon to carry to the limit of its possibilities. Changes during the Pilgrim Century had been dictated by a desire for increased comfort or increased convenience in portability. Changes during the eighteenth and nineteenth centuries were more apt to be called for by a demand for greater elegance or by the whim of fashion. The fundamental change that was taking place in the arts of young America may be compared to that which had already occurred on the Continent as the Renaissance had swept along more than two hundred years before. Design was growing self-conscious, and individuals were soon to step forward to undertake the leadership of public taste. Without doubt such a change as this is always closely connected with an increase in the facility of transportation and the consequent spread of knowledge. The start of the eighteenth century was very decidedly a time of change.

A room of the first quarter of the eighteenth century would have a pretty sturdy assortment of chairs. True, the stiff wainscot chair had long since vanished from sight, and by this time it would be unusual to find a "Carver" or a "Brewster," but the slat back, though getting lighter in construction, was still in vogue, especially in country places. One has to be pretty straight to fit against its uncompromising rails. To the rural colonists, however, this chair was a relative luxury, for the days were hardly out of sight when it was the lot of many of each household to sit on backless forms or stools.

In the finest houses there would be examples of Cromwellian chairs, leather or cloth upholstered, or of beautifully carved Flemish chairs, both relics of the sixteen hundreds, and of the handsome banister backs that seem to have evolved from the Flemish at the turn of the century. Theoretically, a back made of a row of thin vertical sticks or half banisters has more give to it than one made either of slats or of a panel. The switch to vertical members was a fortunate one from the point of style, for it was to lead easily to the grouping of the three, four, or five narrow banisters into a single broad splat, eventually to be pierced and scrolled and carved in exotic woods by Thomas Chippendale and the cabinetmakers that were working a little before and a little after his day.

This room, as we have said, has quite rightly a gate-leg table in the center of it.

It was a time when the demand for ample table space three times a day, in a room that was at other times the center of the day's activity, had just been worked out satisfactorily in the gate-leg table. There were many other beautiful and ingenious types of folding table, most notably the "butterfly." The early seventeenth-century trestle tables that had been constructed to be taken apart after each using, and the long and heavy "refectory" tables too, must have appeared clumsy and undesirable in competition with the new, small table that could spread itself out to entertain as many diners as the room could hold.

It was also the heyday of the light "tavern" table and of the little tables and stands that one might think of as the portable platforms of the establishment—to hold a lighted candle or a couple of mugs of ale. Some of the wealthy colonists at this time could boast of a newly constructed walnut veneer lowboy, or a flat-topped highboy, the latter being the latest development of the chest-on-frame.

Almost any one of the many forms through which the early chest passed in its evolution was being constructed at the start of the eighteenth century, but the character, the proportions, the wood, and the detail would be of the day. A man would build for himself a chest, large or small, with or without any number of drawers, on a frame or not, just as he liked. If he were working in the latest fashion he would quite likely run a little half-round moulding as a decoration around the hole into which the drawers slid—by way of casting a shadow over the inevitable meeting of the drawer with the frame. Soon this half-round moulding gave place to a pair of smaller half rounds—a double arch, as it is called—and as the first quarter of the century passed this double arch in its turn gave way to a little quarter-round "lip" on the drawer itself, usually styled a thumbnail moulding, that extended over the necessary play and became the permanent solution to the problem.

Desks had moved forward along with the tables and chests. At just about this time some desks had become perfectly workable pieces of furniture. The lids in these examples swung toward you on hinges and became flat surfaces to write upon, with knee room below. Inside, until the eighteenth century got under way, it was the custom to put a small sliding door of wood giving access to a shallow space reached from above—the upper "drawer," as it appeared on the front, being merely a dummy. The more common form, however, was still what is known as a desk box, of oak or pine, sometimes painted, frequently carved, with a lid that was more often flat than slanted, as in the example between the windows. Inside one kept the household documents and writing materials, and frequently the Bible.

To stop here in the discussion of boxes would not give a complete picture. There were wooden pipe boxes for long-stemmed churchwarden pipes of clay, salt boxes, and candle boxes to keep the rats from eating up the winter's supply so carefully provided. And also there were shelves, and racks for plates, and spoons, and can-

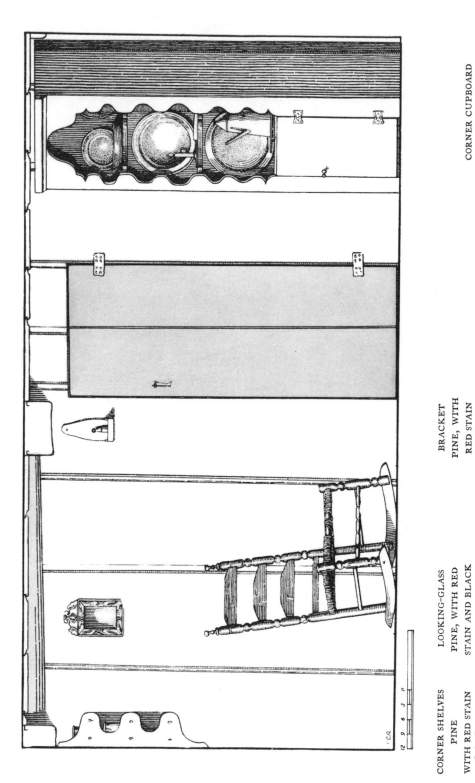

WALL D

CORNER SHELVES
PINE
WITH RED STAIN
18th Century

LOOKING-GLASS
PINE, WITH RED
STAIN AND BLACK
DECORATION
c. 1700

BRACKET
PINE, WITH
RED STAIN
18th Century

CORNER CUPBOARD
PINE, PAINTED RED
Early 18th Century

SLAT-BACK SIDE CHAIR
PINE, PAINTED RED
18th Century (rockers probably later)

dle-holders, all arranged to keep things tidy. Sometimes these were made with much attention and became real ornaments about the room.

It would be a rare thing indeed to find a press cupboard at this date. There never have been many of them. Most housewives during the first century of the colonies contented themselves with corner cupboards similar to the fine red example here, for the display of their polished pewter on the shelves above and the storage of their provisions behind the door below.

Fashionable bedsteads were still slender four-posters, square or turned, simply framed in maple at this period and strung tightly with ropes. From the frame hung a valence and curtains that could be drawn at night for shelter and comfort. There must have been, however, many more "unfashionable" beds without the high posts and the frills, and the occupants considered themselves lucky not to have drawn the more humble lot of sleeping low down among the draughts in trundle beds.

Customarily there were curtains in the windows; occasionally there might be a religious picture or an engraved map or portrait upon the walls; and even in rare instances some local artistic effort with the needle, like "petit-point" or "stump work." Rugs were used on beds and "carpets" on tables. All-covering carpets on the floor did not come into fashion until halfway through the next century, but "floor cloths," or rugs as we would call them, were sometimes mentioned in the inventories of the more prosperous city houses.

Dipped or moulded candles, grease lamps, and in out-of-the-way parts of the colonies rushlights and "candle wood," took care of the illumination, hanging ingeniously from the beams by adjustable trammels, clinging to the backs of chairs, spiked into crevices in the walls, or resting in the normal way on tables. Mirrors of the squarish William-and-Mary style, with handsome crestings, or in the style of Queen Anne, elongated and with the fanciful cresting spilling down over the sides and across the bottom, reflected in an amateurish way the deep tones of the interiors—more as you see yourself in a pewter plate than in the sharp duplication of a modern glass. Wooden or pewter plates and spoons, bone-handled knives, bone-handled forks for those who had learned how to use them—the whole assortment of household utensils was primitive, but there was about it that homemade character which was also by necessity in evidence in the architecture, the furniture, and even the costumes. The result must have given the same aesthetic pleasure as that which we can derive to-day when we stand before the mellow painting of a Dutch Interior —colorful, frugal, orderly, and untainted by even the suspicion of a machine.

CONTEMPORARY DOCUMENTS

Excerpts from the Records of the Town of Concord, Massachusetts, showing the Selectmen attending to Various Problems, especially that of a Town Character known as Cooksay.

November yᵉ 4ᵗʰ 1701 The ſelectmen haveing agreed with peter wright to keep William Cookſay with meat drink & waſhing from January yᵉ 24ᵗʰ 1700/1 untill yᵉ fourteenth of march next enſuing & was to be payd by yᵉ ſelectmen on yᵉ Townes account at three ſhillings pr week wᶜʰ come to 1£ 1ˢ did then order the ſd Wright to procure for ſd Cookſey a ſhirt wᶜʰ come to 6ˢ 6ᵈ & a pare of lining briches 3ˢ 8ᵈ & a pare of ſtockens 4ˢ all comeing to 01£ 15-07 And further yᵉ ſelectmen agree with ſd Wright to provide for ſd Cookſey Cloath for a ſtrait bodied coat & another ſhirt & to be payd out of the Townes Treaſurry

At a meeting of yᵉ Free houlder & other Inhabitants yᵉ 13ᵗʰ of December 1703. Propounded Wheras William Cookſay is a towne Charg we yᵉ Subſcribers do ingage Each of us to keep yᵉ ſd Cookſay with meat drinck waſhing & Loging a Calander month a peece ondly in time of Sikneſs or other Illneſs the Towne to Reimburſe the keepers of ſd Cookſay with neſſefarys ſuttable wiſe providing their be yᵉ number of Twelve perſons Apear in this Caſe

Jonathan Preſcott	*May*	Saˡˡ Davis Senʳ	*Septembr*	Jonathan Hubbor
Jnᵒ Jones	*Jun*	Daniel Pelett	*October*	John Heald
Natˡ Stow	*July*	Natˡ Jones	*November*	Nehemiah Hunt Senʳ
Moſes Wheat	*Oguſt*	Jnᵒ Wheler Virgine	*Aprill*	Saˡˡ Chandler

Concord January yᵉ 3ᵈ 1703/4 then Agreed with Mʳ Samˡˡ Burr by yᵉ Selectmen of Concord to teach ſuch Children and ſervants yᵗ belong to ſaid Town as have Entred into yᵉ Rules of Spelling in Reading writing and Cyphering as alſo in yᵉ Gramm Latine and Greek and yᵉ ſd Samˡˡ Burr begins this third day of january and is to Continue to teach yᵉ School untill yᵉ third day of Aprill next and for his pains and a Reward the Select men or their Sucſeſʳˢ are to pay to him his Hairs or Aſſigns yᵉ ſum of ſeven pounds and ten ſhillings mony as alſo yᵉ keeping of a horſe with good hay and ſtable room during ſaid time

June yᵉ 3ᵈ 1708 At a meeting of yᵉ ſelectmen of Concord yᵉ day aforeſd They did then agree with Danˡˡ Pellit for to ring yᵉ meeting houſe Bell upon all Sabaths, Lecturedayes Court dayes publick meetings all to be done faithfully ſeaſonably, As alſo to ſweep the meeting houſe rub down yᵉ table ſeats, alſo Inſpect yᵉ doars & windows to be done carefully & decently all for the term of one year, Alſo yᵉ ſelectmen have further agreed wᵗʰ ſd Pellit for to keep & give entertainmⁿᵗ unto William cookſy for yᵉ term of one year from this date & onwards, with what is neceſſary (for a man of his capacity) excepting clothing the wᶜʰ the ſelectmen are to ſe yᵗ he is provided for, and the ſd Pellit is to have payd him for his ſervice above mentioned relating to yᵉ Bell & meeting houſe as alſo for his charge in keeping of ſd Cookſy the term aforeſd by ſd town of Concord yᵉ ſum of ſeven pounds in Good paſſable mony. And he ſd Pellit is to be further privilidged to Imploy ſd cookſay in his ſd pellits ſervice, in what he is capable to do & perform yᵉ whole term aforeſd in to yᵉ Bargain only he ſd Pellit doth remitt all yᵗ he might require for giving entertainmⁿᵗ unto ſd cookſy the laſt month paſt. all the above articles & bargains was agreed upon yᵉ day above ſd by yᵉ ſelectmen of Concord and him ſd Danˡˡ Pellit reſpectively, according to true meaning.

The Bofton News-Letter.

Selections from Iffues of 1704-1707.

Windfor, September 14, 1704.

THis day Captain *Trevor*, Commander of Her Majefty's Ship the *Triton*, arrived here; being fent Exprefs by Sir *George Rooke* from the Fleet, with Letters to *His Royal Highnefs*, dated on Board the *Royal Catherine* off of Cape St. Vincent, Auguft 27, O. S. 1704. Which contain the following Account.

On the 9th Inftant, returning from watering our Ships on the *Coaft of Barbary* to *Gibraltar*, with little Wind Eafterly, our Scouts to the Windward made the Signals of feeing the Enemy's Fleet, which, according to the Account they gave, confifted of 66 Sail, and were about 10 Leagues to Windward of us. A Council of Flag-Officers was called, wherein it was determined to lay to the Eaftward of *Gibralter* to receive and engage them; But perceiving that Night, by the Report of their Signal-Guns, that they wrought from us, we followed them in the Morning with all the Sail we could make.

On the 11th we forced one of the Enemy's Ships afhore near *Fuengorole*; the Crew quitted her, fet her on Fire, and fhe blew up immediately, We continued ftill purfuing them; and the 12th, not hearing any of their Guns all Night, nor feeing any of their Scouts in the Morning, our Admiral had a Jealoufie they might make a Double, & by the help of their Gallies flip between us and the Shore to the Weftward; fo that a Council of War was called, wherein it was refolved, That in cafe we did not fee the Enemy before Night, we fhould make the beft of our way to *Gibralter*; but ftanding in to the Shore about Noon we difcovered the Enemy's Fleet and Gallies to the Weftward, near *Cape Malaga*, going away large. We immediately made all the Sail we could after them, and continued the Chace all Night.

On Sunday the 13th in the Morning, we were within 3 Leagues of the Enemy, who brought to with their Heads to the Southward, the Wind being Eafterly, formed their Line, and lay to receive us. Their Line confifted of 52 Ships, & 24 Gallies; they were very ftrong in the Center, & weaker in the Van and Rear, to fupply which, moft of the Gallies were divided into thofe Quarters. In the Center was Monfieur de *Thouloufe* with the White Squadron; in the Van the White and Blue; and in the Rear the Blue; each Admiral had his Vice and Rear-Admirals. Our Line confifted of 53 Ships; the Admiral & Rear-Admirals *Bings* & *Dilks* being in the Center, Sir *Cloudefly Shovel* and Sir *John Leake* led the Van, and the *Dutch* the Rear.

The Admiral ordered the *Swallow* and *Panther*, with the *Lark* and *Newport*, and 2 Fire-fhips, to lie to the Windward of us, that in cafe the Enemy's Van fhould pufh through our Line with their Gallies and Fire-fhips, they might give them fome diverfion.

We bore down upon the Enemy in order of Battel, a little after 10 a Clock, when being about half Gun-fhot from them, they fet all their Sails at once, and feemed to intend to ftretch a-head, and weather us, fo that our Admiral, after firing a Chace Gun at the French Admiral to ftay for him, of which he took no notice, put the Signal out, & began the Battel, which fell very heavy on the *Royal Catherine*, the *St. George*, and the *Shrewfbury*. About 2 in the afternoon, the Enemy's Van gave way to ours, & the Battel ended with the Day, when the Enemy went away by the help of their Gallies to the Leward. In the Night the Wind fhifted to the Northward, & in the Morning to the Weftward, which gave the Enemy the Wind of us: We lay by all Day within 3 Leagues of one another, repairing our Defects, & at Night they filed & ftood to the Northward.

On the 15th in the Morning the Enemy was got four or five Leagues to the Windward of us; but a little before Noon we had a Breeze of Wind Eafterly, with which we bore down on them till 4 a Clock Afternoon: It being too late to Engage, we brought to, and lay by with our Heads to the Northward all night.

On the 16th in the Morning, the Wind being ftill Eafterly, hazy Weather, and having no fight of the Enemy, or their Scouts, we filed and bore away to the Weftward, fuppofing they would have gone away for *Cadiz*; but being advifed from *Gibralter*, and the *Coaft of Barbary*, that they did not pafs the *Streights*, we concluded they had been fo feverely treated, as to oblige them to return to *Thoulon*.

Rhode-Ifland, Octob. 5. On Sunday laft arrived here one *Benjamin Church*, who Sailed hence Mafter of a fmall Sloop bound for *Antigua*, the 8th of Auguft laft, and on the 18th, in the Lat. of 34, met with the fame Storm that the *Jamaica Fleet* met with on faid day, which overfet the Sloop, and the people kept on the Bowfprit from Saturday till Monday when the Sloop righted, but loft her Maft, and through their Induftry they freed her, the Wind hanging Eafterly, they drove afhore on *Cape May*, and fo faved all their lives.

Philadelphia, Auguft 3. Yefterday arrived here Capt. *Puckle* from *London* about 14 weeks pafsage.

Boston, By His Excellency's Direction, Capt. *Tyng* and Capt. *Stephens* with 150 men with Snow Shoes march'd from *Dunstable* eight days ago into the Woods in search of the Enemy.

There are two Mails due from the Eastern Post, and one from the Western, by reason of the great Snows.

Boston, July 3. On Fryday was carried to the Place of Execution seven Pirates to be Executed, viz. Capt. *John Quelch, John Lambert, Christopher Scudemore, John Miller, Erasmus Petersen, Peter Roach* and *Francis King*, all of which were Executed, excepting the last named, who had a Reprieve from His Excellency. And notwithstanding all the great labour and pains taken by the Reverend Ministers of the Town of Boston, ever since they were first Seized and brought to Town, both before and since their Tryal and Condemnation, to instruct, admonish, preach and pray for them; yet as they led a wicked and vitious life, so to appearance they dyed very obdurately and impenitently, hardened in their Sin.

New London, Aug. 3. Yesterday His Honour our Governour went in his Pinnace to *Hartford*, we are much alarmed by reason of a very great Ship and two Sloops said to be seen at *Block Island*, and supposed to be French.

Boston, On Tuesday the 23d Currant, Complaint being made to *Edward Bromfield* Esqr. One of Her Majesty's Council, and Justice of the Peace; of *John Rogers & Son*, of *New-London* in Connecticut-Colony for Profanation of the Sabbath, in Driving of Cattle through the Town of *Dedham* to *Boston* for a Market on the 21st Instant, being the Lords-Day; And opprobriously answering those who disswaded him therefrom; for which being brought before the said Justice, and legally Convicted, he was Sentenced according to the Direction of the Law in that case, to pay the Fine of Twenty Shillings.

Boston, On Wednesday night an English man was kill'd in the Woods at *Groton* by the Indians which were afterwards descryed in the night by the Light of their Fires, by a Person Travailing from *Groton* to *Lancaster*, and judged they might be about Thirty in number; pursuit was made after them, but none could be found.

Marshfield, July 22. Capt. *Peregrine White* of this Town, aged Eighty three years, and Eight Months; died the 20th Instant. He was vigorous and of a comly aspect to the last; Was the Son of Mr. William White and Susanna his Wife; born on board the *May flower*, Capt. *Jones* Commander, in Cape Cod Harbour, November 1620. was the First Englishman born in New-England. Altho' he was in the former part of his Life extravagant; yet was much Reform'd in his last years; and died hopefully.

New-London, Aug. 9. On Thursday last marched from hence Capt. *John Livingston*, with a brave Company of Volunteers English and Indians, to reinforce the Frontiers.

On Thursday night the Reverand Mr. *Gardner*, Minister of *Lancaster* was unfortunately Shot by the Sentinel on the Watch, supposing him to be an Indian climbing over the Walls of the Fortification; of which Wound he dyed in an hours space or little more. (full report in No. 31, p. 2.)

Boston. On Wednesday 21. Came an Express to His Excellency from *Hatfield*, with the Intelligence, That one English man and four Indians, being sent out upon discovery of the Enemy, Travelled 7 days up the River of Connecticut, and discovered some Indians a Fishing, so lay still till Night, and watched where they went to their Wigwam, and Surprized them in the Wigwam, kill'd five of the said Indians being men, took a Squaw alive, who informed them, that the Indians were building a Fort at a place about 50 Miles further up, after further Examination of the said Squaw they kill'd her also, and brought the Six Scalps with them to Northampton: There were two Indians more of the said Company, but they made their escape.

Our People on the Frontiers are in a very good posture to receive the Enemy, if they should come.

Advertisements

CLASSIC COLUMNS REACH THE
NEW ENGLAND VILLAGES

As illustrated by the GREEN DINING ROOM AT THE CONCORD
ANTIQUARIAN SOCIETY *in Concord, Massachusetts*

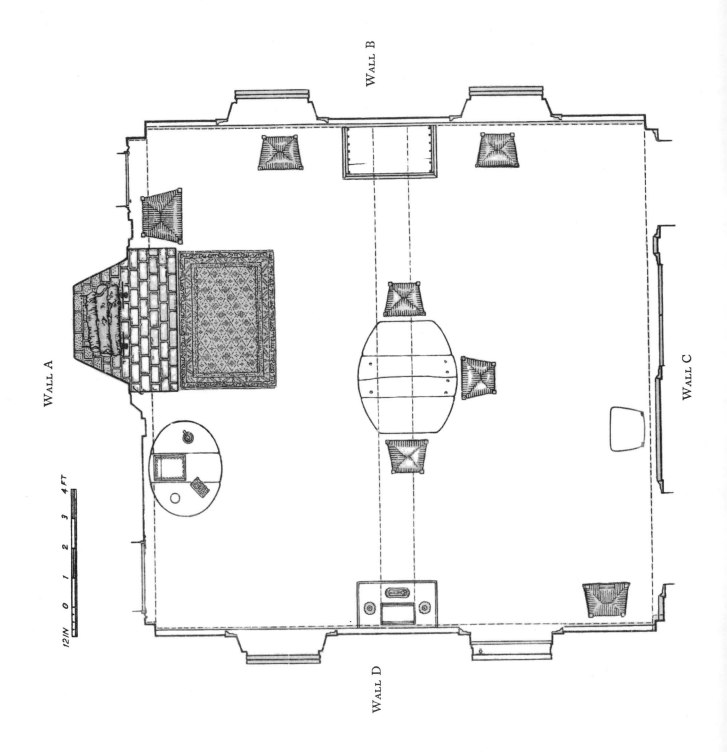

WALL A

WALL B

WALL C

WALL D

12IN 0 1 2 3 4FT

Historical Note

THE first half of the eighteenth century was not a dramatic period in colonial affairs. Stirring events were just before and just behind, but this was Indian summer. Important movements and tendencies were taking shape, but in their early stages they lacked color. Statistics of growth have no surprise for Americans. Of course we grew; of course our population, wealth, and trade increased enormously; and of course we expanded westward. Those things were inevitable, or so they seem to us. We also take for granted the trends toward colonial unity and toward separation from England. Two hundred years of rationalizing the fact that the colonies did unite and declare their independence have made the event seem natural and inevitable. It would be interesting to know just what odds Lloyds or other less dignified sporting establishments would have given, back in the 1740's, that not one of these "obvious" events would ever take place.

But if the general trends of the period lack color for us, there was no such lack in the daily lives of the colonists. To a large extent in the towns and universally on the frontier they were doing creative work and they were doing it for themselves. Clearing forests, building roads and houses, launching ships, starting schools and colleges, most of what they did was new. Life was hard but adventurous. The strong must have found satisfactions that many of us miss to-day. Moreover, there was variety in colonial life. Even in the towns necessity made each man self-sufficient, or nearly so, and variety of employment was as great a blessing to the colonist as to the New England farmer of to-day. In addition the colonist must have been constantly aware that only a short distance westward or northward was unbroken soil promising relief to the unsuccessful and the adventurous alike.

The existence of the frontier was important, of course, throughout our history, but nowhere is it more striking than in the early eighteenth century, when town and frontier lay almost side by side. Here in New England such seacoast towns as Portsmouth, Salem, Boston, and Newport had become settled along conservative lines. An aristocracy, chiefly of wealth, was appearing, and the first half of the century saw greatly increased luxury and display in the towns. The invoices of Boston merchants showing large importations of broadcloth, silks, and satins, the increasing number of private carriages, the elegance of many houses and their furnishings, the inventories giving the extent and scope of private libraries, all show the existence of a prosperous, settled society somewhat more worldly than is sometimes supposed. The third generation in America had forgotten much that the first generation had held dear. The established church was gaining converts even in Boston and Salem, and the liberal revolt within the Puritan church itself could not be stopped. In the larger towns Puritan America was disappearing.

Only a short distance inland was the frontier. There the people struggled

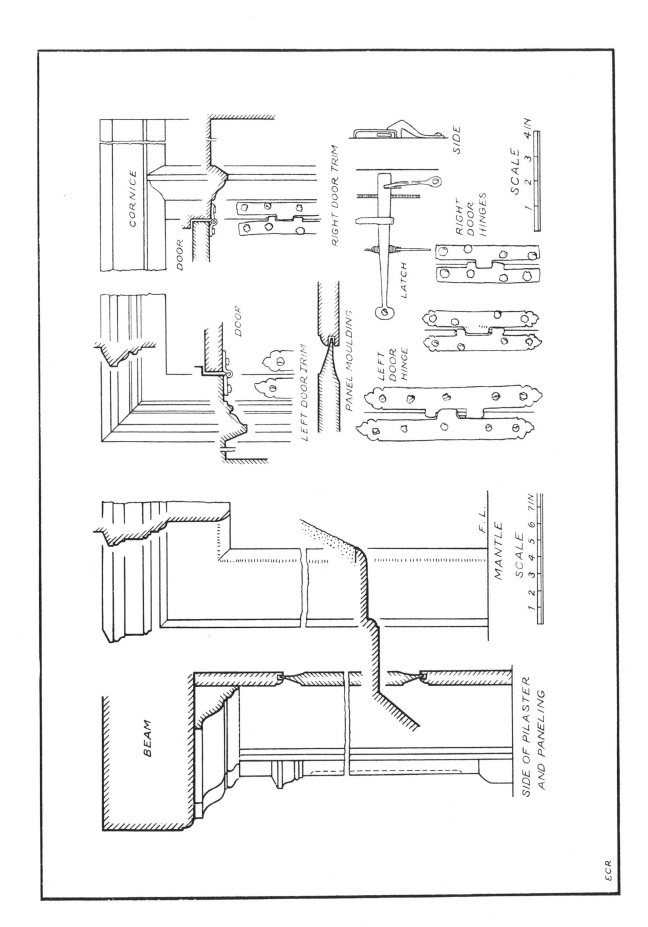

CORNICE

DOOR

RIGHT DOOR TRIM

SIDE

RIGHT DOOR HINGES

LATCH

SCALE
1 2 3 4 IN

DOOR

LEFT DOOR TRIM

PANEL MOULDING

LEFT DOOR HINGE

BEAM

MANTLE

F. L.

SCALE
1 2 3 4 5 6 7 IN

SIDE OF PILASTER
AND PANELING

ECR

against as great odds and lived as frugal an existence as had the settlers along the seacoast in the previous century. It is difficult for us to appreciate how short a distance and how great a difference separated the frontier from the wealthy and orderly towns. In 1702 the Indians killed an Englishman in Groton, thirty-five miles from Boston. In 1705 Lancaster was attacked by the Indians. Between 1728 and 1736 the Provincial Treasurer paid bounty on twenty-two hundred wildcats in Massachusetts. In 1734 Worcester was much troubled by wolves, and as late as 1757 Essex County was complaining that wolves and bears made sheep raising impossible. In Boston at about this time, Pelham's dancing school was flourishing, traffic regulations were being drawn up, streets were being paved, provision for oil street lamps was made, several booksellers had popular circulating libraries, and a Captain Goelet was attending the "consort" of four small violins, one bass violin, a German flute, and "an indifrent small organ."

Concord, twenty miles from Boston, must have been mid-ground between the old and the new at this time. It was near enough to the coast to keep in touch with the world of affairs and it was old enough to have passed through the crudities of pioneer days. Yet it was so close to the wilderness as to see and know it well. Probably it was fairly typical of the hundreds of small villages of the interior. In it would have been found a few houses of well-to-do people (in one of which the "Green Dining Room" of the Concord Antiquarian Society might have been found) and several houses little less primitive than those of the pioneers a day's ride to the west. During Revolutionary days and after, Concord acquired special dignity, but before that time there is little trustworthy evidence to distinguish her from other small towns similarly placed.

In describing a few details of life in rural New England, therefore, it should be remembered that they are probably as applicable to Concord as to other communities. Many European travellers of the early eighteenth century mention the vast amount of alcoholic drinks consumed by the colonists. One town of forty families put up three thousand barrels of cider in 1728. Another account states a minister was allowed forty barrels of cider for the winter. Those who could not afford cider, which cost only three shillings a barrel in Boston in 1740, made spruce, birch, or sassafras beer or concocted out of honey the popular metheglin. Some of the 1,260,000 gallons of rum made annually in Boston in the 1740's must have found its way inland together with smaller quantities of imported wines for the well-to-do. In their blissful ignorance of what constitutes safe drinking-water, perhaps they instinctively took the wiser course.

Smoking was almost universal in the colonies. In towns the long clay pipes called church wardens were most used, but in the country wooden and corn cob pipes were common. Cigars were little used before the end of the century, but the taking of snuff among the upper classes was general. In some towns smoking in public on Sunday was forbidden, but a more common regulation was to prohibit smoking within five miles of a church on the Sabbath. In one colony, a man making a journey of ten miles, presumably to church, was permitted to smoke one pipe in public.

Towns were required to have at least one tavern. On one occasion Concord was fined because no public accommodation for travellers had been provided. It was customary to establish the tavern close beside the church for the convenience of churchgoers between the morning and afternoon services. That the warmth and cheer of the tavern offered a pleasant contrast to the frigid meetinghouse is shown by the fact that some sextons were charged with the duty of emptying the tavern before the afternoon service began, and in other towns the tavernkeeper was required to close his bar a half hour before church began.

Most of the churches were more bare within than without. Neither light nor heat was permitted in New England churches before the end of the century. A few of the less hardy souls took foot warmers to church. One of these boxes of coals left in the church burned the First Church in Roxbury in 1747. Some ministers would not permit such luxuries, holding that "sinful indulgence of the body would tend to weakness of the soul."

Fireplaces were the only means of heating dwellings, but in 1744 Franklin's "New Invented Pennsylvania Fireplaces" were put on the market. The following extract from Franklin's advertisement of his new stove, though often quoted, is worthy of repetition:

In these Northern Colonies the inhabitants keep Fires to sit by, generally Seven Months in the Year. Wood, our common Fewel, which within these 100 years might be had at every Man's Door, must now be fetch'd near 100 Miles to some Towns, and makes a very considerable Article in the Expence of Families. The large open Fire-places used in the days of our Fathers had generally the Conveniency of two Seats, one in each Corner. These Fireplaces almost always smoke, if the Door be not left open. The cold air so nips the Backs and Heels of those that sit before the Fire, that they have no Comfort 'till either Screens or Settles be provided to keep it off; which both cumber the Room and darken the Fire-Side. Our Ancestors never thought of warming rooms to sit in. All they purpos'd was to have a Place to make a Fire in when acold. . . .

Franklin not only told the advantages of the new stove, but proceeded to refute the argument that sitting in a warm room would make one subject to take cold on going out. The whole pamphlet is well worth reading.

Private carriages were becoming more numerous, but they were still considered luxuries and therefore probably sinful. Reverend Joseph Emerson of Malden wrote in his journal in 1735:

Some talk about my buying a Shay. How much reason have I to watch and pray and strive against inordinate affection for the Things of the World.

A week later he wrote that he had bought the chaise for £27 10 s., but that his parishioners smile as he is drawn by in his magnificence.

The eighteenth century saw, along the seaboard at least, an interest in sport that a century before would have been considered ungodly. New England never devoted as much attention to horses as did the southern colonies, but one of the most famous breeds of colonial days was the Narragansett pacer of Rhode Island and Massachusetts. These horses were in great demand throughout the colonies and were even exported to England. Fishing in the seventeenth century had been largely a matter of necessity, and the Indian methods of spearing and netting were chiefly used. In the eighteenth century people gave more attention to angling, much of the tackle being imported from England. In 1732 "The Colony in Schuylkill," an angling society of thirty Philadelphians, was formed. Snares and traps were sometimes set for getting game, but gun and dog were more frequently used. Rifles were common, double-barrelled guns not uncommon, and several gunsmiths were experimenting with repeaters of one kind or another. Elk and buffalo were then found as far east as the Carolinas, though they had disappeared by the end of the century. Crévecoeur, just before the Revolution, complained of the absence of game in Ulster County, New York, and wrote of the good old days when game was everywhere abundant. In 1708 New York provided for a closed season to protect the heath hen on Long Island. The disappearance of game is not surprising, considering the slaughter that had been going on for a century. Cockfighting, then commonly called "cock-scaling," was not as common in New England as farther south, but Cotton Mather felt called upon to denounce it as one of Boston's principal iniquities in 1705. There are fewer mentions of card playing in New England than in southern accounts but, if the number of packs imported by Boston merchants is any indication, New Englanders knew one card from another. Shuffleboard, quoits, bowling, billiards, cricket, and several varieties of football were all popular games. Dancing was still frowned upon in many parts of New England, but in the larger towns, at least, dancing teachers seem to have had plenty of employment. There was much interest in music and considerable instruction was offered, but the ban on the theatre was not lifted in New England until around 1800.

Other conditions and customs of the period might well be mentioned, if space permitted, but perhaps these illustrate as well as any others the curious contrasts of the time. Along the coast prosperity and politics were supplanting religion in people's minds. The old forms persisted, but the spirit of Puritanism was dying. In the back country, however, in many places only a day's ride away, men were fighting the Indians and fearing the Lord as had the first New England settlers a century before. Their meetinghouses had their "foundations laide in ye fear of ye Lord, but their walls were laide in ye fear of ye Indians." The Green Dining Room is symbolic of the comparative prosperity and security of that section of provincial America which was just inside the slowly advancing crescent of log cabins and frontier conditions.

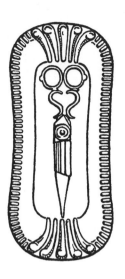

WALL A

KNIFE-BOX
BLACK LEATHER. PROBABLY ITALIAN

GATE-LEG TABLE WITH OVAL TOP
BEECH
Last quarter of 18th Century

BANISTER-BACK ARMCHAIR
MAPLE WITH ASH STRETCHERS
PAINTED BLACK
1st quarter 18th Century

Classic Columns Reach the New England Villages

THE old panelling from Burlington, Massachusetts, in the charming Green Dining Room at the museum of the Concord Antiquarian Society is dated, on grounds of style, between 1720 and 1750. The long panelled side of the room has been reconstructed very well, and beautifully repainted in the original color. Its proportions are unchanged. Opposite, the wall has necessarily a utilitarian character and does not correspond to the original layout in Burlington; the short unpanelled sides between correspond only in a general way to the original, yet the interior space of the room is characteristic in effect. The lighting is arranged to show the old panelling to the very best advantage, and bring out the excellences of the fine old furniture.

What are the peculiarities of this room? At first sight it appears as a formal design, with a touch of that delightful primness which the eighteenth century knew so well. A moment's inspection shows, however, that there is no real symmetry in the design, and that the classical-looking pilasters do not in fact conform to the classic norm. While it is perfectly true that there is a citified eighteenth-century air about the pilasters, they still have a clinging trace of Gothic freedom about them, and the same may be said of the panelling. The relationships there are not classic; the odd little diagonal reveal beside the fireplace is not classic. This room is, then, a rustic example of the combination of two great traditions—the Gothic not quite extinguished, and the Renaissance version of the classic not yet well understood—a stage reached in England a century and a half earlier, and in Italy three centuries earlier.

It will be worth while, perhaps, to consider the state of architecture at the period when the Green Dining Room was first built, for there was a most interesting interplay of styles at just that time, and an interesting lesson may be read from the relationship of this vernacular work to the more sophisticated examples.

A place is being made in architectural terminology for a "Gothic survival." The phrase covers just such unconscious reminiscences of mediaevalism as are traceable in this dining room. Here the Gothic is only a vague influence, discernible in proportions, oddly shaped panels, and unconventional mouldings; but in contemporary Europe there were much more fully characterized examples. The rebuilding of Orléans Cathedral is an excellent case in point. Gothic vaulting was still being built, unconsciously, in remote districts of France, England, Spain, and Spanish America; it was a degenerate, but a natural and unsophisticated continuation of the mediaeval. Obviously the main current of architectural style flowed far from these backwaters. To the great designers of the early eighteenth century the struggles between Gothic and classic were a remote memory. Brunelleschi, who created the early Renaissance in Italy, had been in his grave for nearly three centuries. Masterpieces like the Farnese Palace, the Massimi Palace, and the central parts of St. Peter's in Rome were already old buildings, and the reconquest of classical form and imperial grandeur represented in them had been the possession of the great exponents of the Renaissance for two centuries. The Baroque style initiated by Michelangelo had come to its gorgeous climax in the work of Bernini two or three generations previously—had indeed reached its very limit in the careful but extravagant and almost psychopathic work of the gifted Borromini. France, slow to abandon Gothic, had seen the Renaissance style established by the notable work of J. H. Mansart and his precursors, and so solidly established that the graceful French version of the Renaissance style became dominant in Europe as the eighteenth century advanced.

In England, where the Renaissance style was even tardier than in France, the great work of Jones and Wren was already accomplished, for St. Paul's in London was finished when the Green Dining Room was built. But from the very fact that the Renaissance came later to England, the Gothic tradition remained stronger there. Wren, in St. Paul's Cathedral, sought to "reconcile the Gothic with a better manner of architecture."

And interestingly enough, England saw the beginnings of a genuine Gothic revival in the early eighteenth century, before the last reminiscences of the old Gothic had quite died out. Hawksmoor, one of Wren's followers, designed All Souls College, Oxford, in the 1720's. The "Gothick" here was degenerate enough, but in the manner of its creation quite definitely to be distinguished from the unconscious Gothic survival work. Though surrounded by authentic examples of mediaeval collegiate Gothic, Hawksmoor attempted (like so many later revivalists) to build in a sort of cathedral architecture at All Souls—the two strange towers make that clear. There was a whole century of endearing absurdities like the older "Gothick" garden temples, the Batty Langley designs, Strawberry Hill, and Fonthill Abbey before the revived Gothic became a practical rather than a romantic part of the tradition of modern architecture.

It is easy to reproach the eighteenth-century attempts at Gothic for shallowness and decorative artificiality. But the reproach, if just, is equally to be levelled at the contemporary Renaissance architecture. It is axiomatic in architectural development that decorative formulas are generated from structural inventions as the styles successively run their course. Since the Renaissance had no really new structural problem of its own, its artists had to borrow their decoration, as the Romans had done before them in the corresponding phase of classic architecture. The great Italian Renaissance architects naturally borrowed Roman decorative elements to replace the mediaeval when the imported and half-understood Gothic structural system was cast aside. The inventive energy which would have created a new styl-

WALL B

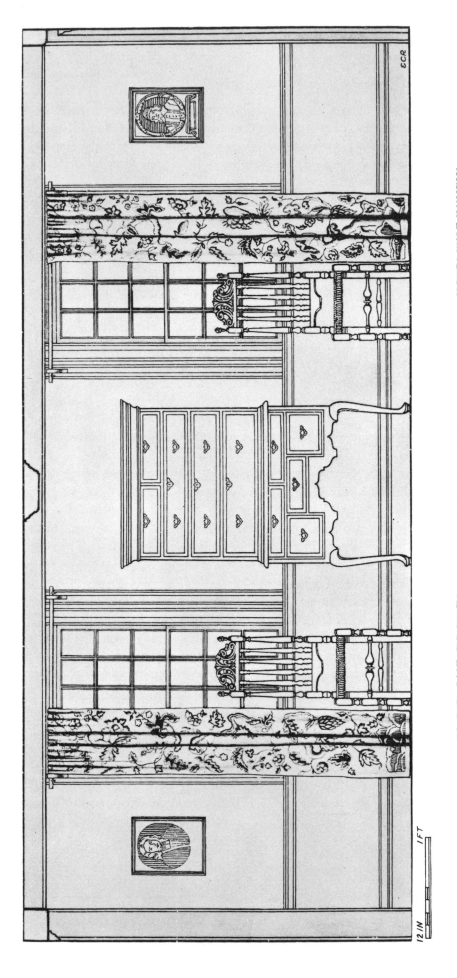

ECR

BANISTER-BACK SIDE CHAIRS
WITH CARVED CRESTINGS
1st quarter 18th Century

HIGH CHEST OF DRAWERS
WALNUT VENEER
c. 1720

CREWEL WORK HANGINGS
REPRODUCTION OF JACOBEAN EMBROIDERY

12 IN

1 FT

istic formula if there had been a new structural problem, produced instead the wonderful flowering of Baroque architecture. The superficiality of this style was in the very logic of the situation, and is in no sense a reproach, for this very superficiality made the marvelous decorative freedom possible. Once these possibilities began to be exhausted, however, it was inevitable that the architects and decorators should begin to seek other material to borrow. With increasing knowledge of architectural history (and the eighteenth century was an encyclopaedic age), the eclecticism of the nineteenth and early twentieth centuries followed as night and day. How widely is it known that Fischer von Erlach, perhaps the first man to design in the neo-classic style, produced an album of Egyptian, Chaldaean, Hebrew, and Greek, as well as Roman designs? The album was published in 1725.

Clearly, in European architecture of the Renaissance, the style developed through energetic contributions from individual men. The development did not proceed by constant minor improvements (although these did occur) but rather by the creative activity of an artistic élite. These men formed the successive styles by inventing the paradigms. The rules followed as a natural consequence, indicating the manner in which the creative inventions might suitably be applied. The great men affirmed their greatness by original work outside of and beyond the accepted formularies.

The process by which the Green Dining Room was produced, however, was quite a different one. In a simple, rustic, or folk art the rules of formularies have become a mere habit, and development is very slow, for commanding personalities rarely confine themselves to vernacular art. This art is a possession rather than a creation of the artist. The savorous fruit of generations of modest good craftsmanship and experience is to be found in a characteristic piece of folk art. The beauty of a well-made haystack, shelter, or cabin, and that of a well-thatched cottage represent practical and artistic impulses tempered by centuries of habit, judgment, and steady discipline. Any one who understands the simple people who make these things realizes that they are aware of beauty in them. So, on a somewhat higher scale, was the artisan who made the Green Dining Room from Burlington. The charm of that room is the charm of traditionally good and satisfactory volumes, proportions, and details, rooted deep in the building habits of these colonies. Into this complex, really a folk-art complex stemming from the folk-Gothic of early colonial days, we see the absorption of a sophisticated outside element, the pilaster. Whether it be considered that the room's pilasters represent Jacobean England, or an influence from the already citified architecture of the contemporary colonial centers, the same observation may be made: namely, that the sophisticated element loses something of its sophistication, and drops away from the accepted paradigms of formal architecture when it becomes a part of this vernacular design.

The whole kaleidoscope of styles which eighteenth-century Europe begot had its reflection here in America. Successive impulses came from abroad and affected our formal architecture. But the old colonial wood-framed style persisted as an indigenous tradition which absorbed, only to transform and modify (sometimes to vulgarize), the incoming motives. Our generation has thought that the homey mansion of the 1840's, the battened Gothic farmhouse, the "Hudson River bracketed," the strange mid-century "Americanese," and the shingled Richardsonian, were *not architecture*. Formal architecture they are not, indeed, but they were the citadel of the architecture which was genuinely our own. They were the basis and background of our American contribution to the new architecture. Wood framing used for all sorts of buildings, in the American way, prepared our architects and engineers to develop metal framing for ordinary structures, and thus to make a vital contribution to the new architecture. The unclassical freedom which the vernacular retained, while responsible for many uncouth designs, did in fact lead the way to the recognized new methods of architectural composition based on organically interpenetrating space-cubes.

Thus the Green Dining Room stands in a curiously interesting relationship to its contemporaries and to later architecture. It is still touched with the Gothic survival at a time when the Gothic revival is well begun in Europe. It timidly accepts the Renaissance pilaster at a time when neo-classic columns, Greek and Roman, begin to displace it in advanced European work. In so far as the pilasters represent a concession to the current formulas, they point toward the battle of styles which distinguished nineteenth-century formal architecture. But the vernacular part of the design is a link in the chain which led to Sullivan and Wright, men of real genius who transformed (or rather transfigured) our vernacular, and found in it rich gifts for an entirely new architectural style.

One is not always tempted to such far-flung ruminations when one visits this room in Concord. Its placid beauty, and the jewel-like light which plays through it, invite one to examine the room and its furnishings for their own sake and to live awhile in the period of the 1740's. To help us do this let us read the items of the inventory of Dr. Simon Tufts, of Medford, Massachusetts, whose estate was appraised in 1747. If we keep in mind the fact that he was far more than ordinarily supplied with worldly goods—for any man who owned thirty-eight chairs was running quite an establishment—we will get a very complete picture of the times without losing sight of the fact that in the average household frugality still dominated the scene.

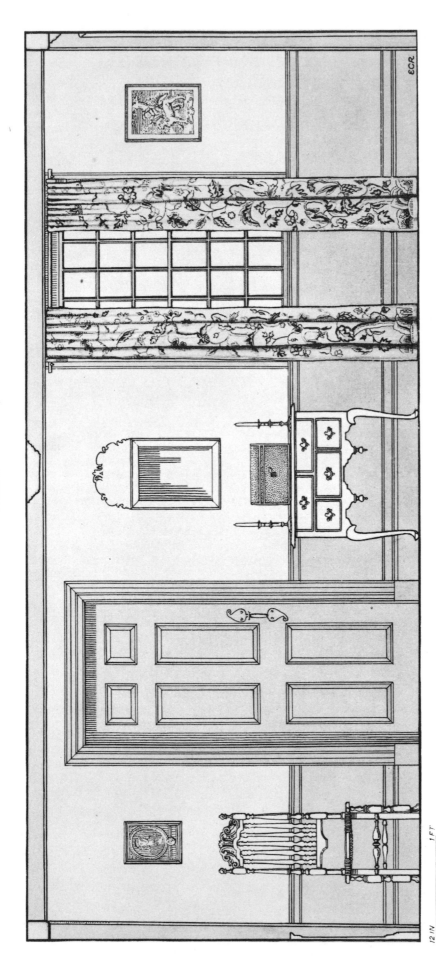

WALL D

LOOKING-GLASS
WILLIAM-AND-MARY STYLE, PROBABLY ENGLISH
WALNUT VENEER ON PINE
c. 1700

TRINKET-BOX, WITH RED ITALIAN VELVET COVER
ENGLISH. 16*th Century*

DRESSING TABLE
MAHOGANY AND MAPLE
1*st quarter* 18*th Century*

BANISTER-BACK SIDE CHAIR
MAPLE AND BEACH WITH
ASH STRETCHERS
1*st quarter* 18*th Century*

12 IN   1 FT

An Inventory of the Estate of Dr. Simon Tufts apprizd:

to a large dwelling house and barn with land adjoining the same in Medford near the bridge. Valued at the sum of — 2350— 0— 0

to a piece of land called the farm about ninety-five acres with a dwelling house and barn thereon, valued, together with a right in a wharf it being also in Medford, at the sum of — 2800— 0— 0

to a piece of land adjoining the burying place. About 2 acres — 200— 0— 0

to a piece of salt marsh about ten acres. Valued at the sum of — 400— 0— 0

to a Negro man named Pompey 250—0—0, another Abraham 150—0—0 — 400— 0— 0

to a watch 35—0—0, a large black walnut table 9—0—0, one less (large) 8—10—0, old one (table) 2—0—0 — 54—10— 0

to a chamber table and case of drawers 36—0—0, a small square table 0—18—0, an old table 0—5—0 — 37— 3— 0

to an oval table 3—0—0, square one 1—10—0, both in kitchen. Tobacco tongs 1—0—0 — 5—10— 0

to a fire shovel 1—0—0, two pair of tongs 1—10—0. Six old chairs in the upper chamber 2—8—0 — 4—18— 0

to a woolen wheel 1—0—0, a box 1—0—0. Fire shovel and tongs 1—0—0. Andirons a pair 1—0—0. Five maps 2—10—0 — 6—10— 0

to a gilt framed picture 0—10—0. Book shelves 0—5—0, five carved top black chairs 6—12—0 — 7— 7— 0

to a gilt framed looking glass 9—0—0, glassware 2—0—0, fine ware 1—10—0, tea pot 0—18—0, box 0—15—0 — 14— 3— 0

to an earthen case for knives 1—0—0, great chair 1—0—0, a trunk 1—5—0, pair of cards 0—16—0 — 4— 1— 0

to a case of drawers 4—0—0, a white chest of drawers 3—0—0, clothes hook 3—0—0, book case 3—0—0 — 13— 0— 0

to a desk 9—0—0, small table 1—0—0, six chairs white 2—0—0, great chair 0—15—0, child's chair 0—15—0, cradle 1—0—0 — 14—10— 0

to nine chairs 2—5—0, a wheel 1—0—0, great chair 1—0—0, seven throwback black chairs 3—0—0 — 7— 5— 0

to a round backed chair 0—18—0, a gun 6—10—0, a large looking glass 15—0—0, a standing candle stick 4—0—0 — 26—18— 0

to a pair of brass candle sticks and snuffers 1—10—0, six iron ones 1—5—0, eight pair andirons in middle room 0—50—0 — 5— 5— 0

to brass topp'd andirons 1—10—0, a pair of old andirons in the kitchen 2—0—0, two trambells 2—10—0 — 6— 0— 0

to two spits 1—14—0, a jack 16—0—0, bellows 1—0—0, dripping pan 1—0—0, a tender and flesh fork 0—10—0 — 20— 4— 0

to two forms 0—8—0, large brass kettle 15—0—0, a middling kettle 2—10—0, a small one 2—5—0 — 20— 3— 0

to three brass skillets 3—0—0, skimmer 1—0—0, a trivet 0—15—0, two gridirons 0—15—0, toaster 0—5—0 — 5—15—0

to a frying pan 1—5—0, an iron skillet 0—8—0, sieve 0—7—0, half bushel 0—10—0, three iron pots 4—0—0 — 6—10— 0

to two iron kettles 2—0—0, two pails 0—5—0, washing and brewing tub 0—14—0, steel yards 2—0—0 — 4—19— 0

to a warming pan 4—0—0, earthenware 1—0—0, glass bottles five dozen 8—0—0, five meat tubs 2—10—0 — 15—10— 0

to a churn 1—0—0, old casks and dozen chests 5—0—0, two cider barrels 2—0—0, three hogsheads 0—50—0 — 10—10— 0

to an old warming pan 0—15—0, old iron 3—0—0, knives and forks 4—0—0 — 7—15— 0

in the upper chamber—coverlet 4—0—0, rug 2—0—0, sheets 0—28—0, featherbed and bolster 23—0—0, underbedstead and cord 0—75—0 — 34— 3— 0

in the kitchen, a featherbed, bolster and pillows 23—16—0, underbed 0—35—0, bedstead and cord 0—25—0, blankets 6—0—0	32—16— 0
to a coverlet 5—0—0, two pillow cases 0—18—0	5—18— 0
little chamber coverlet 3—0—0, rug 2—0—0, green blanket 0—10—0, sheets 0—45—0, featherbed 16—16—0	24—11— 0
underbed 1—10—0, bedstead and cord 0—25—0	2—15— 0
in the west—rug 8—0—0, striped coverlet 0—30—0, blanket 0—15—0, sheets 3—10—0, bed 23—0—0, pillows, bedstead cord 0—50—0	39— 0— 0
in the front—counterpane 4—0—0, blankets 6—10—0, sheets 8—0—0, bed 23—12—0, underbed 0—48—0, bedstead rods 5—10—0, curtains 30—0—0	80— 0— 0
Negro's bed, bedding, bedstead, and cord	8—10— 0
to nine sheets 18—13—0, six table cloths 11—15—0, six diaper napkins 3—0—0	33— 8— 0
to three damask 0—25—0, seven pillow cases 4—9—0, twenty yards of Valdararaio 22—10—0	28— 4— 0
to a silver tankard and other vessels of silver 76—0—0, pewter dishes, plates, porringers 19—0—0	95—19— 0
to a lignum vita mortar 3—0—0, box irons and heaters 2—0—0, lanthorn 0—8—0, wheelbarrow 0—30—0, axe 0—35—0	8—13— 0
to an old chaise 20—0—0, great shovel 0—15—0, hoe 0—8—0, cane 0—30—0, wedges 0—30—0, broad hatchet 1—0—0	25— 3— 0
to a cart, wheels and ladder 12—0—0, large plow 4—0—0, a chain 2—0—0, two yokes 1—0—0, a sleigh 5—0—0, sled 0—30—0	25—10— 0
to a horse plow 3—0—0, two forks 0—12—0, four rakes 0—12—0, crow. 0—30—0, a morticing axe 1—0—0, spade 0—30—0	8— 4— 0
to a narrow axe 0—33—0, a great shovel 0—12—0, grindstone 3—0—0, two hoes 0—15—0	6— 0— 0
to a pair of old oxen 50—0—0, a young pair 42—0—0, cow and calf 20—0—0, a red cow 15—0—0, a brown cow 11—0—0	138— 0— 0
to a red and white cow 10—0—0, a large bay horse 45—0—0, little horse 20—0—0, colt 12—0—0, gray mare 12—0—0	110— 0— 0
to a velvet harness 3—0—0, two saddles and two bridles 12—0—0	15— 0— 0
to apothecary's drugs, pots, glasses, and with instruments for chirurgery	148— 3—10
to books	34—17— 0
to a pew in Medford meeting house	50—80— 0
	7294— 8—10

Apprizd by:
Capt. Brooks
Lt. Ste. Hall
Jos. Tufts*

May $\stackrel{e}{y}$ 26
1747

The Green Dining Room may be taken to represent just the sort of aristocratic household as was apparently that of Dr. Tufts. The spacious and well-fitted hearth, a powdering closet close beside it (now serving to store a collection of porcelain), and an old American banister-back armchair, still very grand in spite of cut-down arms and legs, make a pleasant group; the oval gate-leg table with its knife-box, the dressing table with its trinket-box dating from Queen Elizabeth's time, the high chest, the gate-leg center table, and the prim banister-back side chairs all add their meed of interest and charm to the ensemble, as do several old engravings, a fine old mirror, and the beautiful new curtains so carefully made in the eighteenth-century style.

* This inventory is in the possession of the editor.

CONTEMPORARY DOCUMENTS

Groton, Massachusetts, a Frontier Town, successfully implores the Aid of Governor Dudly in her Spiritual and Financial Difficulties in 1704.

To his exalancy Joseph Dutly esquir captain genarall comander in and over hur maiesties provines of the massacheusits bay in new Ingland and to the honorable counsil and raprasantitifes in genarall court asambled at boston this Instant desember 1704:

The humble patition of the Inhabitants of the town of groton in the county of midlsax in the provians aforesd humbley sheweth

1 That wharas by the all desspofing hand of god who orders all things in infinit wisdom it is our portion to live In such a part of the land which by reson of the enemy Is becom vary dangras as by wofull exsperiants we have falt both formarly and of late to our grat damidg & discoridgmant and spashaly this last yere having lost so many parsons som killed som captavated and som ramoved and allso much corn & cattell and horses & hay wharby wee ar gratly Impoverrished and brought vary low & in a vary pore capasity to subsist any longer As the barers herof can inform your honors

2 And more then all this our paster mr hobard is & hath been for above a yere uncapable of desspansing the ordinances of god amongst us & we have advised with the Ravrant Elders of our nayboring churches and thay advise to hyare another minister and to saport mr hobord and to make our adras to your honours we have but litel laft to pay our deus with being so pore and few In numbr athar to town or cuntrey & we being a frantere town & lyable to dangor there being no safty in going out nor coming in but for a long time we have got our brad with the parel of our lives & allso broght very low by so grat a charg of bilding garisons & fortefycations by ordur of athorety & thar is savral of our Inhabitants ramoved out of town & others ar providing to remove. axcapt somthing be don for our Incoridgment for we are so few & so por that we canot pay two ministors nathar are we wiling to liv without any we spand so much time in waching and warding that we can doe but litel els & truly we have lived allmost 2 yers more like soulders than other wise & accapt your honars can find out som bater way for our safty and support we cannot uphold as a town ather by remitting our tax or tow alow pay for building the savarall forts alowed and ordred by athority or alls to alow the one half of our own Inhabitants to be under pay or to grant liberty for our remufe Into our naiburing towns to tak cor for oursalfs all which if your honors shall se meet to grant you will hereby gratly in coridg your humble pateceners to conflect with the many trubls we are ensadant unto

whar fore your humble pationars humbly prays your axcalancy & this honared court to tak this mater into your seares confedration and grant releef acordingly and your pationars shall as in duty bound for evr pray

by ordur of the town of groton

JONAS PRESCOTT
JAMES NUTTING
JOSEPH LAKEN
SAMUEL PARKER

Jan^ry 2^d 1704 *Read.*

In the House of Representatives.

Jan^ry 3, 1704. In Anſwer to the Petition on the other ſide

Reſolved That there be allowed, and Paid out of the publick Treaſury, the ſum of Twenty Pounds, to the Town of Grotton to Encourage & Aſſiſt them in Procuring[?] another Miniſter, to help them under the preſent Diſability of their Paſtour Mr. Hubbard, & Ten Pounds more be allowed & Paid out of the publick Treaſury, to Jonathan Tyng Eſq. & Mr. Nathan^ll Hill, to be by them proportionably diſtributed to ſuch of the ſd Town, as in their judgment have been greateſt ſufforers, in the late outrage, made upon them by the Enemy

Sent up for Concurrence.   Jam^s Converse *Speaker*

    In Council.

4th January, 1704   *Read and concurred*

                 J. Addington *Secry.*

[Mass. Archives LXXI, 107, 108.]

The *Boston*-Gazette,

AND COUNTRY JOURNAL.

Selections from Issues of 1719-1725.

BY Letters from Paris of the 30th of March, we have an Account, that the Princess of Modena, Daughter to the Duke of Orleans, was so well recovered of her Distemper, as that it was thought fit she should begin her Journey for Italy. Tho' in regard to her being but weak, after so violent a distemper as the Measles had been to her, she should rest every third day, besides Sundays.

It was not thought proper that she should take her Leave of the King, for fear of the Distemper, by any remains of it about her, should affect his Majesty; which however was a very sensible Affliction to her. It is impossible to describe the Affliction which all the Ladies and Princes of the Blood appear'd in at their taking leave of her. The Princess fainted away three times in the Arms of those that came to kiss her and bid adieu; and particularly when Madam de Monpensier, her Sister, embrac'd her, she was long insensible.

The Regent her Father, could not bear the Passion she appeared in, and resolved not to take his Leave among the rest; but sent her word he would go the first days Journey with her, (viz.) to Essonne; which he did. The Princess parted the 11th, after Dinner, in one of the King's Coaches, drawn by eight Horses; the Dutchess of Villars Brancas being in the Coach with her. Her Retinue is the most magnificent and most numerous of any, that has been known in some Ages, except of a Daughter of France, as they call the King's Eldest Daughter; she is attended thro' the whole Kingdom, even to Antibes, by a strong Detachment of the Guard Du Corps, who are plac'd in Relays on the Road, to relieve one another. She has near a thousand Horses in her Retinue, including the Guards and their Baggage; and they tell us, the Expence of her Journey will amount to 1800000 Livres, including 400000 Livres which the King gives to the Dutchess that attends her, to bear her charges to Italy and home again. She is to be attended at Antibes by two Great Gallies and three Men of War, who are to land her at Geneva, or at Civitta Vecchia; as the Weather and her indisposition shall permit.

The same Letters from Paris give a long Account of the fall of the publick Credit there, and that their Stocks are now sunk almost 700 per Cent. nor has all the Wit and Art of Monsieur Law, upon whom they depended as infallible in those Cases, been able to support it. It is no wonder to have their Letters as full now of the lamentable Circumstances of Families, who now lose by the fall of the Stocks, any more than it was formerly to hear of the raising and Riches of others, by the first and sudden rising of the said Stocks; and if they go on and continue to fall, the Numbers also will be very great.

They continue to talk of great things which Mr. Law is to do, and today one thing is started, to Morrow another; but they come to nothing: And if it be only politickly withheld for a time, 'tis a very dangerous Policy, and Monsieur Law may chance to stay so long, till most of his Friends are undone by it.

That Gentleman is besieg'd daily by the importunities of the People to save them, if it be possible, from the ruin which threatens them; and he gives them good Words, and appears himself in the greatest Tranquillity imaginable; from whence some infer, that he is so absolute Master of those Things, that he is able to raise the Humour and Fancy of the whole Nation, at what time, and in what manner he pleases. But this present distemper of affairs seems to be above his Reach.

The Government of France have now brought their confus'd Projects in relation to raising and lowering their Coin, to a Point: The use of Money in France seems to be very much wearing out of Fashion; all the Gold Coin is cry'd down, and nobody is allowed either to take or receive it, or to keep it by them in Bulk; so that, in short, Gold is but Dirt in the literal sense, for we do not see of what use it is like to be in France; it is not only not to go as Coin, but not to stand still as Metal: No man is allowed either to keep it by him, or send it abroad; so that the poor people are like to be in more Jeopardy for having some Gold than the poorer part that are undone for want of it. It is almost the like in Silver, and in a word, by this new Edict or Arret, there is not a piece of money current in France, bigger or of more value than half a Crown; but then it is true, that to make amends they have sunk the Value of this small mony by degrees to such a low Ebb, that at last the Coin will be reduced as low as before the first rising of the Money by the late King; and if this be done while the Bulk of the Species is in the

Hands of the Government, it feems as if the Lofs would be borne by the Government, which is fomething extraordinary.

PARIS, Octob. 19, 1719.

There is much talk of an Expedition for attacking all the Spanifh Colonies along the Coaft of Mexico, beginning with Vera Cruz, and thence quite up to the River of Miffiffipi. Eight thoufand Land Forces are appointed for this purpofe, with as many Voluntiers of Louifiana as will go; and 'Tis thought this project will prove equally eafy and advantageous in its Execution.

Octob. 13, 1722.

The Small Pox continuing very mortal, they talk of inoculating them as they do in England. Some Doctors of the Sorbonne having been confulted about it, were of different Opinions, and the Sorbonne themfelves, when told of it, declared in general againft the Practice; neverthelefs we are affured that it will be put into Practice.

LONDON, Octob. 12, 1723.

Robberies are very frequent not only here, but everywhere throughout Europe.

PORTSMOUTH, New Hampfhire, July 8, 1720.

The Hon. Lieut. Governour Wentworth, and feveral Gentlemen that attended him, have had a Treaty with the Indians at Arrowfick about the death of a Penobfcot Indian, fuppofed to be murdered in this Province, and has by a prefent after the Indian Fafhion made up all Differences and Demands about that matter; and by the performance of feveral Rites and Ceremonies after the Indian manner, have entirely buryed the Indian, and blotted out the remembrance of that Affair.

LONDON, March 21, 1724.

The Watermen, who ply on the River Thames, being grown very numerous of late, occafion'd (as it is thought) by a long Peace, and their taking too many Apprentices, have petitioned the Parliament for fome Regulation in their Company, many of them being fcarce able to fubfift themfelves and their Families. According to fome Accounts, their Numbers (including Lighter Men) amounts to 9741 Men.

PARIS, May 12, 1722.

The Marquis de Lede has not appeared in Publick, neither at Court, nor elfewhere fince his Arrival in this City. Monfieur le Blanc, whofe Father was Harbinger to the King, having been ruined by the Miffifippi Bubble, attempted laft Week to make way with himfelf, by jumping into the River, but having been immediately taken out and Blooded, 'tis hoped he will recover : Such great Numbers of People have gone diftracted on Account of the Like Loffes, that we have not Mad Houfes enough to contain them all.

LONDON, September 24, 1724.

The Society for propagating the Gofpel in Foreign Parts, have purchafed a large Number of Common-Prayer Books, and other Books of Devotion, to be fent beyond Sea, for the Ufe and Meditation of the Reform'd Chriftians.

RHODE-ISLAND, Feb. 5.

Some of our Narraganfet Men have been out a Whaling and have met with good Succefs: laft Week they kill'd a Cow and a Calf; the former is believed to be worth between 4 and 500 l. which has given great Encouragement to others there to proceed on the like Undertaking.

LONDON, June 25, 1724.

The Duke of Bedford and the Lady Mary his Sifter, who lately had the Small Pox innoculated upon them; are both perfectly recovered, but the Dutchefs Dowager, their Mother, has the Natural Small Pox, & lies dangeroufly ill.

The River of Thames is fo fhallow, on Account of the dry Seafon of the Year, that People frequently ride over it on Horfe-back at Twittingham.

THE EARLY DAYS
OF THE CONNECTICUT COLONY

As illustrated by the LIVING ROOM OF THE ROSE HOUSE

North Branford, Connecticut

now in the Gallery of Fine Arts at Yale University

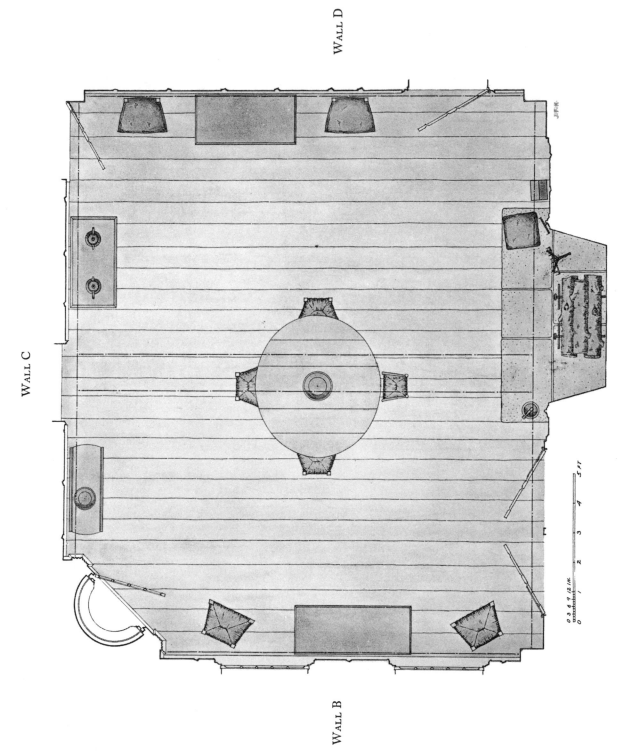

WALL D

WALL C

WALL A

WALL B

Historical Note

THE early days of the Connecticut Colony may be briefly summarized by the words struggle, perseverance, and courage. The first Connecticut settlers found a hostile wilderness inhabited by savage men and wild animals. To subdue this wilderness while protecting themselves from the Indians and the wolves was an undertaking that might easily have daunted the bravest of men. There is a well-known type of man, the pioneer, who is never at rest with himself except when blazing a trail across new frontiers. Usually he is a soldier of fortune who cannot adjust himself to any social group but who always must search beyond the horizon for adventure. The Connecticut settlers, however, were not of this type, for they were largely of the yeoman farmer class of England. Interspersed with this group were a few merchants and professional men, of whom the latter were mostly clergymen.

At first glance it would seem that a group of farmers led by clergymen would not be able to cope with the harsh conditions which faced the first settlers of Connecticut. Some strong emotion must have stirred them, to leave their English homes and venture their lives and fortunes, as well as the lives of those dear to them, in what must at times have seemed to them an almost foolhardy adventure. This emotion was a religious fervor which burned so strongly in the hearts of the leaders that it supplied courage and inspiration to most of the followers. They felt that they were the children of God and that it was their privilege as well as their duty to establish the Kingdom of God in this world and to live in accordance with God's will as recorded in the Bible. So strong was their zeal for the world to come that this world became a matter of small importance to them. They believed that the term of years which God granted them was only a period of probation during which time they were to prepare themselves for the rewards of paradise. The greater the hardships they were forced to undergo, the greater would be their merit in the sight of God. These impulses were the same as those which caused the great migration of the Puritans from England to Massachusetts in the decade from 1630 to 1640.

In considering this migration it is necessary to be cautious in one respect. While most of the settlers of Massachusetts and Connecticut were guided solely by religious emotion, there were a certain number who were also influenced by hopes of economic betterment. Most of this group heartily approved the religious convictions of the leaders, but they had an interest in this world as well as in the next and, while saving their souls, saw no sin in improving their financial positions. It is to be hoped that they were more successful in saving their souls than in their other ambition, because for many years after the founding of Connecticut hardship fol-

I~I

H~H

G~G

J~J

K~K

L~L

F~F

A~A

B~B

C~C

D~D

C

Elevation   Section

0 3 6 9 12 IN.
0   1   2   3 FT.

0   1   2   3   4   5   6 IN.

J.F.K.

lowed hardship and most attempts at trade and commerce were dismal failures. In the end almost every one had to turn to agriculture in order to provide enough food for himself and his family.

All of the original settlers of Connecticut came from England by way of Massachusetts. Several reasons can be given as to why these men were not satisfied with life in Massachusetts and why they made this second migration. As Massachusetts had been settled several years before the men who were to found Connecticut arrived there, they discovered upon arrival the best of everything already taken. The best fields for planting and grazing had been allotted to the earlier arrivals. The churches were already well supplied with ministers. The government had become a closed corporation which was reluctant to admit the newcomers to a voice in its management. Thomas Hooker, whose ideas of government did not agree with those of Governor Winthrop, was one of the first of the leaders to become dissatisfied with life in Massachusetts. He wished to work out his own ideas in his own way and to be independent of all authority except that of God. His followers agreed with him and, after a year of argument with the leaders of Massachusetts, permission was granted his group and the groups that founded Windsor and Wethersfield to migrate to the Connecticut River Valley.

John Davenport and Theophilus Eaton were the leaders of another group which also wanted freedom to develop its own religious and civil institutions. After a short stay in Massachusetts this group moved on to found the independent colony of New Haven. It is interesting to notice that this desire for self-expression continued after the original Connecticut settlements were made, and resulted in groups leaving the towns soon after they were settled and founding new towns. This splitting off of groups from established centers is one of the most characteristic developments in early Connecticut history and accounts for the growth in Connecticut of many small communities rather than the concentration of population in a few large centers. With miles of wilderness open to them for the asking, these men, possessors of determination and assurance, could see no reason for remaining in any environment with which they were not in perfect harmony.

Groups of small settlements cannot hope to have commercial or social intercourse either with each other or with the outside world unless adequate means of communication are provided. In early Connecticut transportation by road was impossible, the roads not even being worthy of the name. Commerce was limited to the rivers and to the seacoast, but as there was little money in the colony with which to build ships, even this means of intercourse never became as important a factor in the life of this community as in the neighboring colonies. Each town became, to a great extent, self-sufficient. Contact with the outside world was limited to cases of necessity. In the same way each family tended to produce only that which was needed for its own consumption, since the cost of transporting and marketing a sur-

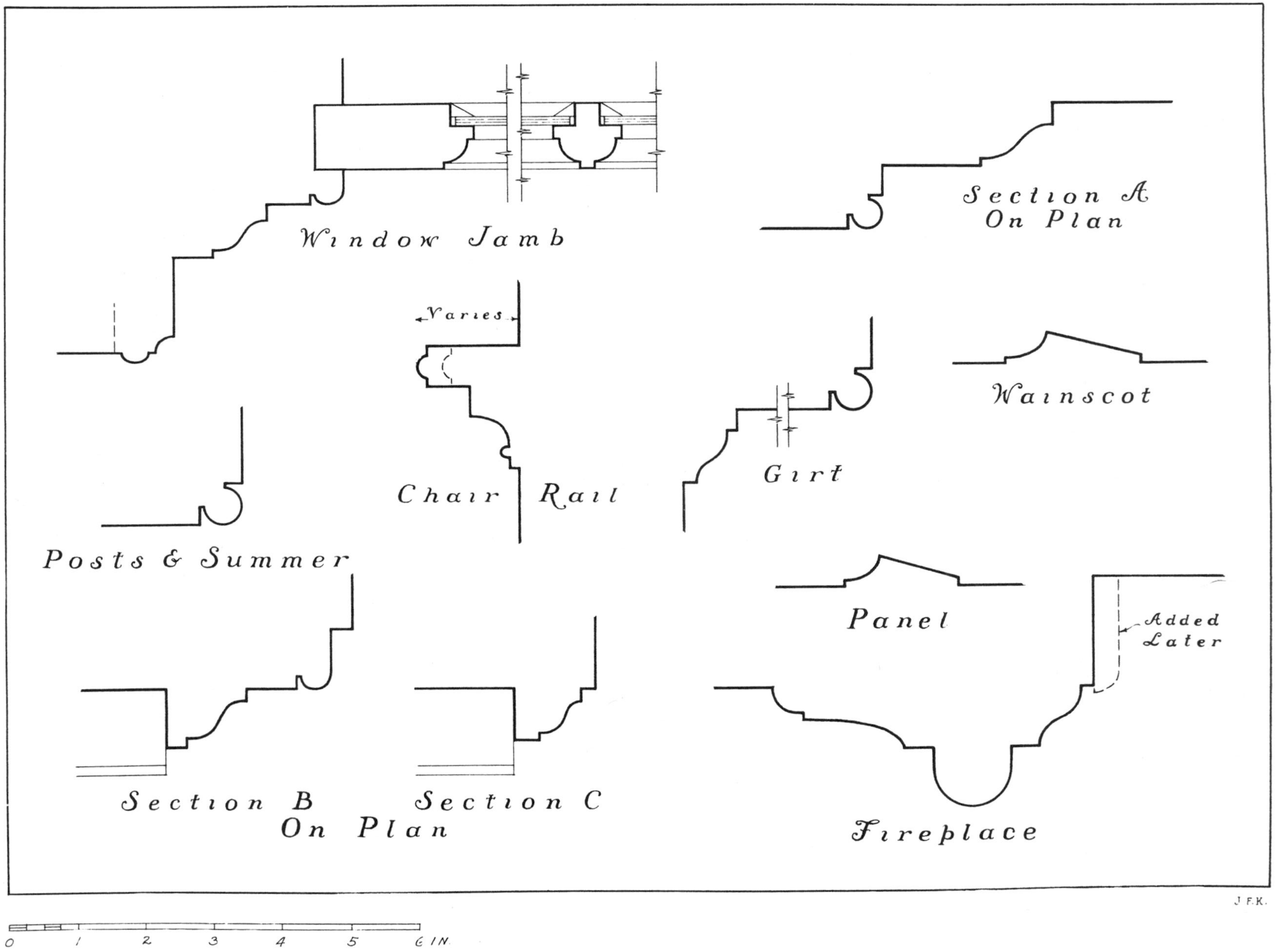

Section A
On Plan

Wainscot

Girt

Panel

Added
Later

Fireplace

Window Jamb

Varies

Chair Rail

Section C

Posts & Summer

Section B
On Plan

J.F.K.

0   1   2   3   4   5   6 IN

plus eliminated any worth while profit. Even if the problem of transportation could have been solved, it would have been difficult to produce a surplus because of the nature of the land under cultivation, which, except for that in the river valleys, was rocky and unfertile.

The unifying factors in the life of early Connecticut were the church and, to a lesser extent, the central government. The importance of the church cannot be overemphasized. Although many people had to walk five or more miles from their homes to the meetinghouse, every one was required to be present at services on Sundays as well as on other special days ordered by the General Court. In winter this requirement worked great hardship, somewhat lightened, however, by the fact that the period between the morning and afternoon services was the only time when friends could meet and enjoy social contacts. The remainder of the week was spent in hard work on the farms or in the homes. Aside from the social interval, the church services must have been grim affairs. For many years there was no heat in the churches, and the sermons were long drawn out.

As only the fit could survive the sufferings endured by the early settlers, there developed in a few generations a remarkably hardy group of men and women; and this is one of the reasons why Connecticut, in proportion to its size, has been able to produce so many outstanding men—men who have written their names across the pages of the history of the United States.

As a unifying factor, the central government was rather ineffective; yet it also played a part in the life of Connecticut. Its first important act was to declare war on the Pequot Indians, raise a military force, and provision it. The war, completely successful, ended in the practical extermination of the Pequots, thus permanently ending the Indian menace within the boundaries of Connecticut. All future Indian wars were fought outside Connecticut territory. The central government proved useful in other ways: by protecting isolated towns near the border from being absorbed by neighboring colonies, acting as a court of appeal to settle arguments between the towns; by granting permission for the creation of new towns; and by acting as the custodian of the charter granted by Charles II in 1662. Taking it by and large, the central government left as much power to the local authorities as was consistent with a stable government. In local matters the towns could do pretty much as they pleased, provided they could agree upon a sound policy of local control.

As this is a foreword to the Branford Room, a few words should be said about the settlement of the town of Branford. As soon as the followers of Davenport and Eaton arrived at New Haven they saw the wisdom of providing for future expansion. In consequence, on December 11, 1638, a tract of land between New Haven and Guilford was purchased from the Indians for "eleven coats of trucking cloth, and one coat of English cloth made after the English manner." The deed of sale was signed for the Indians by Montowese and Sausounck, John Clarke acting as agent and interpreter for the New Haven Colony. The following year Samuel Eaton, a brother of Theophilus Eaton, obtained a grant of this land from the Court and soon after sailed for England to organize a group of colonists for the settlement of this district. But owing to the conditions in England he was unsuccessful in obtaining followers, and for several years the territory, still unsettled, was used by the New Haven colonists for hunting and fishing. By 1643 a dispute in the church in Wethersfield had reached such a point that the migration of the minority group offered the only hope of settlement, whereupon this group, in the search for a new home, in October, 1643, purchased from Samuel Eaton his claim to this undeveloped portion of the New Haven Colony for an amount between twelve and thirteen pounds in excess of the previous sale. This district had been known as Totoket before the arrival of the Wethersfield settlers, but soon after the name of the settlement was changed to Branford, possibly after the town of Brentford in England from which some of the original settlers may have come.

It is interesting that Branford, which until 1663 was part, not of Connecticut, but of the New Haven Colony, was settled by men from the Connecticut Colony. Evidently the struggle in the Wethersfield church had become so bitter that the defeated group wished to leave Connecticut as well as Wethersfield, but they enjoyed their isolation only about twenty years, for the New Haven Colony was absorbed by the Connecticut Colony three years after the granting of the Connecticut charter, an act of aggression which was resented by the inhabitants of Branford and caused some of them to migrate to eastern New Jersey.

By 1710, the date given for the Branford Room, this feeling between Branford and Connecticut had died out, and it was mutually agreed that, as one strong colony was much better able to defend itself than two weak ones, the union of the New Haven and Connecticut Colonies had been beneficial to both.

The Branford Room is on exhibition in the Gallery of Fine Arts at Yale, a most appropriate place for it, for it was in Branford in 1701 that took place the founding of what later became Yale University. Tradition has it that each of the clergymen present at the ceremony, September, 1701—all of whom were to contribute a number of books as a nucleus for the college library—in turn placed his books on a table, declaring, "I give these books for the founding of a College in this colony." While Yale never was organized in Branford, being first in Saybrook and finally in New Haven, yet it is most fitting that this Branford Room, most likely very similar to the room in which so long ago the books for the Yale foundation were donated, should be preserved in the Yale of to-day.

WALL A

TIN CANDLE SCONCE

0 3 6 9 12

BANISTER-BACK SIDE CHAIR
MAPLE AND ASH
PAINTED BLACK
c. 1700

UPHOLSTERED WINDSOR STOOL
1720-1730

The Early Days of the Connecticut Colony

THE panelled and sheathed room from the Rose House in North Branford, Connecticut, and now in the Gallery of Fine Arts of Yale University, is of exceptional interest because it reflects certain radical and far-reaching changes that were taking place in the Connecticut house of its time. Its ascribed date of *circa* 1710 places the house from which it was taken in the fore part of the third period of Connecticut's domestic architecture; the two earlier periods extending from 1635 to 1675, and from 1675 to 1700 respectively. The outstanding characteristics of the first- and second-period work were its mediaeval quality and the domination of construction over ornamentation, which was altogether absent or sparingly used. With the advent of the third period in 1700 the use of ornament or decorative forms—begun in the preceding period—continued in a freer way, and the craftsmen of that time began to exhibit in their work a quality of architectural design that hitherto had been lacking. The Rose House room clearly illustrates this change, and shows as well the first uncertain groping toward the use of classic forms, for Georgian influence was just beginning at this time to find its way from old England to the shores of New England.

The room we are discussing—the parlor—was the "best room" in an unusually large house of lean-to type built upon a central-chimney plan. The room itself is large, accordingly, for a Connecticut house of its period, its dimensions being 16 feet, 5¾ inches, by 19 feet, 5 inches. We must regard it, then, not as a typical room of its time, but as one of more than usual pretensions. Indeed, its windows alone indicate this, for while they contain glass of the conventional 6 by 8 inch size, the sash are five rather than the usual four lights in width. The story-height of 8 feet, 1 inch, from finish floor to plaster ceiling is, as well, somewhat greater than might be expected in a room of this date. On the other hand, the use of plaster on the ceiling only is a bit difficult to account for, in view of the fact that this means of finish superseded wainscot very early in the New Haven Colony, within the jurisdiction of which this house stood. In fact, the records show that in May, 1641, a court order established prices "by the yeard" for plastering side walls and ceilings in New Haven.

The outstanding architectural feature of the room is its exceptionally fine corner cupboard, which occupies the conventional position, i. e., the left-hand corner as one stands with his back to the fireplace. Here it is apparent that the craftsman who conceived and built it was attempting—with no inconsiderable degree of success—a deliberate venture in the field of design. He was not satisfied to produce a mere shelved niche for displaying and storing articles of the household, he was determined to make it beautiful as well as useful. While the presence of slender, fluted pilasters, and mouldings, for the most part classic, impart an unmistakably Georgian flavor to the composition as a whole, it is apparent that its designer either failed to understand the conventional use of classic forms, or else was working from an imperfect memory of them. A lingering hint of Elizabethan times may be seen in the carved Tudor roses that adorn the pilasters—six-petaled as usual in Connecticut—and the beak-shaped moulding that appears in the group below the glazed door. The three broad bands of mouldings— at the level of the floor, the counter, and above the arched door—are singularly effective in tying together and unifying the whole design. Arched or "coffin-head" panels such as the lower doors display are typical, but the central light in the upper part of the glazed door, in the form of an inverted heart, is unique in Connecticut. Inside the upper portion, delicately fluted and reeded pilasters displaying carved rosettes form stops for the ends of the curved shelves, and show a graceful attenuation of form that appears to be surprisingly early.

Another Georgian note is evident in the handsome panelling of the fireplace wall, an unbalanced arrangement due, as usual, to the position of the chimney stack, but an altogether satisfactory one nevertheless. The arched fireplace opening —rare in Connecticut—is repeated in form by the broad bolection moulding that surrounds it, and still displays the generous dimensions of seventeenth-century work. The use of raised panelling on this wall necessitated the same treatment for the two doors which form a part of it, and this in turn, for the sake of uniformity, obviously determined the design of the other doors opening into the room. Otherwise, we might expect them to be of batten construction and made of the same matched wainscot as the walls in which they occur.

Another feature of the room is worthy of comment. The student of Connecticut's early architecture knows that in the beginning the structural members of oak, such as posts, girts, and floor beams, were frankly left exposed. Later, they were given a decorative treatment by means of beading or chamfering cut into them. Finally, they were hidden from view by a casing of pine. The builder of this room, having definitely embarked upon an architectural scheme of considerable elegance, found himself committed to an arrangement of cased structural members, although they still projected into the room beyond its finished surfaces. Accordingly, the corner posts, the girts, and the summer beam are all encased. The time had not yet come, however, to add mouldings to the girts and the summer beam, as became customary later.

The room is floored with oak, laid in unbroken lengths. The lack of greater width in these boards—which have never been painted—is difficult to account for, in view of the comparatively early date of the house. All the other items of interior finish are of white pine, no doubt of native growth. The paint that now covers the wood was found after the removal of many superimposed coats of other colors. The

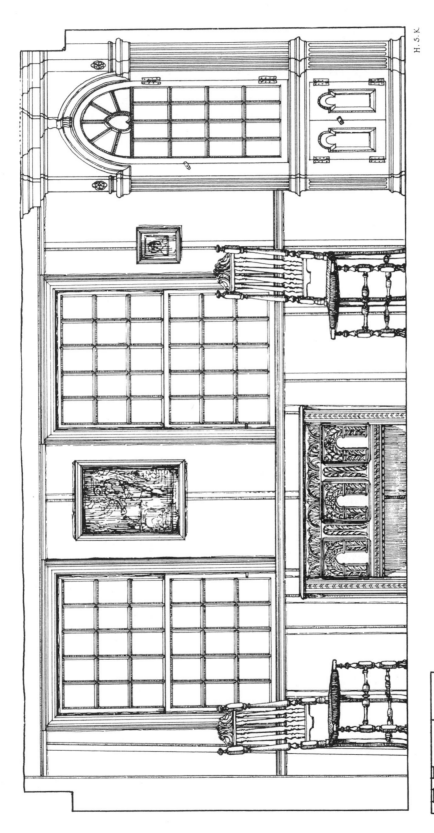

WALL B

PAIR (OF FOUR) BANISTER-BACK
SIDE CHAIRS
MAPLE AND ASH
PAINTED BLACK
c. 1700

CARVED AND PANELLED CHEST
OAK WITH PINE LID
c. 1675

BUILT-IN CORNER CUPBOARD
PAINTED THE COLOR OF THE
WALLS WITH TOUCHES OF RED

H. S. K.

window sash are white, the pilaster rosettes and the interior of the upper portion of the corner cupboard a pure vermillion. All else is painted a mellow greenish blue, possibly produced by adding a small amount of burnt umber or "Spanish brown" to cobalt blue. Whether this painting was done when the house was built or sometime later is a point that cannot be definitely determined. While we are aware that painting was, as a general thing, conspicuously absent from the interiors of seventeenth-century houses, there is no way of telling to-day when its general use began. In fact, even after the use of interior paint became common, certain builders failed to use it due to a want of means, and in such cases it was applied, perhaps, by a later generation.

Although the furniture that the room contains was gathered from other sources, it is of the sort that the house would probably have contained when built. For the better part it was staunchly made, and while oak, pine, and maple were the woods that entered principally into its construction, the use of cherry was beginning to creep in—a forerunner of the later and more elegant mahogany. Placed in the center of the room is a large gate-leg table with handsomely turned legs and stretchers; surrounding it are carved Cromwellian chairs with rush seats. Ranged against the walls are other chairs of the same sort, a smaller butterfly table, carved oak chests with pine lids, and an impressive court cupboard of oak. While oaken chests and cupboards such as these were no longer being made at the time the house was built, they were carried over from the seventeenth century and looked upon as household treasures due to their beauty, usefulness, and the sturdiness of their construction. The constant use of more than one generation was required to wear out such pieces of furniture as these. Although the floor is bare of rugs or other covering, a few engravings in simple frames adorn the walls. Here and there are items of pewter: a pair of lidded flagons, a great charger, smaller dishes, and basins. Two lanterns, such as are displayed in the room, are of the sort then in use; one is of tin and the other of wood, but both contain glass and burned tallow candles. The andirons and implements of the fireplace are iron, and it seems not improbable that they may have been forged at the very "bloomery" that was located not far from the house, at the foot of Lake Saltonstall. This forge was established with the help of the younger Winthrop in 1655, and continued in operation there for some thirty years. This equipment of the fireplace, like every other item and article in the room, bears the unmistakable appearance of being handmade. Door hinges and latches were of hand-wrought iron, and nails were forged out, one by one, on the smith's anvil. Mouldings were run by hand, with special planes made for the purpose. Despite the fact that the sawmill made its appearance during the seventeenth century in Connecticut, the practice of pit-sawing by hand persisted for many years. But by whatever means boards were made, they were always planed by hand until a very late date, and this method of finishing imparted a quality and texture to their surfaces that can be obtained in no other way.

One who enters the room cannot escape its atmosphere. Here is straightforward, honest construction; an air of simple dignity; the evidence of man's eternal quest for beauty. While the court of the "Sun Monarch" was blazing in false splendor in Versailles, against a background of gilt and mirrors and crystal, the men of Connecticut, such as those who built the Rose House, were gravely going about their task of hewing homesteads from the wilderness and helping to lay the foundations of a great Republic.

WALL D

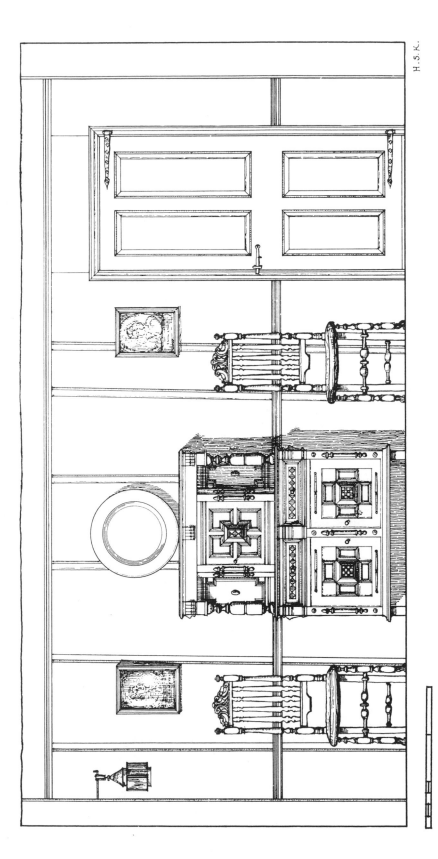

H. S. K.

TIN CANDLE LANTERN

PEWTER CHARGER
22 IN. IN DIAMETER

PRESS CUPBOARD
OAK, WITH INLAY AND
APPLIED SPINDLE DECORATION
Mid 17th Century

BANISTER-BACK SIDE CHAIRS
MAPLE, PAINTED BLACK
c. 1700

CONTEMPORARY DOCUMENT

*Selections from the Picturesque Report of the Governor and Council of Connecticut in
1680 in answer to the Twenty-Seven Questions asked them by His Majesty Charles
II's Committee for Trade.*

Our cheif Trade, for procuring of cloathing, is by fending what proviffions we rays to Bofton,
where we buy goods with it, to cloath us.

The trade wth the Indians in this Colony is worth nothing, for by reafon of warrs they have
wth other remote Indians they get little peltry.

Our principle Townes are Hartford upon Conecticutt river, New London upon Pequot River,
New Haven and Fayrefield by the fea-fide, in which townes is managed the principall trade of
the colony. Our Buildings are generally of wood, fome there are of ftone & Brick, many of them
of Good ftrength and comelynefs for a wildernefs, both thofe of wood, ftone & brick (many 40
foot long & 20 foot broad: & fome larger three & four ftories high)*

The Comodities of the country are wheat peas Ry Barly Indian corn & porck beif woole Hemp
flax cyder perry & Tarr deal Boards pipe ftaves horfes but to fay the yearly value of what is exported or fpent upon the place we cannot. The moft is Tranfported to Bofton & there Bartered
for cloathing. Some fmall Quantities directly fent to Barbadoes Jamaicah & other Caribia Iflands,
& there Bartered for fugar cotton wool & rumme, & fome money, & now & then rarely fome veffells
are laden with Staves peafe porck & Flower to Maderah and fyall & there Barter their comodities
for wine. we have no need of virginia Trade moft people planting fo much Tobacco as they fpend

Our wheat having been much blafted & or peafe fpoyld with wormes for fundry yeares paft
abates much of or trade

for the Materialls for Shipping here is Good Timber of oak pine & Spruce for mafts oake
Boards & pine boards & Tarr & pitch & hemp. (Some fayle Cloth is allready made in thefe parts,
but no great quantity.)*

The value of the comodities imported yearly we cannot compute, but poffibly it is 8 or 9,000 £.

In or colony there are about 20 petty merchants Some trade only to Bofton fome to Bofton
& the Indies, others to Bofton & New York, others to Bofton, the Indies & Newfoundland. As
for forraighn merchants, few & very feldom trade hither.

There are but fewe Servants amongft us & Lefs Slaves not above 30, as we Judg in the
colony.... & for Blackes there comes fometimes 3 or 4 in a year from Barbadoes: and they are
fold ufually at the rate of 22 £ apeice, fometimes more & fometimes lefs according as men can
agree with the mafter of veffells or merchants that bring them hither.

As to the eftates of the merchants we can make no guefs of that: but as for the eftates of the
corporation in generall it doth amount to 110,788 £. Houfes are fo chargeable to maintaine
that they are not valued in the above mentioned fumm.

it is rare any veffells com to trade with us but what come from Maffachufets Colony or N.
yorke, but fundry of their veffells doe come & Tranfport or proviffions for or Merchants to
Bofton.

Selection from Connecticut Archives, *Document 19, Volume I, Series I.*

---

* The words in parentheses are crossed out in the original document.

Newbury Burks, Septemb. 4, 1714

The Duke of Marlborough passed by us on the 12th of August in his way to Bath to see the Duchess of Sunderland. About 40 or 50 Horses met him Three Miles out of Town, and Rode with him a quarter of a Mile beyond Hungerford, in all about Ten or Twelve Miles. The Duke stop'd his Coach for 'em to take leave of him; and then the Reverend Mr. Joseph Standen the Present Pastor of the Dissenting Congregation in Newbury, Address'd his Grace in the following Words.

My Lord Duke of Marlborough.

I Hope your Grace will Pardon our attending you in so disorderly a manner, but tis something natural for Joy to be a little Tumultuous. We have taken the Liberty of waiting on you so far, to do an Honour to our Selves, much more than to your Grace. We are Overjoy'd (Contrary to the Reports we had Heard) to find your Grace in so good a State of Health, and to see you again amongst us, My Lord, at such a Critical Time, when if our Old Enemy should attempt to disturb us; Your Grace's Name alone would be Superior to any Force he will be able to send against us. We wish Your Grace a Continuance of your Health and a Long and Happy Life: But should we wish your Life as long as it is glorious, we should wish you never to Die. But you will live in the Hearts of Honest Men after all the Monuments that shall be Erected to your Memory shall be Moulder'd into Dust.

His Grace Answered,

I hope my Intentions have been Sincere for the Good of My Country. I desire you to give Thanks to those who have taken the Pains to come along so far with me.

At Bath the Duke was met by about a Hundred Gentlemen, well Mounted, Four or Five Miles out of the Town.

St. James, April 17, 1714

The following Address from the Colony of *Connecticut*, was presented to Her Majesty by the Right Hon. the Lord Viscount *Bolingbroke*, One of Her Majesty's Principal Secretaries of State.

To the QUEEN's most Excellent Majesty.

The Humble Address of the Governour and Company of Your Majesty's Colony of *Connecticut* in New-England.

May it please Your Majesty

We Your Majesty's most dutiful Subjects, having in obedience to your Command, Proclaim'd the Peace Your Majesty has made with France, humbly beg leave, on so joyful an Occasion, to approach Your Sacred Presence with our most dutiful Acknowledgements of Your Majesty's great Wisdom and Goodness, which have so bright an Appearance in the Happy Fruits of this great Blessing to Your People.

In the midst of Your Triumphs over the utmost Force and Power of Your Enemies. Your Majesty has prefered the Ease and Tranquility of Your Subjects to those Increasing Glories of Your Arms.

While we adore the Favour of Heaven, which has inspired Your Majesty's Councils in this great Affair, and crown'd them with a Success so Desirable and Glorious; We come with a profound Devotion to render at Your Feet, our Tribute of Gratitude and Obedience for the tender Regard Your Majesty has therein shewn, to the most valuable Interests and Prosperity of Your People.

This must remain a Testimony to all the World, of the Satisfaction Your Majesty has in the Weal of Your People.

And there is now no greater Blessing for us to wish ourselves, than that Your Majesty may long enjoy the Comfort of so Divine a Pleasure, Increas'd by the fervent Zeal of Your Happy People, to express, with the greatest constancy, a most entire Acquiescence in Your Majesty's consummate Prudence and a most Cheerful Obedience to Your Government, as the only way to perpetuate so great an Happiness.

For this we make our incessant Vows to Heaven, and are with a most devout and resolved Fidelity, Madam, Your Majesty's most dutiful and most obedient subjects.

Which Address Her Majesty received very graciously.

Boston, On Thursday last the 22nd Currant, a Countryman brought to Town a Cart load of Turnips to be sold, and at the Dock in Boston before the Warehouses, one of the Merchants observed the Country mans half Bushel not to be agreeable to the Standard the Law directs in that behalf, complaint whereof being made to one of Her Majesties Justices of Peace, the Country man's Measure was ordered to be broke in pieces, and the Turnips that were unsold to be given to the Poor, which was accordingly done.

Pokanoke, Maryland, May 19. There is an Old Woman near a Hundred Years Old, call'd Widow Quillin, born in England, who has lately Three very Fair Teeth sprung up in her Mouth, where she has not had one for above Twenty Years before. (What is here inserted comes from a Credible Hand, and attested by some now in Boston.)

Simon Harcourt Esq. (Son to the Right Honourable Simon Lord Harcourt, Lord Chancellor of Great Britain) is gone over to Montpellier in France for the benefit of the air.

Here also follows a Remarkable Piece of News from London in July Last.

We have now alive and in good health at the Merchant Taylors Alms-House on Little Tower Hill Anne Schrimpshaw the Daughter of Thomas Schrimpshaw Wool Stapler. She was born in the Parish of St. Mary Le Bow London, April the 3rd Anno Domini 1584, being now 127 years of Age, and so great a Rarity that Her Majesty was pleased to make her a Visit.

Yesterday morning George Chesley of Oyster River was Intercepted as he was going to Mill by 7 Indian Enemies that appeared, who first shot his Horse, wounded himself, and then knock'd him in the Head; and for haste to fly into the Woods, being a little space off the Garrison, they left his Arms lying by his side.

Our Rivers are all Froze up, so that we have no Vessels arrived, nor Entered and Cleared this Last Week.

By his Excellency, Joseph Dudley, Esqr. Captain General and Governour in Chief, in and over her Majesties Province of the Massachusetts Bay, in New England: A Proclamation.

GENERAL FAST.

Upon Consideration of the Vast Importance of the Affairs of the present Summer in Europe, referring to the further Prosecution of the War, or Treaty of Peace; and of the Distresses of this Province by the Calamitie of War, and the present sore Drought and Worms, awfully threatening the Fruits of the Earth, as a just punishment for our Unfruitfulness, of refusing to be Reformed.

I have thought fit by & with the Advice of her Majestie's Council, and at the Instance of the Representatives of the present Session, to appoint a General FAST to be observed throughout this Province, upon Thursday the Fifteenth of June currant, strictly forbidding all Servile Labour thereon; and Exhorting that Ministers and People in their respective Assemblies on the said day, with humble penitential Confession of our manifold Sins and Transgressions and sincere and fervent Supplications to Almighty God, implore the Divine Mercy for the following Desirable Blessings. That is to say, that the Sacred Person of our Sovereign Lady the QUEEN may always be under the Divine Protection, and preserv'd against all ill attempts and Conspiracies, Her Life long continued, and Her Majesties Just Arms with those of her Allies be crown'd with glorious Victories and Successes; and all overtures for Peace be graciously directed; That Her Majesties Commands for the Provinces may speedily arrive to us, and be attended with Success, that our Frontiers & Sea-crafts may be under the Protection of Heaven; Infectious mortal Sicknesses be kept out from us; that our Prisoners in the hands of the Enemy may not be poysoned with the Romish Religion, but soon Returned home; That God graciously pity us with respect to the Drought and Devourers; speedily and plentiful Rain for refreshing the thirsty Earth, revive the languishing Fruits thereof & Rebuke the Worms and Insects; Grant His gracious direction to the Government, and his Blessing on all their just Administrations; That the Spirit of Grace may be poured out upon all Degrees and Orders of persons among us; that the true Protestant Religion may be propogated throughout the whole Earth.

Given at the Council Chamber in Boston upon Friday the Second of June 1710. In the Ninth Year of the Reign of Our Sovreign Lady Anne by the Grace of God, of Great Britain, France and Ireland QUEEN, Defender of the Faith, etc.

By order of His Excellency,
with the advice of the
Council & Assembly,
Isaac Addington Secr.   J. DUDLEY

God Save the Queen

Advertisements.

THis is the last day of the second quarter since the Revival of the News-Letter the first of January last, which had been dropt for eight Months after five years experience, for want of any Tollerable encouragement to support it; which was again set on foot at the desire of several in this and the Neighbouring Provinces, particularly of the Town of Boston, in hopes of meeting with a far better reception both from public and private hands, for its present support, and future continuance which hitherto it has not met with; However the Undertaker intends to carry it on till January next (Life permitting) for a further tryal, and such who have not already paid in their first and second Quarters payment, are now desired to pay or send it; and all such who have a mind to encourage the said Letter of Intelligence may agree either by work or Writing with *John Campbell*, Post-Master of New-England, at Boston, who shall favor them on reasonable terms.

RAn-Away from his Master *Robert Rumsey* at Fairfield in Connecticut Colony, on the 27th of March last, a negro man call'd *Jack*, a tall thin fac'd Fellow, exceeding black, a considerable scarr on his face, can play on a Violin, he hath carried his Fiddle with him, and a considerable bundle of Cloaths. Whoever shall apprehend the said Runaway Negro man, and him safely convey to his said Master, or give any true Intelligence of him, so as his Master may have him again, shall be sufficiently Rewarded, besides all necessary Charges paid.

THE RICH DETAIL
OF THE CONNECTICUT VALLEY

As illustrated by the PARLOR FROM NEWINGTON, CONNECTICUT

now in the Metropolitan Museum of Art in New York City

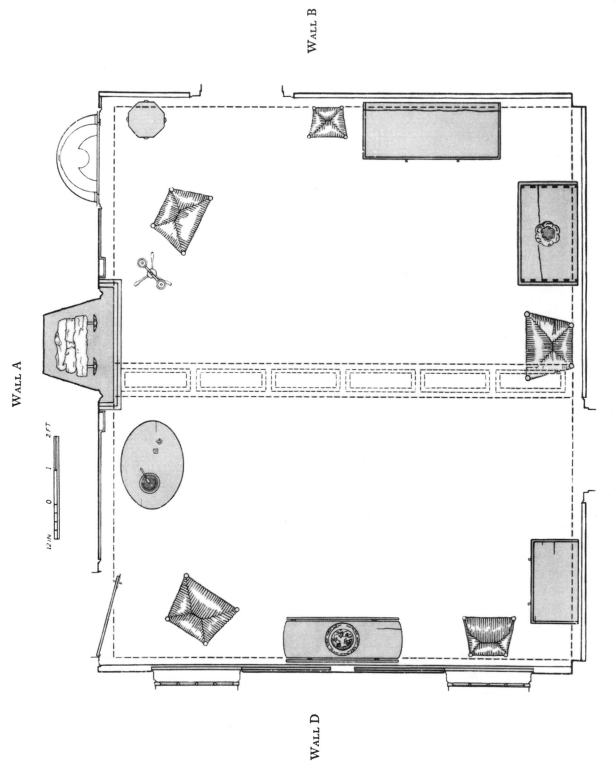

WALL A

WALL B

WALL C

WALL D

12 IN   0   1   2 FT

Historical Note

IN reading the various histories of Connecticut, written in the last century and a half, one is impressed by the emphasis given to particular periods. That from the founding of the colony about 1635 to the granting of the Connecticut charter, in 1662, has been adequately covered. The attempt at the suppression of the charter by Governor Andros and his final discomfiture, from 1686 to 1689, have been discussed by many writers; also the part played by Connecticut in the Colonial and Revolutionary wars has been carefully recorded. Yet between the downfall of Andros in 1689 and the beginning of the Revolutionary War in 1775 lies a period of almost ninety years, of which little has been written, save for the part played by Connecticut in the French and Indian War.

The reason for the neglect of this period is easy to discover. Until recent times historians have been more interested in dramatic events such as wars or violent changes of government than in the social or cultural life of peoples; whereas the history of Connecticut through the first seventy years of the eighteenth century was devoid of dramatic incidents. During all these years no wars were fought on Connecticut soil, nor was there any change of any importance in the form of government. The life of the average Connecticut family changed but little between 1700 and 1775. A few persons acquired greater economic security as the years passed, but less change occurred in Connecticut than in Massachusetts and Rhode Island, where Boston and Providence became important commercial centers and wealth was accumulated through trade with England and the other colonies. During this period Connecticut was gaining for herself the reputation as the land of steady habits.

The government of Connecticut during the eighteenth century was controlled by a small group of men whose rule was not questioned by the majority of the people. At its head was the governor, who had limited power but exercised considerable personal influence. He was chosen by the freemen for a term of one year but was almost always re-elected until either serious illness or death ended his career. Without exception, the governors of Connecticut were men of integrity against whom there was never a breath of scandal. They were required to be church members; also they were of the extremely conservative type who believed in the established order and not in experimentation. In a large degree the Connecticut colonial governors typified the spirit of colonial Connecticut. The great mass of the Connecticut people, religious, God-fearing, and opposed to sudden change of any kind, found in their governors their civil ideal as they found their religious ideal in their clergymen.

The governor was aided by a council composed of the deputy governor and a

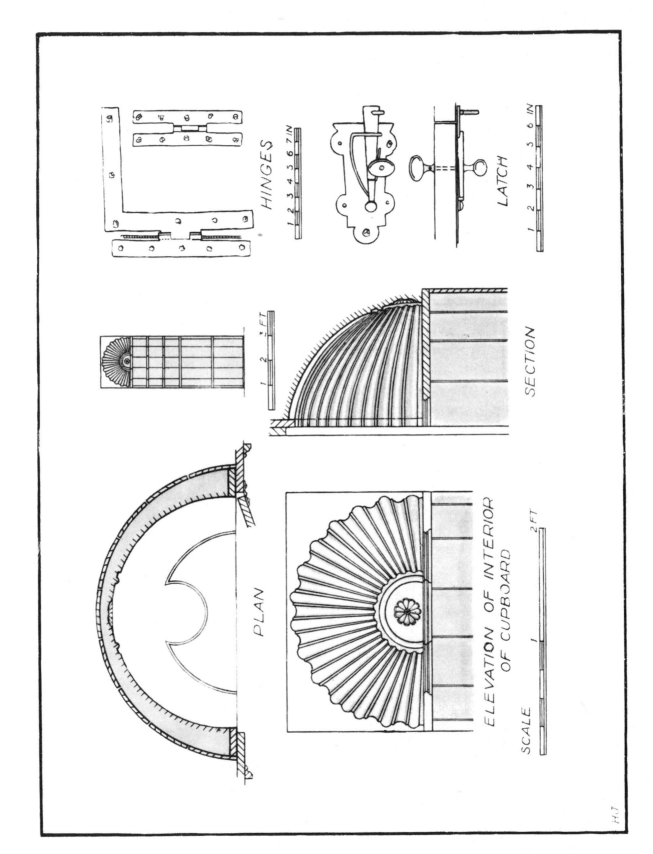

HINGES

1 2 3 4 5 6 7 IN

LATCH

1 2 3 4 5 6 IN

SECTION

1 2 3 FT

PLAN

ELEVATION OF INTERIOR
OF CUPBOARD

SCALE 1 2 FT

group of men known as assistants or magistrates, elected in the same manner as the governor, the number of whom was usually ten but varied from time to time. When the governor died, the new governor was chosen from among the assistants. Usually the deputy governor was promoted to the governorship, while the senior assistant, in point of length of service, became the new deputy governor. The deputy governor and assistants were re-elected year after year without question and without the political struggle of modern times. There was only one political group in colonial Connecticut, the orthodox conservative group, and it was taken for granted that the members of this group would govern the colony honestly and to the best of their ability. In this expectation they did not disappoint the people of Connecticut.

The franchise, as applied to colonial officials, was very limited. Only those who could meet a property qualification and who would take the freeman's oath, which declared a belief in the doctrine of the Trinity, were qualified to become freemen; and only freemen could hold colonial office and vote for colonial officials. Thus it is evident that colonial Connecticut was not a democracy, but a religious oligarchy ruled by a small group composed of the ablest men in the community, members of the Congregational church.

Besides the governor and assistants there was another group of colonial officials known as deputies. They were elected by the freemen of the towns, each town electing one or two deputies. The entire group of deputies composed the lower house of the colonial legislature, while the assistants composed the upper house. To pass any measure it was necessary to obtain an affirmative vote from both houses. As it was often difficult to obtain an agreement between the two houses, much legislation which would have proven of value to the colony was never enacted. On the other hand, the necessity of an agreement between the houses prevented any sudden or ill-advised legislation.

There is little to be said of the history of Connecticut in the eighteenth century. By 1700 the form of government under the charter was well established. Almost the only contacts Connecticut had with England were with respect to the charter and to matters of trade and commerce. During this period several attempts were made in England to vacate Connecticut's charter and to reduce her to the status of a royal colony with an English appointed royal governor. It is interesting to notice that of all the English colonies in North America, some of which had been founded as royal colonies, some as proprietary colonies, and some as corporate colonies, only Connecticut and Rhode Island were able to preserve their charters until the outbreak of the Revolutionary War. The English government wished to unify the colonial governments of the various colonies, and usually succeeded in its attempts to do so. The reason why the Connecticut charter was not vacated was due partly to the fact that Connecticut made itself as inconspicuous as possible in the sight of

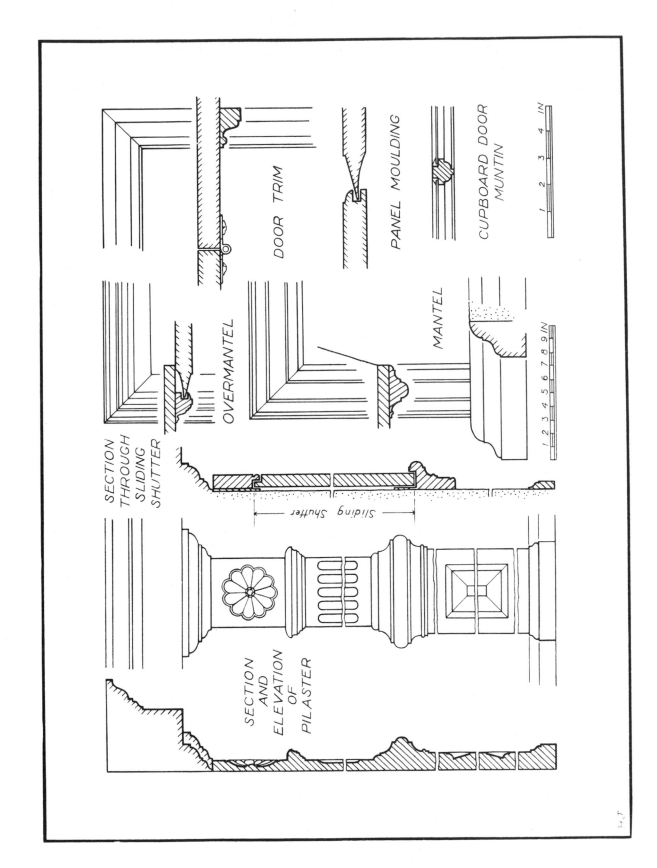

DOOR TRIM

PANEL MOULDING

CUPBOARD DOOR
MUNTIN

1 2 3 4 IN

OVERMANTEL

MANTEL

1 2 3 4 5 6 7 8 9 IN

SECTION
THROUGH
SLIDING
SHUTTER

Sliding Shutter

SECTION
AND
ELEVATION
OF
PILASTER

the English government and also that during this period a strong feeling grew up in the English Parliament against tampering with chartered rights, except in cases of the utmost gravity. Furthermore, when a chartered colony changed its status to that of a royal colony, the power of the king was by so much increased at the expense of Parliament, a fact that also played an important part in the preservation of the chartered rights of Connecticut.

And no wonder Connecticut valued her charter highly, because under it she had almost entire local self-government. The only English appointed officials on Connecticut soil were the customs collector and the naval officer at New London. Every other public official in Connecticut was a native of Connecticut and derived his power from the local Connecticut government. In consequence of this internal independence, Connecticut, when the Revolution came on, was the only English colony which continued under its same governor and under the same form of rule. The only change was the denial of any allegiance to the English government and the elimination of the English customs collector and naval officer, who were replaced by Connecticut men.

The district which now composes the town of Newington was originally part of the town of Wethersfield, and its development is typical of the growth of many of the Connecticut towns. Sowheag, an Indian chief, sold to the Wethersfield settlers the vacant land between the towns of Farmington and Wethersfield, and this tract remained unsettled until committees from these two towns established a boundary line. In 1671 the inhabitants of Wethersfield divided what is now Newington into seventy-six shares or lots, one for each of the "householders of the town that lived on the west side of the river." Another division of public lands was made in 1694. By 1708 the settlement of Newington had progressed to such a point that its inhabitants petitioned to have the privilege of a separate church. This was not granted, but in 1710 permission was given to hold church services during the winter months. By 1712 the demand for their own church had reached such strength that it had to be granted and the doing so brought on the only conflict in the local history of Newington. A difference of opinion arose as to where the meetinghouse should be built, owing to the fact that there had grown up within the limits of Newington two small villages, each of which wished to have the building as near it as possible. The difficulty was finally settled by permitting a part of the Newington parish to secede and join the main parish of Wethersfield. In compensation, a certain part of Farmington was annexed to Newington.

Newington throughout the colonial period remained part of the town of Wethersfield and, as we have said, its history was typical of many of the small Connecticut towns. Agriculture was the chief interest of its inhabitants and a peaceful life on a moderately fertile farm was the general rule. An amusing story which gives an insight into the type of man who lived in Newington in the colonial period is that of a Mr. Andrus. He was of the God-fearing type, who had enough of the old-time Puritan spirit within him to fear that his life was too pleasant, that he was thinking more of this world than of the world to come, and that he had not experienced unhappiness in this life to be worthy of eternal rewards. Therefore, after considerable thought he determined to marry the most disagreeable woman he could find and so through unhappiness in this world find salvation in the next. After his marriage his friends asked him why he had married such a woman. Andrus told his story which in time was repeated to his wife. Whereupon she in a spirit of anger and revenge stated that her bad temper could not be used as a means to salvation for her husband and became one of the most pleasant and thoughtful of women. Whether Andrus was satisfied with this change in his wife is not known.

This story is interesting in that it shows, even in the middle of the eighteenth century, how strong in Connecticut was the Puritan faith and how much progress towards a happy and contented life had been made there since the period of settlement. In the century from 1635 to 1735 the land had been cleared and farming had proved itself profitable in the river valleys. Danger from the Indians had been eliminated. In the settled parts of the colony the wild animals had been exterminated, and as the years passed a slow but steady growth of population was accompanied by economic improvement. Houses became larger and more comfortable, although until the invention of the Franklin stove they must have been bitterly cold in winter.

During the last twenty years of the colonial period there was a marked increase in population and foreign trade in Connecticut. In 1756 the population of Connecticut was about 130,000, while by 1774 this had increased to 200,000. During this period the export trade with Great Britain had increased from £130,000 annually to £200,000, which was in exact proportion to the increase in population. The import trade, however, increased more rapidly. In 1756 it was estimated to be about £50,000 annually, while by 1774 it had reached £200,000. Evidently the people of Connecticut began to spend more freely in this period. It would seem to have been a period of economic expansion in Connecticut, to be accounted for by the fact that money became more plentiful, due to the credits paid by Great Britain for help given her by Connecticut in the French and Indian War. Probably a large part of this money found its way back to Great Britain through the purchase of British manufactured goods, and the conclusion may be drawn that it was necessity, rather than desire, which made the Connecticut colonial so noted for his frugality.

The eighteenth century in Connecticut showed a slow but continuous progress toward the consolidation of a stable government under which there were no extremes of wealth or poverty and little if any social injustice. By 1775 Connecticut was ready to play its important role in the struggle for independence.

WALL A

SLAT-BACK ARMCHAIR
MAPLE
2nd quarter 18th Century

"TAVERN" TABLE
MAPLE
Early 18th Century

The Rich Detail of the Connecticut Valley

N the Connecticut River Valley, a few miles from Hartford, lie the towns of West Hartford, Wethersfield, Farmington, and New-ington, whose first settler John Andrews migrated thither from Farmington. We know that, because of fear of attack from the In-dians, his home was fortified, and proved thereby a refuge for set-tlers and their families in time of need. From what actual house in Newington came the room now in the Metropolitan is no longer known, but a de-tail such as the inside panelled shutter made to slide across the windows is good evi-dence that even by the second quarter of the eighteenth century the protection af-forded by a fortified house such as John Andrews' was a memory still expressed, if only in this somewhat vestigial feature of house construction.

The fireplace wall of this room is original, the other three walls, posts, girts, and summer beam having been reconstructed from contemporary models of similar character. There is added interest in the fact that this fireplace wall is one of the first pieces of American panelling to be shown out of its original setting, and its exhibition in the Hudson-Fulton celebration of 1909 did much to arouse that na-tion-wide interest in the surroundings of our ancestors that has led to the intelli-gent preservation today of so much Americana which might otherwise have been lost to us.

In this room, probably originally that just to the right of the front door, we have a fine example of a transition period, always charming in itself, which is a logical step in design after that of the Rose House of North Branford. The same round flower, a detail so typical of Connecticut work, which we find on the pilaster of the corner cupboard of the Rose House, appears here also. But it is more delicate in treatment, even as the pilasters on which it is carved have a smaller and more in-timate scale, and the whole interior is characterized by a mastery of design which in subtle fashion sloughs off the last trace of mediaevalism and seems definitely to turn towards the contemporary ways of life of England. Timid it may seem com-pared with any work of the mother country, but within the simple means at the builder's command, an effect has been gained wholly appropriate to the living con-ditions of its owner.

Architecturally, taste developed here with less ease, perhaps, than it did in the case of articles, sufficiently portable so that actual examples of them could be brought from England. We have, therefore, in this room of the second quarter of the eighteenth century a type of panelling based definitely on the treatment usual in the reign of Queen Anne and the early years of George I as king—a period slightly earlier than the house's construction. Queen Anne feeling is particularly evident in the arched panels of the fireplace wall and sliding shutters, while the crossed stiles in the doors and lower wainscot are a feature distinctive of much of the best work of this period in Connecticut River towns. All the panels are of the typical bevelled type, bordered with the slightly flattened "quarter-round" cut on stiles and rails. An exception to this is the raised panel above the fireplace surrounded by a small scale bolection moulding. The fireplace itself, still lacking a mantel-shelf, is framed by a similar moulding but much larger in scale and more vigorous in its profiles—another English heritage from the time of William and Mary and Queen Anne. The delicately fluted pilasters, not more than five inches wide, on either side of the fireplace acknowledge English inspiration even while their essential character gives evidence of the simplification proper to the translation of the classical idea from the land of its origin and renascence via Northern Europe to the remote Connecticut River Valley. Each pilaster is set upon a panelled podium, and each has incised below the surface of its "cap" the eleven-petalled flowers—a far cry surely from the conventionalized leaves of the Corinthian order, or the idealized geometry of the Ionic cap. One cannot but admire, however, the craftsmanship of our ancestors who could, with the few crude chisels and gouges at their command, produce an effect at once so unpretentious and so appropriate to the soft native pine always at hand. The raised hearth of the Connecticut brown sandstone so generally used, and a fireplace lining of the same material, add a color note harmonious with the unpainted pine of the wall.

Balancing the solid door to the left of the fireplace is a cupboard recessed behind a door, the upper half of which is glazed like the windows of the room, and here may be seen to great advantage the display of a series of shelves of household pewter. The semicircular recess at the top of the cupboard is decorated with a carved shell of fine quality in the center of which the incised flower again appears.

Elsewhere in the room the wood treatment is simpler: a small moulding nailed to the surface of a flat board forms the door architrave; girts, summer beams, and posts are, as was common at this date, encased in wood, the soffit of the summer beams being decorated with six panels; while a simple chair rail and baseboard are set against the uneven texture of the plaster, and a few mouldings added as a decorative "cornice" beneath the casing of summer beam and girts. Floor boards of random width put down with hand-wrought nails maintain the brown tone of the room. The omission of sheathing or panelling in three walls in favor of plaster again gives evidence of the increased skill of the New England craftsman. Lack of limestone for masonry had long been for him a problem solved early in the eighteenth century often by the use of clam and oyster shells as a base for plaster work. The tendency was more and more towards confining panelled work to the fireplace wall, while the other walls might have low panels to chair-rail height, or, as in this case, simply a chair rail applied directly to the plaster surface. By 1725 paint and stain were coming into fashion, the Connecticut colors most often used being still

WALL B

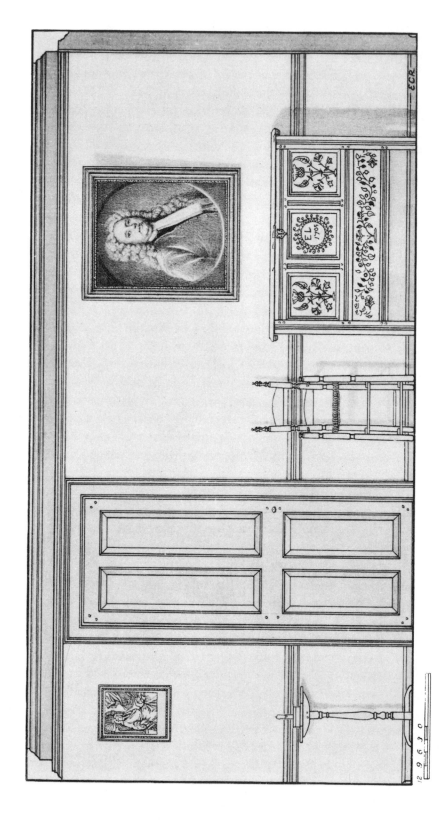

MEZZOTINT OF THOMAS HOLLIS
BY PETER PELHAM
BOSTON. 1754

CANDLE STAND
MAPLE
Early 18th Century

CHILD'S SLAT-BACK CHAIR
MAPLE WITH ASH STRETCHERS
Late 17th Century

PORTRAIT OF NATHANIEL BYFIELD
BY JOHN SMIBERT

OAK CHEST WITH PINE LID
PAINTED DECORATION
Dated 1705

the blue-green of the North Branford rooms, or a rusty red applied with a buttermilk or egg base which on that account wore off in large part, leaving a charming mixture of natural wood color with added traces of red. Even in rooms still wholly unpainted, such as the Newington room, the plaster walls give a more modern flavor and afford a background against which the more delicate forms of William and Mary and Queen Anne furniture appear to great advantage.

By 1725 furniture in the colonies had definitely lost the last vestiges of the Gothic construction and ornament characteristic of the work of even the latest seventeenth-century furniture makers. Styles were reaching America more quickly, thanks to the increasingly frequent passage of ships across the ocean, though designers were still ten to fifteen years behind the styles of England and not for another fifty years were the cabinetmakers here to be working in a manner thoroughly contemporaneous with that of the mother country. The last decade of the seventeenth century and the first quarter of the eighteenth brought forth a mass of architectural volumes in English accompanied by plates, and these were responsible in no small measure for the high standard of house construction and building design in general in the colonies. But it was not until almost the end of the eighteenth century that books on furniture design became available to any extent, though there were undoubtedly copies of Chippendale's *Gentleman's and Cabinet Maker's Director* of 1754 imported into the country by individual connoisseurs and exceptional craftsmen. For the first fifty years of the century, however, new ideas were brought in by the colonists who travelled, by those who sent over actual pieces of English manufacture, and by new colonists, particularly those cabinetmakers among them who may have brought in sketches wrapped up with their tools.

In England by 1725 the walnut styles of William and Mary and Queen Anne had largely given way to the late baroque and rococo design which later reached new heights in the work in mahogany of Thomas Chippendale. In America, however, the craftsmen of the early eighteenth century were more slow to master the art of veneer upon which the William and Mary style depended, and consequently the dates of this style are later than in England, approximately 1700-1720, and those of the Queen Anne style roughly 1720-1740.

Handsomely matched panels of finely grained wood, such as walnut, veneered most often on a carcass of soft wood, were an innovation in this country and gave a decorative effect appropriate to the new leisure which the more prosperous men and women were beginning to enjoy. Some respite from labor for the amenities of life called for a more sophisticated type of furniture, and soon small tea and coffee tables began to appear, and the new form of chest we call the highboy for the more convenient storage of linen. Chairs were more ample, and the wing chair, infinitely graceful forerunner of our elephantine overstuffed furniture, offered within its handsome and vigorous baroque curves the first really luxurious haven of daytime ease, while the "day-bed" gave evidence of a comfort which would have amounted almost to slothfulness early in the Pilgrim Century. Translated into simpler and more linear terms Flemish baroque features appeared in stretchers of chairs, tables, highboys and lowboys, as well as on the arms and back of chairs. The cabriole leg marked around 1730 the definite desertion of the severely vertical and horizontal lines of mortise and tenon construction in favor of a design which, in its essential function of support, contained curves expressive of a resilience hardly to be suspected in these light members used increasingly in the construction of furniture. For these new variations as well as for the more old-fashioned pieces, a variety of woods were used—pine, oak, and ash for the conservative country pieces, but for the newer fashions mostly walnut, maple, and, particularly in Connecticut, cherry, the fine grain of which would give that satiny texture so appropriate to the new mode.

In a small Connecticut town, not on the seacoast, however, what kind of furniture would be apt to be in a house built near the beginning of the second quarter of the century? Certainly the latest fashions from England could not yet be keenly felt here. One must expect the flavor of past generations to linger longer in Newington than in Boston or Philadelphia. Nor is it proper to suppose our ancestors to have been devoid of some inheritance in the form of furniture when they branched out into a new house and founded a family unit of their own.

It is not surprising, therefore, to find here that a predominating portion of the furniture harks back to the turn of the century both in style and construction. Chairs, including a child's high chair, are mostly of maple with ash side stretchers of the type called the slat back. They vary little save in small details in turning, the earlier examples having more bulbous turnings on the front stretchers. The rush-bottom seats have on them flat pads covered in yellow damask—one of the few luxuries of the times. One chair has at the top of the front posts the so-called "mushroom" terminations in which shallow holes have been bored to hold candles for reading.

A maple "gate-leg" table, a small oval-topped "tavern" table, and two candlestands, one of which has arms arranged to revolve around the center post and so adjust the height of the light, all are of maple and show traces of the red stain so characteristic of Connecticut.

A one-drawer lift-top chest of oak shows construction features typical of the Guilford region. Stiles and rails are painted a mottled light and dark brown, the two end panels decorated with stiff sprays of thistle, carnation, and tulip blossoms, while the middle panel bears within a circular wreath the date 1705. Like the mortise and tenon construction, the colors of the painted designs are mediaeval in their feeling: red, black, and white.

The Flemish feeling introduced by Charles II after his return from exile to France, and reaching maturity under the reign of William and Mary (William

WALL D

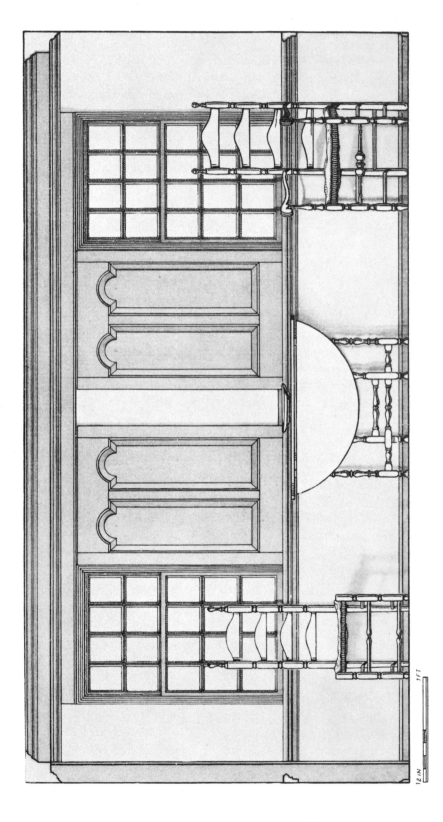

SLAT-BACK SIDE CHAIR
MAPLE AND HICKORY
c. 1725

GATE-LEG TABLE
MAPLE, PAINTED RED
Late 17th Century

SLAT-BACK ARMCHAIR
MAPLE
1725-1750

III being himself a Dutchman), is represented here by a fine four-legged highboy, the drawer fronts of which are finished in burled walnut veneer. Trumpet turnings, neat turnip feet, crossed stretchers with Flemish curves, double-arch mouldings between the drawers, and imported brass "tear drop" handles, all proclaim this a provincial piece of about 1720, worthy to be compared with its English prototypes. Other articles of interest include a small spice box in the form of a miniature highboy, and a lowboy which instead of the conventional type of legs has simply turned posts and stretchers like a tavern table.

Significant of the era of this room are a few additional touches solely for decorative purposes which appear on the walls. Up until 1700 pictorial representation for its own sake was rare in any form and preserved for honoring occasional outstanding figures, such as the governor of a colony or a person of great wealth and influence in an individual community. A portrait of a man such as this is that of Nathaniel Byfield (1653-1733), one of the four proprietors of Bristol, R. I., by John Smibert (1683-1751), which hangs on the wall above the Guilford chest. Here we have a portrait by one of the earliest known painters in the country, a Scotchman who studied Venetian painting in Italy and who had come with George Berkeley, Dean of Derry and later Bishop of Cloyne, to be a professor of fine arts in the ill-fated college which Berkeley proposed to found in Bermuda for teaching the natives. The Italian influence is clearly evident in the flesh tones, just as it is in Smibert's famous portrait of Dean Berkeley and his household painted in 1729 during Berkeley's sojourn in Newport. This portrait, the first group portrait ever painted in America, now hangs at Yale in the gallery adjoining the North Branford rooms.

Smibert, who remained in America for the rest of his life after his ecclesiastic patron had returned to Ireland, was also a seller of painters' materials and prints. Advertisements in the newspapers of 1734-1735 listed a collection of engravings "after the finest pictures of Italy, France, Holland and England," which may also have included prints such as those found in the Newington room.

Over the fireplace appears an engraved map of Boston, so rare as to be possibly unique, by Thos. Johnson, a native-born American. It is dedicated to His Excellency Wm. Burnet, governor of Massachusetts, and shows some artistic pretension in the emblematic vignette bearing the legend "Boston N. Eng. Planted A. D. MDCXXX, engraved by Thos. Johnson, Boston, N. E." It was published by Will Burgis in 1729. Elsewhere in the room appear three mezzotints by Peter Pelham (1684-1751), an English engraver who came to Boston following the death of Cotton Mather in 1728 to engrave a portrait of the deceased. A superb impression of this mezzotint, the first to be executed in America, is accompanied by similar portraits of the Lord Protector Oliver Cromwell and of Thomas Hollis, a benefactor of Harvard College. These represent the earliest type of portraiture available to the ordinary man at reasonable prices. Their present-day rarity is explained by the fact that out of the many engravings listed in inventories few seem to have been framed and glazed, and so have been lost to us.

In these prints, however, we have another evidence of the changes the eighteenth century was bringing into the lives and surroundings of the American colonist. Much of the severity of seventeenth-century living is still evidenced in the Newington room, but in it also are beginning to be seen traces of the prosperity and more leisurely life of the eighteenth, and these are here preserved for us in the peculiarly charming and naïve terms which inevitably usher in the changing customs and manners of a new era.

CONTEMPORARY DOCUMENTS

An Indian Chief's Anxiety over the Effect of the White Man's Strong Liquors upon His Own People.

To the Honourable
JOSEPH TALCOTT Esqr.
Governour of Connecticut
Now at New Haven.

The Petition of Ben=Uncus Sachem of the Mohegan Indians
To the Honourable General Court now Sitting In New Haven

Your Petitioner is Abundantly thankful, for the Care that has been taken Many Years past, In the [instructing of?] him and His People and Especially that It has pleased the Gentlemen of Boston to send us A Minister, whose Continuance Among us is greatly Desired by us, that we might be acquainted with the Principles of Religion, which our Fathers for Generations past have been greatly Ignorant of: I my Self would Gladly have waited upon the Honourable Court, If I were able, But having been of Late Sick, and now being A Cripple I am not able to Doe It.—I find that notwithstanding the Care that has been taken of us, yet we are under Sorrowful Circumstances, our Good is greatly obstructed By Reason of Strong Liquors being brought In Such great Quantities into our town—(Cyder by the Barrel, and Rhum by the Gallon) English Men often bring great Quantities of Strong Liquor up the River to us, and whatsoever we have that they want they purchase with It, and our Indians often Buy great Quantities of Strong Drink In the Neighbouring Towns.—And my Humble Petition is that there might be Some way found out whereby the Evil Practise might be Suppressed.

[Oct. 1733]   *Ben=[Sign] Uncus*

Connecticut State Library—*Indian Archives*, Series I, Volume I, page 161.

Ame Hide, of Norwich, must Mend her Ways at Sunday Meeting.

To Elijah Backus of Norwich in New London County Esqr. one of his Majestys Justices of the Peace for Said County; Comes Thomas Waterman & Benjamin Huntington Ju^r. both of Said Norwich, two of the Grand Jurors within and for Said County; and upon Oath present and inform That Ame Hide of Said Norwich Single Woman Not having the fear of God before her Eyes but being mooved by the Instigation of the Devil on the 15th Day of this Instant October (it being Saboth or Lords Day) Did Laugh and play in the Meeting house in the first Society in Said Norwich in the time of Publick Worship in such a manner as to Disturb Sundry of the then Worshipers in said house; all which doings of the Said Ame is a Breach of Sabboth and against the Peace of our Sovereign Lord the King his Crown and Dignity and Contrary to the Laws of this Colony — Dated Norwich October 30th A D 1769 — and in the 10th year of his Majestys Reign.

For Witness's take   *Benj. Huntington Ju^r.* } *Grand*
Lucretia Thommas   *Thomas Waterman* } *Jurors*
Margaret Waterman
Mary Waterman

A manuscript owned by Philip A. Johnson, Esq., of Norwich, Connecticut.

CONTEMPORARY DOCUMENT

The Indians beg Relief from the Englishmen's Encroachments on their Land.

To the Honble JOSEPH TALCOTT, *Eſq^r.*

Petition of the Pequot Indians.

Groton, [Conneɛticut] Sept. 22, 1735.

Honorible and worthy Sir Gove^r Talcot Sir after our humble Reſpeɛts to your honnor theſe are to inform your Self of the wrongs and diſtreſs that wee me[et] with by Some People that make Poſeſſions of our Land. They deſtroy So much of our timber for fencceing and for other ueſſes that wee ſha[nt] In a Little time have a noſe [enough] for fire wood and Eſpechely for fenſing for we find it is in vane to Plant within thare enchloſers for we planted tha[re] Laſt Spring and our Corn was Deſtroyed by the Engliſh Cretors and by fenſing in of our Land thay take away in a Great meſure the Privile[dg] of our orcherds for thay Let there own Swine go in and eat up our apples and bed Down and if our Swine accidenttoly get in thay Commit them to the Pound, which wee cold not ſubſiſt without Ceepint ſome Cretors. Wee ſhold be glad if wee cold have more of the Produſe of the Land to Ceep oather Cretors.

And they Removed a great part of our Gennerrell feild fence to arreɛt Thare own fence weich is Grately to our Dammage, for Some of it had ben Planted but two years and the Engliſh bild houſen upon our Land and put Tenants in them and one of them makes habbuck of our appels in makking Sider, and for oather uſe, and thay Sowe whet upon our Land. In as [much?] as wee Sea Plainly that thare Chefeſt deſire is to Deprive us of the Privilidg of our Land, and drive us of to our utter ruin, it maks us Conſerned for our Children what will be Com of them for thay are about having the goſpell Preched to them, and are a Learning to read, and all our young men And women that are Cappell [capable?] of Lerning of it and thare is Some of our young men wold be Glad to bild houſen upon it, and Live as the Engliſh do Cold they have a Sufficiency of The Produſe of the Land wee Crave your Pacience and wee will acquant your honnor a Little farther. The oather of their tennant Puts Cattle a nite into our Gennerall feild ammongſt our Corn and take them out in the morning And when wee teell them to take Care and Ceep out their Cretors thay Thretten us if wee dont hold our tongs to beat our Brains out and he threttens us that wee Shant Plant thare anoather year and Some people Cut our Stoaks [stalks?] ſome time when the Corn is in the milk, we Shold be Glad if thare Cold be a Stop Put to it the Stoaks being our own Labbour wee Shold be Glad to have them for our own uſe for wee find that wee Cant very well Subſiſt with out Ceeping Some Cretors and wee Shold Be very Thankfull if thare Cold be Some ways found out and taught of wherein our Land and the Privilildge thereof Be Reſtored to us again I Think wee have Given your honnor a true annecount as near as our memory Serves but a Great deal might be added but wee wold not be Two Tedis to your honnour and So wee Remain Your Servants To Command

Sam nees	Moſes Chonk	Charls
young achquet	Ben onneſon	Abner
John Chonk	Robin onneſon	Simon
young Charls	David toby	Sox
John neco [nees?]	Zacriah waquondam	Little Gorge
	Sambo	Great Gorge
	Peter Shocket	Tobey
	Samson Shocket	Palpy [?]
	Peter toby	Daniell quatch
	Gorge [?]	Peter Sox
	John [?]	Sam [?] Sox
	[?]	young Simon
		tom quatch
		Simon quatch

[A mark follows each name.]

[Indorsed] *Memoriall Pequott Indians, Oɛt^r., 1735.*

Conneɛticut State Library—*Indian Archives*, page 227, Volume I, Series I.

The NEW-ENGLAND
Weekly JOURNAL;

Containing the moſt Remarkable Occurrences Foreign & Domeſtick.

Selections from Iſſues of 1727-1730.

London, Nov. 4.

THEY write from the *Bath* that the King's Birth-Day was uſher'd in as follows, with this Proceſſion;

At four a-Clock in the Morning the Bells ſtruck out, a Bonfire was lighted, and a whole Ox ſet a roaſting, with a Quantity of Liquor, and Huzza's to his Majeſty's Health: At 6 the Drums beat the young Gentlemen Voluntiers to Arms; by 8 an Hundred and Sixty aſſembled themſelves together at the Colonel's Houſe; by 10 they were ready to march, but firſt every Man drank a Glaſs of Brandy to his Majeſty's Health; the Officers were extreamly rich in their Apparel, Velvet, Embroidery, Gold and Silver Lace; the Men with fine Caps, Cockades, Holland Shirts, Silver and Gold Ribbons, Shoulder-Knots, fine Scarlet Cloth Breeches richly lac'd, white Stockings, red Tops to their Shoes; the Slings to their Pieces had this Motto, *God ſave King* George *the Second*: By 12 they marched through the beſt part of the Town, with two Sword-Bearers, a Sett of Morris-Dancers, and Martial Muſick before them; then came to the Market-Place, where they drew up in Order for Fire; Wine was brought, and every Officer charg'd his Glaſs; the King, Queen and Royall Family went round diſtinct, with a Volley at each Health; the Glaſſes were thrown over their Heads, and in other Parts of the Town they did the ſame; then Captain Goulding repeated this Verſe *Extempore*:

In ſpight of Legions of Infernal Devils below,
To ye Powers above, Supream Divine,
Let George *in the Center our Standard be,*
And his Queen the Great Caroline.

One Colonel Edward Collins that keeps the White-Hart Inn, & Capt. Thomas Goulding Jeweller in the Walks, Capt. James Warriner Bookſeller in the Walks, Lieut. Collins Woolen-Draper in the Churchyard, Lieut. Taylor Sword-Cutler in the Churchyard, and three more young Gentlemen of the Town-Officers, which makes 8 in Number, that gave the Ox and all the Charges thereto: They drew to the Beef when roaſting, with Handfuls of Silver each Officer, and obliged the Cook to ſtuff it into the Shoulders and Neck; and Captain Gould-ing, Jeweller, ſtuffed above an Hundred true Stones into the Buttocks of the Ox, ſeveral Diamonds, Rubies, Saphires, Emeralds, Garnets, Amethiſts and Topaſſes. At Two the Ox was ready brought to the Table, put into a Diſh 12 Foot long, and 6 wide, made on purpoſe: They din'd in the publick Market-Houſe; but the Stuffing made the Mob ſo furious that they flung themſelves over the Heads of the Officers, into the Diſh, and ſtood over their Shoes in Gravy, and one was ſtuff'd into the Belly of the Ox, and almoſt ſtifled with Heat & Fat; the Greaſe flew about to that Degree, which made the Officers quit the Table, or all their Cloaths muſt have been ſpoil'd; they ſtopt and look'd on their Proceedings till Three, then they all march'd to the Colonel's, and ſtaid till Four; they went out again on their Proceſſion; at Five the Candles began to light; at 6 the Town was illuminated; they beat into the Colonel's Quarters near Seven, with Huzza's, *King* George *for Ever*: Where there was great Quantities of Wine and Beer drank to his Majeſty's Health, and all his loving Subjects in his extended Dominions; at Eleven the Drums beat *Go to Bed Tom*, and all departed in Peace after Pleaſure.

OBSERVATIONS on the CASE *of the Provinces of the* Maſſachuſetts-Bay *and* New-Jerſey, *and the Colonies of* Connecticut *and* Rhode-Iſland, *and* Providence Plantations, *with reſpect to the Bill now depending in the Honourable Houſe of Commons, Intitled,* A Bill for Preſervation of His Majeſty's Woods in America, *and for the Encouragement of the Importation of Naval Stores from thence, &c.*

THE Prohibition as to Cutting or Felling any White Pine-Trees in general, ſeems to be attended with ſtill worſe Conſequences than that relating to Iron; the Bill prohibiting the Cutting or Felling any white Pine-Trees, but ſuch as are within Fence or actual Incloſure.

WITHOUT all Diſpute, a due Care ought to be taken for the Preſervation of the King's Woods, with regard to ſuch Trees as are neceſſary for Maſting the Royal Navy; but at the ſame time, the Inhabitants ought not to be debarr'd from making uſe of ſuch Trees as they want, either for their own Uſe, or for the Supply of the *Britiſh* Iſlands in *America*; or laſtly, such Trees as are requisite, and might be imported to *Great Britain*, for our own Use: it being very plain and evident, that we have now vast annual Supplies, both of Firr-Timber and Boards, as well as Masts, from other Countries, at very dear Rates; and by the Bill now depending, instead of Encouragement for the Importation of them from our own Plantations, it totally defeats it.

BOSTON.

On Fryday last the 27th Currant, was the Annual *Commencement* at *Cambridge* for this Year, (it being the Third in order of the more Private *Commencements*.) when the following Persons, had their Degrees given them, after they had held their Publick Disputations in the Church of that Town, as they are in the Printed *Theses* and *Questions*, viz.

Bachelors in Arts.

Simon Frost	Abiel Howard
Benjamin Walton	Job Parker
Richardus Clarke	Enoch Freeman
Henricus Welsteed	Philemon Robbins
Nathaniel Walter	Samuel Mawdsley
Ward Cotton	Zecharias Hicks
Johannes Cushing	Johannes Shaw
Johannes Loring	Elisæus Eaton
Gulielmus Williams	Timotheus Brown
David Parsons	Amos Main
Josephus Lee	Solomon Page
Ephraim Keith	

Masters of Arts,

Simeon Stoddard Mr.	Thomas Goodridge Mr.
Gulielmus Clarke Mr.	Eleazer Allen Mr.
Josephus Pynchon Mr.	Jonathan Parker Mr.
Guilielmus Willoughby Mr.	Daniel Dwight Mr.
Richardus Hall Mr.	Jeremias Fisher Mr.
Thomas Greaves Mr.	Jedidias Jewet Mr.
Henricus Gibbs Mr.	Johannes Emerson Mr.
Isaacus Lothrop Mr.	Atherton Wales Mr.
Nathan Stone Mr.	Jonathan Stedman Mr.
Josephus Green Mr.	Thomas Prentice Mr.
Edvardus Jackson Mr.	Theodorus Coker Mr.
Thomas Cheesebrough Mr.	Isaacus Richardson Mr.
Jacobus Bridgham Mr.	Stephanus Huse Mr.
Jeremias Condy Mr.	

We also hear from New-London, that at the Superiour Court Holden there the 30th of March last, one William Watkins was Tried for Thieft, found Guilty, and Sentenc'd to be Branded, and his right Ear cut off, which was done the same Day: He intended to have had his Ear put on again, but being unskilful in Surgery, he kept it till it was dead, that it was attempted in vain: so that as the poor man could not do as he *wou'd*, he must e'en do as he *can*.

Burials in the Town of BOSTON, *since our last*, Seventeen Whites ; One Black.
Baptiz'd in the several Churches, Nine.

Philadelphia, February 10.

On Saturday last an unhappy Man, one Sturgis, upon some Difference with his Wife, determined to drown himself in the River; and she, (kind Wife) went with him, it seems, to see it faithfully performed, and accordingly stood by silent and unconcerned during the whole Transaction: He jump'd in near *Carpenter's* Wharff, but was taken out again, before what he came but was th[o]roughly effected, so that they were both obliged to return home as they came, and put up for that Time, with the Disappointment.

Whitehall, Nov. 10.

His Majesty hath been pleased to appoint John Montgomery Esq; to be Governour of New-York and New-Jersey in America, in the room of William Burnett Esq; who is appointed Governour of the Massachusetts Bay and New-Hampshire in America, in the room of Samuel Shute Esq;

Bristol April 19.

The Press still continues, taking all the Hands out of the Vessels that come in the Road. The Captains of the Outward bound Ships, to prevent their Men from falling into the Hands of the Press Gang, let the Pilots proceed with their Ships as far as the Holmbs, while their Men march by Land down the Country, and are fetched off by the Pilot's Boats.

ADVERTISEMENTS.

THE HOSPITALITY OF A NEW ENGLAND INN

As illustrated by the BARROOM AT THE WAYSIDE INN

South Sudbury, Massachusetts

WALL B

WALL A

WALL C

WALL D

PLAN

Scale

0   2   3   4 ft.

Historical Note

TO those who for various reasons find information and pleasure in turning back the pages of American history, no other word brings so many associations as "tavern." From the village "ordinary" of the Puritans, through the stagecoach and Revolutionary tavern days, to the six-horse-sleigh inns of our grandfathers, these gathering places "for man and beast" provide a wonderful background against which to study our forebears. Though the Puritan was alleged to be dour and straight-laced, we shall find him relaxing a bit over his beer at the ordinary. Our minute-man uses more unguarded words over his flip than in his speech at town meeting. And grandmother, who looks so prim and sedate in the daguerreotype, coquettes gaily at the dance after the tingling moonlight ride to the country inn.

The ordinary or tavern was here as early as the English settlers. The founding of a village meant the establishment of a tavern. The Cambridge, Massachusetts, town record is typical, viz.:

Sept. 20, 1648. It is ordered, that there fhalbe an eight peny ordinary provided, for the Townfmen, every fecond munday of the mo. uppon there meeteing day, and that whoever of the Townfmen faile to be prefent with in half an houre of the Ringing of the Bell (which fhalbe half an houre after elven of the clocke) he fhall both lofe his dinner & pay a pinte of facke or ye vallue, to the prefent Townfmen, and the like penalty fhalbe payd by any that depart from ye reft with out leave, the charges of ye dinner fhalbe payd by the Cunftables out of the Towne ftocke.

The next reference is,

The Townfmen do grant liberty to Andrew Belcher to sell bears and bread for entertainment of ftrangers & the good of the Towne.

The "meeting day" was town-meeting day, held once a month in the meeting-house, that is, in the church; for church government and town government were to all intents a single interest. In the winter months, we may be sure, the town meetings would be held in the taverns. The cheer of the open fires and the landlords' brew was more enticing than the deathly chill of the unheated church. All meetings of town officials were held in private houses or in the taverns. This custom endured for many years, and the liquor consumed by the selectmen was paid for by the taxpayers without question.

Ordered the clerk to pass a bill to the Town Treasurer for 2 pounds 4 shillings 7 pence to pay Mr. John Muzzey for entertaining the selectmen in 1724.

That is, the selectmen met that year at Muzzey's Tavern and lightened the drudgery of running town affairs by generous samples of the tavern brew.

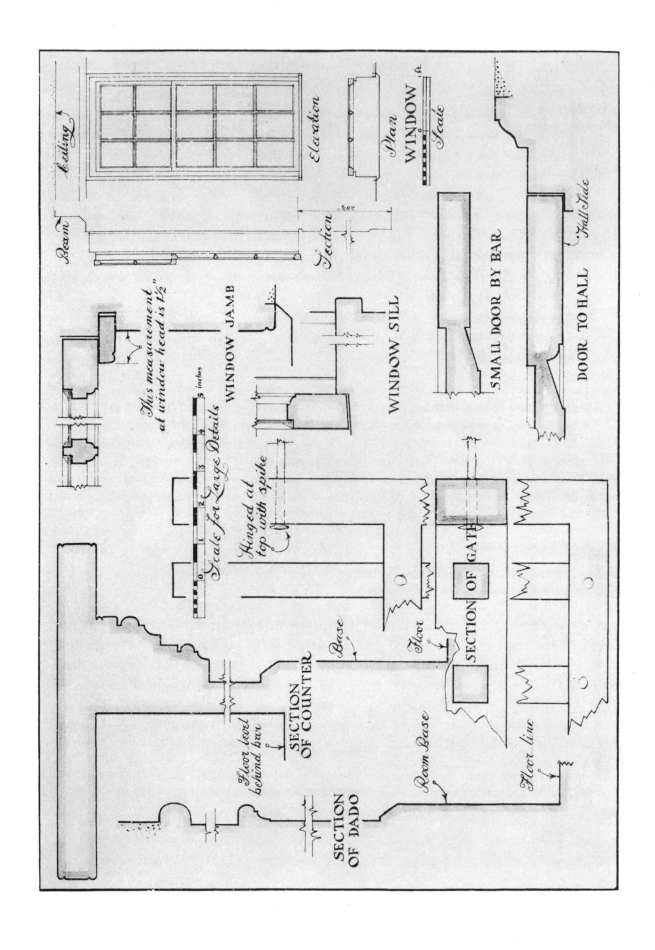

Historical Note

What tales the tavern walls could tell as to what took place at these meetings! The discipline of the youth of the village, for our selectmen then enjoyed certain privileges now delegated to the courts. The disposal of minors who, without consultation as to their desires, were bound out until their majority. The sale (vendue) of paupers or insane to the lowest bidder. The disposal of vexing matters of the church: whether or not to have any singing during the service; the purchase of a baptismal basin; the qualifications of a new minister. All topped off with liberal drafts of "Mine Host's" best.

The tavern keeper was usually an important and prosperous citizen; and well he might be, for, in addition to town-meeting days, there were "lecture days" once a month, and no Puritan with any thought of his soul would think of staying away— and there were training days and muster days for all able-bodied men. Sunday was an especially busy day for the landlord and his family. Churchgoing consisted of a long service in the morning and an equally long one in the afternoon. During the noon hour all would repair to the tavern. The best bedroom would be used as a parlor for the women that they might be beyond earshot of the levity of the taproom. Perhaps there had recently been a shift wedding in the village!

Even the funeral of a pauper meant business for the tavern. There would be a good turnout of town officials—a long-standing custom. At a meeting of the selectmen, July 6, 1728, in the town of Lexington, occasioned by the death of Thomas Paul's wife (a pauper), these officials "then received seven quarts and one jill of rum for her funeral."

The first ordinaries were the small dwellings of early settlers, perhaps of four or five rooms. Business was mostly local, and the occasional traveller could be accommodated in the spare bedroom. With settlements springing up away from the coast and the establishment of well-defined "paths" between the larger towns, travel increased, until the roads were filled with a colorful procession toward the tavern doors. There would be oxcarts, high wagons with two or three horses hitched tandem, pedlars, flocks of turkeys, and the stagecoaches. The old taverns were enlarged —"sprawled out" would better describe their appearance—and large barns were built, placed parallel to the highway.

With many strangers—both drovers, and gay folk with fine clothes—our tavern takes on a livelier air. We must look over the letters left on the bar to be called for. Pedlar Joe will have some new calico and be rich with gossip; we must be on hand when he unties his pack. Or perhaps it will be a "peepshow" with amazing scenes from foreign lands. To-night there are so many gay travellers that there will be a dance; and when the dance is over, the landlord will let down the temporary partition which transforms our ballroom into the necessary two bedrooms.

If all was gay within, the teamsters and drovers were equally merry in the tavern yard. There was always rivalry between the back-country teamsters and the villagers. "Pull-up" matches and impromptu wrestling bouts provided a summer evening's sport. The well-to-do would of course have bedrooms to themselves, but at the taverns which catered to the drovers and teamsters, two or three beds in a room were customary and, oftentimes, two or three in a bed. Late comers would have to sleep on the hay in the barn.

Tavern days reached their pinnacle upon the visit of some national hero. It would seem that Washington or Lafayette ate or slept in every tavern in the colonies. The interesting and human story of many a tavern is to-day boiled down into the single phrase, "Washington once slept here." The stir and bustle created by such a visit fill many a page, and make delightful and instructive reading. Historian and housewife both exclaim over James Phinney Munroe's famous letter describing Washington's stay at Munroe Tavern in Lexington. We will quote three paragraphs of it here, for though it is a fictitious document written in 1889, its picture must be exceedingly accurate. Mr. Munroe was a real scholar, and, being a great-grandson of the Colonel William Munroe who was proprietor of the tavern at the time of George Washington's visit, he was the possessor of a wealth of very direct evidence in the form not merely of document and letter, but also of furnishings, costume, and family anecdote.

Mr. Washington seemed something sollem at first, but soon waxed livlyer and asked many questions, they told me, of the fight. He would, moreover, see the houses round about, and when he enterred Mr. Buckman his tavern, I was in a great figget 'till he come out, fearing lest Mr. Merriam, who is but just approbbated as a taverner and knows nought about the bisness, might entreat him into eating there. At last it being close onto two of the clock, the hour set for the dining, we set out, the President and the rest riding and walking at the head, and the coach and the townsfolk tagging after, huzzaring and waving kerchefs. 'Twas a pitty we gave him no set speach as 't was did in many towns no bigger than ours, and your Father could have writ it exselent. When we come to the house, there stood my Father and Step-mother at the taproom door, Anna and the naybors skulking in the parlour. My Father looked grandly in his rejimentels, and proud indeed was I of him as he led the way to the dinner-room prepar'd for Mr. Washington in the upper room, looking towards your house. 'T was arrang'd that my Step-mother dish the vittles in the kitch'n, yours should bring them to the stares (the short way, thou knows't, thro' the shop & the tap-room) and then my Father should serve them to the guests. 'T was permited me to stand in the corner betwixt the windows, to give what help was needed. We had a right fine feast, I can tell you, and much of it; roasted beef, a showlder of pork, chickins, pyes, puddings, syllybubs, and, best of all, some fine young pigens sent in by the Widow Mulliken. Mr. Washington would have none but plane things, however, saying, as my Father handed the others to him, That is to good for me. When the pigens, of which there was but few, were served, the President said, Are all these fine kickshores for my servents too? My Father stamering that he had not tho't to give them such, his Highness bade the dish of squobs be divided in half that his black men, forsooth, might have the same as him. During the dining he talked of little other than the vilenes of the roads, calling them as blind and ignorent as the directions of the

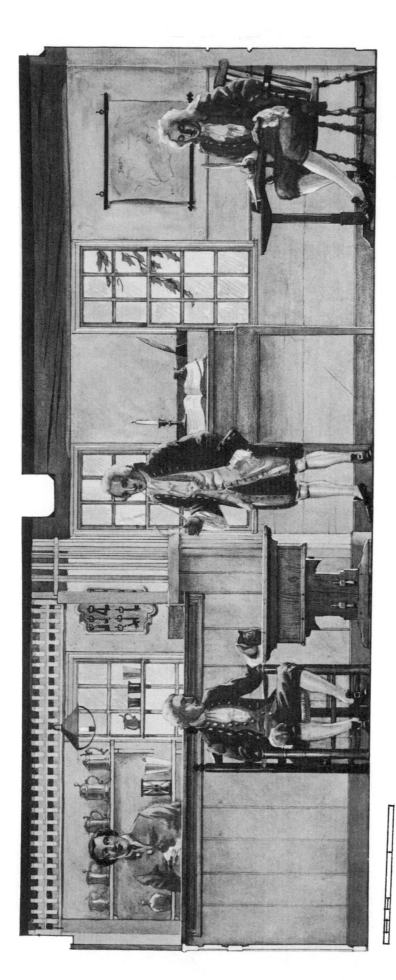

WALL A

WRITING-ARM
COMB BACK WINDSOR
MAPLE, PAINTED RED
*3rd quarter
18th Century*

CANDLE STAND
OAK AND MAPLE
WITH PINE TOP
PAINTED RED
Early 18th Century

PINE DESK
1st half 18th Century

HUTCH TABLE
OAK AND PINE WITH
WALNUT TOP
PROBABLY EUROPEAN
17th Century

"PILGRIM SLAT-BACK"
ARMCHAIR
MAPLE AND ASH
c. 1700

inhabitents. He had more to say than was seemly, to my thinking, of the Ladyes, how hansome he found them, their black hair being to his liking. He was exceeding frugall in his drinking, as well as in his feeding, for he took but one mug of beer and two glasses of wine during the whole meal. After the second glass he rellated sundry aneckdotes, but with such gravyty & slowness that none durst smile. He told us that Mr. Franklin, having been much vexed in England by the British complaneing that the Yankees, as they term us, took a wrong advantage on the 19th of April, in firing from behind stonewalls, the great philosofer had retort'd 'Were there not two sides to the walls?' The only other storey I mind his telling is of his having come to a Tavern where the host was away and where they had to arowse the mistress, she being in bed: on hearing that the President was below, seeking shelter, she would have nought to do with him, believing him to be but the President of the little Yale College in Conn. . . .

The sun being now low, Mr. Washington entered his carriage, and started off to-wards Watertown, having denied a mug of flip which my Father, with much pains, had prepar'd. Messiers Tobyas Lear and Jackson and the black men did not say him nay, tho', I warrant you.

I have burned 3 dips, which is sinfull, & have set up long beyond bell-ringing to send you this, so now must I stop.

Your ever afectionate

SALLY.*

If the Revolution was born in Sam Adams' town meetings and the virtues of liberty nurtured in the New England pulpits, the tavern provided a place for the intimate and frank discussion of these weighty matters. The Boston newspaper would be on the bar, the latest appeal from the selectmen of Boston tacked on the wall, the landlord filled with the latest news brought by his guests. At the taproom bar one could talk freely with a group of neighbors. The will to resist British tyranny expounded in pulpit, press, and town meeting was welded strong over mugs of steaming grog at the tavern table. Resting sure in the loyalty of the landlord toward the cause of the colonists, the tavern became the secret meeting place of the most ardent patriots. Paul Revere, Dr. Warren, and Samuel Adams, with their "Sons of Liberty" meeting at the "Green Dragon" in Boston, made but one such group helping to make our taverns secure in history, as the newspaper section of this chapter makes very clear.

The stories of the taverns have been written, and good reading they are; and the best known of all is Longfellow's *Tales of a Wayside Inn*. (Howe's Red Horse Inn in South Sudbury, situated on one of the busiest highways in the colony, had its reputation for hospitality well established before 1716.) Its door has opened to Puritan, to minute-man, and to an unusual list of notables. An architectural, literary, and historical monument, the door of the Red Horse Tavern now opens to you.

* Courtesy of the Lexington Historical Society.

The Hospitality of a New England Inn

THE power of even gentle poetry is often productive of unexpected and far-reaching results. The most authentic of our old inns—the Wayside Inn in South Sudbury, Massachusetts—was originally and for many years in the eighteenth century known simply as Red Horse, or the Red Horse Tavern, and travellers would break their journey where "the red horse prances on the sign." It took Longfellow's poem, *Tales of a Wayside Inn*, to replace the original time-honored name, redolent of so many an old English inn, with the appealing bucolic-sounding title of the Wayside Inn. Here, according to the poet, gathered a group of congenial souls representing varied walks of life—but in the upper strata—and while the boisterous wintry blasts rattled the windows from without, all was genial within, where, before the impelling urge of the "blazing fire of wood," each guest revealed his claim through music, legend, or theology to the interest of the moment.

This flight of poetic imagination was sufficient to fasten unalterably on the hostelry its present fortunate appellation. It represents what is with us a rare instance of the evolutionary process by which appropriate designating names arrive and attach themselves to objects and localities in a leisurely manner that was usual in our mother country, and is in sharp contradistinction to our hasty, impatient methods of name selection to-day.

It was as early as 1670 that the section which is now near by Marlborough to the west had its ordinary, kept by the first John Howe, an honored and illustrious family of this region. Quite possibly it was here that his grandson David found his first interest in the role of innkeeper that led him later to build the present Wayside Inn on his 130-acre grant from his father, and eventually to become innkeeper there himself in what was the fifth inn on the Boston Post Road going west within the township's early borders.

It was Colonel Ezekiel Howe of Revolutionary fame, however, who hung out the sign "Red Horse"; and after his reign as landlord had come to an end, he turned the business over to his son, Adam, who carried on for forty years. This tavern undoubtedly went through the various progressions from ordinary of common entertainment, to the tavern of refreshments and amusements, and on to the inn which should combine these offices with that of the traveller's temporary home.

Whatever the architectural form of the first building, it must have been far different in size and outline from the present traveller's domicile. From the beginning, the magnificent oaks, which lend an English parklike air of age and dignity to the immediate landscape, intensified the homelike atmosphere. With the physical accessories of an inn of the period, the establishment made an intri-

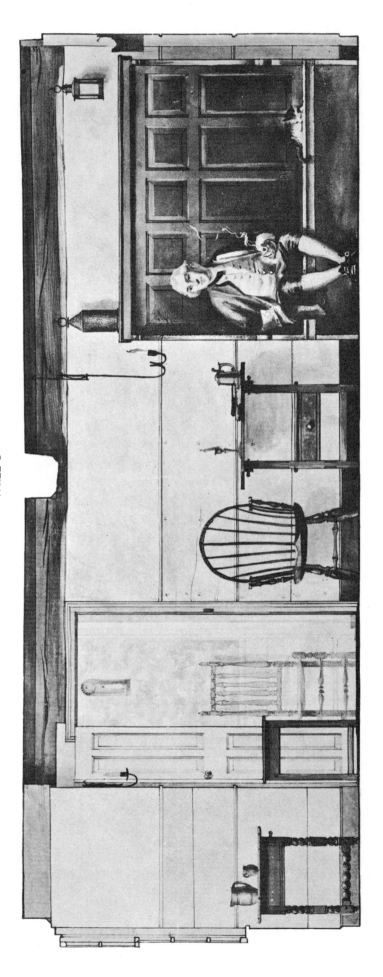

WALL C

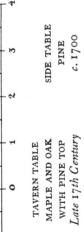

TAVERN TABLE
MAPLE AND OAK
WITH PINE TOP
Late 17th Century

SIDE TABLE
PINE
c. 1700

BOW BACK
WINDSOR ARMCHAIR
*3rd quarter
18th Century*

CHAIR-TABLE
OAK, WITH CURLY
MAPLE TOP
Late 17th Century

PINE SETTLE
18th Century

guing stopping place for what must have been the traveller's chronic condition of cramps on arriving in an uncomfortable coach over rough roads.

Sudbury, as a frontier town, was prominent in the annals of the Colonial Wars against the Indians and was subject to attack by them until well after King Philip's (Metacomet) War, toward the close of the seventeenth century, when the earliest unit of the Wayside Inn was built. Marlborough, to the west, had been burned, and, as an indication of the remoteness of the region from anything like population, it is therefore probable that more than ordinary credence can be given to the legend that, during the erection of the inn, the workmen nightly took refuge in a neighboring garrison house.

It is pleasant to-day to picture for the arriving guest the face of the hostelry bathed in the south sun, with the sturdy weatherbeaten walls and wide-spreading gambrel roof, fluently expressing the anticipated cheer within. In such an ensemble, the many and irregular outbuildings attaching themselves to the main body were of picturesque uncertainty of height and form, with ample stable, coach house, storage sheds, primitive ice house, sheds with feeding troughs, and the all-important woodyard with quantities of cut wood of varying lengths laid up in neat piles or in conical formations, or put carefully under cover for dryness, while exposing the ends. Then there was, of course, the inevitable poultry house and adjoining yard, probably placed at a distance from the guests' rooms to mitigate the early matutinal cadences of the feathered tribe. Somewhat nearer the house would be the slightly less noisy but vastly more picturesque dovecote. Other attendant features of the usual farm in the way of corn cribs, cowsheds, piggery, and intangibles —for a remote country inn had to be, in a measure, of farm-supporting sustenance —would be relegated to more distant quarters.

Where the curved drive entered from the main road stood the signpost, with the sign hanging from the crosspiece, indicating that here would be found Entertainment, and on its attractive outline would be whatever scrolls and embellishments in painting the local artist or itinerant artist-traveller might supply. Hard by the entrance door was always the mounting block for assistance in overcoming, with probably varying degrees of success, the insecure footing of arriving or departing guests.

In that busy period of wringing a livelihood from the soil under primitive conditions, there could not have been much in the way of horticultural decorations, but certain plants and shrubs, such as lilacs, cinnamon and damask roses, and that hardy variety known as the Gallica rose, or by the dubious appellation "apothecary rose," were inevitable and are still found existing near the rough stone footings of the entrance doorway of many a house long ago burned or deserted.

Extending from the more formal quarters of the inn was the vegetable and small-fruit garden, and somewhat apologetically but none the less determinedly, interspersed as a questionable luxury, whatever the busy hostess might be able to command in the way of flowers and cherished plants.

No apology was needed for the attendant herb garden, which of yore was looked upon as an indispensable requirement, and therefore incapable of becoming, as now with us, the expression of a refined taste in gardening approaching the status of a cult. Hedged about by encroaching vegetables and small fruits, it would be frequently drawn upon for lavender and rosemary for making fragrant the linen closet; thyme, tarragon, and chives for flavoring the salads; rue, sage, and savory for the vegetables; mint for ameliorating meats and drinks; dill for fish sauces and pickles; anise for pastries and confections; and perhaps even balm and coriander for flavoring liqueurs. And somewhere, in an inconspicuous but convenient corner, would grow the lusty stalks of costmary, where the broad and fragrant leaves could be quickly gathered on a Sabbath morn to serve as markers for designated passages in the Scriptures, thereby acquiring the title "Bible leaf."

All these dependencies and accessories of an inn of the period would be variously interesting to the individual guests as they sought to while away the time of an enforced or prolonged extension of the inn's hospitality.

Crossing the entrance threshold, one came directly under the very personal care of a man of much importance in his community—the innkeeper himself. In him there would be evidenced a unique type of landlord as compared with the English standard. Vastly different conditions in our new land had caused the development of a more assertive and less cringing type than is pictured in much of the inn lore of the mother country. Men like Colonel Ezekiel Howe, for instance, were inured to greater hardships and had been forced to a far more rigid self-development than would have been the case if they had grown up along one of the stagecoach lines that spread out from London in all directions.

The landlord presided over the entire enterprise. His vantage point was unquestionably behind the counter of the barroom, but he mingled genially with his guests wherever he thought he could add to their pleasure or comfort, and of course was in the courtyard to greet and speed the stages.

Sudbury was no exception to the general practice of the times in its approval of and indulgence in spirituous liquors, and the average new arrival probably headed at once for the bar. By good fortune, the elaborate serving arrangements of the Wayside Inn barroom—a section that has so generally been destroyed—have here been left intact.

In the small taproom, located between the dining room and the bar so that it could respond equally well to the demands of each, were kept the bulk of stores of beer, ale, wine, rum, cider, and the like, in bottles, kegs, and barrels. It must have been a crowded little room, for an inn of the eighteenth century did much boasting about its choice and extensive stock.

WALL D

THREE
TODDY
IRONS

PIPE BOX   WARMING
PINE   PAN

PIPE
TONGS

0 1 2 3 ½ FT.

The Hospitality of a New England Inn

Opening directly from the taproom was the narrow run between the bar counter and the shelves of mugs and flip glasses and minor seasonings. It was from here that the landlord held his sway—a monarch of his realm—with a small slant-top desk for the inn's accounts, a drawer for cash beneath it, a handsome keyboard for the inn's brass keys hanging in orderly rows.

Although the day of the brass foot rail had not arrived, the broad counter must, nevertheless, have upheld countless heavy elbows during its two centuries of service. There were also small tables for the sociable but less eager drinkers, and we even see at the Wayside Inn to-day a writing-arm Windsor chair set in a far corner, away from the fireplace group and away from the noisy bar, for that exclusive sort of individual who has found that he can mix his ale with a little writing or a book more pleasantly than he can wrangle over it in a crowd of men of different opinions and tastes from his own.

The wooden fencing, with its down-swinging gate, that encloses this busy corner of the inn suggests that quite naturally all bottled and kegged goods could not be left safely out in the open when the house had retired for the night. Quite possibly, though, there was another use for the fence and gate. One notices that when the grille falls in locked position there is still a slit just high enough to push back and forth a mug of beer underneath. This makes one wonder if the gate might not have been shut toward the end of a rough session on a Saturday night, to keep the singing, arguing, boisterous crowd from taking too much liberty with the master of ceremonies, or even with his pretty daughter, if she were doing a turn behind the counter at a busy time.

The jog beside the entrance to this barroom contains a steep staircase, just recently restored, that, according to both tradition and record, was used as a quick and inconspicuous means of helping up to their rooms those guests who were ready to call their day sufficiently full.

One feels that the architecture of a room of this sort is of secondary importance to the furnishing dictated by the main business of it. A fireplace wall, wainscoting or a dado, and door and window trim—these would be simple, straightforward designs, varying with the current styles and preferences; the shelves and counter remained as changeless as the need and the appetites that they were filling.

The inn, and especially the barroom, acted as a clearing house for news items and rumors. Events were eagerly discussed by the natives as well as by those who tarried through the night under its roof, and who undoubtedly brought welcome additions to the store of news as they arrived from the important centers.

Such burning events as the raising of soldiers for the expedition to Lake Champlain and Maine; the cessation of hostilities between England and France, which left Canada no longer a factor to be reckoned with; the appearance of the question of the local holding of slaves, which early raised its envenomed head in the colony; * the ominous vote of the town in 1771 to select a site to build a powder house —these and many other subjects lead us on to the high points of interest in the approaching Revolution. The growing unrest of the colonies under the unreasonable treatment by the mother country; the resentment of unjust taxation; the arrogance of official representatives of the Crown; and finally, the culmination in the definite breaking away from maternal restraint—all these phases were discussed vigorously at every turn: in the stable yard, at the table, and, most of all, in the barroom, where pounding fists went far in condemnation.

The first step in making it possible to reconstruct this picture of the romantic days of the Wayside Inn, came when a former owner, who was an ardent collector of antique furnishings, put the building back into sound condition. In fact, it was he who really saved the entire property from ruinous neglect, and he acquired the inn more as an attractive background for his belongings than from any desire to become a landlord—an office which was apparently thrust upon him.

This step was succeeded by the opportune discovery of the Wayside Inn by the present owner, whose deep appreciation of its importance as a rehabilitated old-time inn has opened it again for our present-day enlightenment and enjoyment.

The picturesque reminiscences that the old inn recalls present a sorry contrast with the drab background of modern hotel lobbies and their smugly efficient clerks. Much has been lost since the remote day of the pine-finished walls, the high stool and desk with its compartments for mail, and the accompanying ledger which openly told of many a private account. Undoubtedly there are compensating factors in the acceleration of to-day, living as we do at least a half dozen lives in comparison with those of recent passage, but it may be well to give pause and consider, as we are able to in the environment of the Wayside Inn, some of the aspects of a more leisurely life, when, returning to the poet,

> . . . men lived in a grander way,
> With ampler hospitality.

* To-day mute evidence of kindly consideration and appreciation for services rendered exists in the early burial-ground in East Sudbury (now Wayland), where apparent slaves, "Peter, a colored man," and "Flora, a colored woman," lie across the feet of their lord and master.

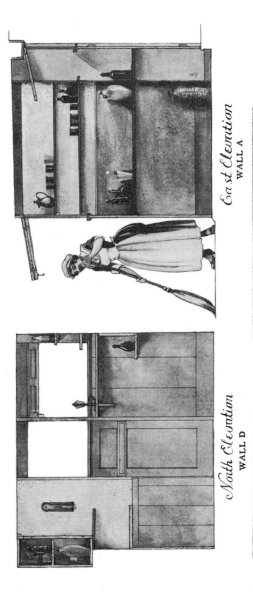

East Elevation
WALL A

South Elevation
WALL B

ELEVATIONS OF
TAP ROOM

Scale

North Elevation
WALL D

West Elevation
WALL C

CONTEMPORARY DOCUMENTS

An English Traveller comments on American Fare in 1807

" It is the custom in all American taverns, from the highest to the lowest, to have a sort of public table at which the inmates of the house and travellers dine together at a certain hour. It is also frequented by many single gentlemen belonging to the town. At Gregory's upwards of thirty sat down to dinner, though there were not more than a dozen who resided in the house. A stranger is thus soon introduced to an acquaintance with the people, and if he is travelling alone he will find at these tables some relief from the ennui of his situation. At the better sort of American taverns very excellent dinners are provided, consisting of almost everything in season. The hour is from two to three o'clock, and there are three meals in the day. They breakfast at eight o'clock upon rump steaks, fish, eggs, and a variety of cakes with tea or coffee. The last meal is at seven in the evening, and consists of as substantial fare as the breakfast, with the addition of cold fowl, ham, &c. The price of boarding at these houses is from a dollar and a half to two dollars per day. Brandy, hollands, and other spirits are allowed at dinner, but every other liquor is paid for extra. English breakfasts and teas, generally speaking, are meagre repasts compared with those of America, and as far as I observed the people live with respect to eating in a much more luxurious manner than we do. Many private families live in the same style as at these houses; and have as great variety. Formerly pies, puddings, and cyder used to grace the breakfast table, but now they are discarded from the genteeler houses, and are found only in the small taverns and farm-houses in the country."

Selection from Stage Coach and Tavern Days, *Alice M. Earle.*

There were Social Distinctions even in the Good Old Days.

Rules of this Tavern

Four pence a night for Bed
Six pence with Supper
No more than five to sleep in one bed.
No boots to be worn in bed
Organ Grinders to sleep in the wash house
No dogs allowed in the Kitchen
No Razor Grinders or Tinkers taken in

Valentine's Manual, *Vol.* 7, *p.* 261.

CONTEMPORARY DOCUMENT

Nathaniel Ames uses his Almanacs of 1751 *and* 1752 *to advertise his Inn, "At the Sign of the Sun," and incidentally replies to Slanderous Critics.*

Advertiſement.

1751

*T*HESE *are to ſignify to all Perſons that travel the great Poſt-Road South-Weſt from* Boſton, *That I keep a Houſe of Publick Entertainment Eleven Miles from* Boſton, *at the Sign of the* SUN. *If they want Refreſhment, and ſee Cauſe to be my Gueſts, they ſhall be well entertained at a Reaſonable Rate,*

N. Ames.

Courteous Reader,   1752

WIth the Year 1740 all the Ephemerides of the Planets Places then extant expired; and however cheap and contemptible a Thing an Almanack may ſeem to be, it annually coſts me much Time and hard Study to prepare one for you; and your chearful Acceptance of my Labours, for theſe *Twenty ſeven* Years paſt has encouraged me more to continue in this your Service than the Reward I receive for it.

The Affairs of my Houſe are of a publick Nature, and therefore I hope may be mentioned here without Offence to my *Reader*: The Sign I advertiſed laſt Year by Reaſon of ſome little Diſappointments is not put up, but the Thing intended to be ſignified by it is to be had according to ſaid Advertiſement. And I beg Leave further to add, that if any with a View of Gain to themſelves, or Advantage to their Friends, have reported Things of my Houſe in contradiction to the aforeſaid Advertiſement, I would only have thoſe whom they would influence conſider, that where the Narrator is not honeſt, is not an Eye or Ear Witneſs, can't trace his Story to the original, but it is only by Hear-ſay, a thouſand ſuch Witneſſes are not ſufficient to hang a Dog: & I hope no Gentleman that travels the Road will have his Mind bias'd againſt my Houſe by ſuch idle Reports.   *N. Ames.*

Selections from The Almanack of Nathaniel Ames, *Massachusetts Historical Society.*

The *Boston*-Gazette,

AND COUNTRY JOURNAL.

Selections from Issues of 1767-1775.

NEWPORT, January 11. [1768]

ON Friday the 1st Instant, being New-Year's Day, a Number of respectable Ladies of South Kingstown, Narragansett, were invited to the House of a Gentleman of the first Rank and Figure in the Town, to celebrate the New-Year Anniversary in a festival Manner, where they all appeared in homespun Manufactures, (except one from Boston, who appeared in the Habiliment of Tabby:) And though a most genteel Repast was the entertainment of the Company, yet no foreign Tea, either Bohea or Green, was set before them, nor was it even expected. The whole Evening was spent in a very mirthful, yet in the most decent, frugal and innocent Manner.—This Intelligence is published as an Example to all Lovers of Decorum and Oeconomy.

LONDON, September 23. [1767]

They write from New-York, that the roads at the back of that province, New England, and Virginia, have been so greatly improved, that they had established public caravans & stage-coaches, for the accommodation of passengers.

The Merchants and Traders in the Town of Boston, are desired to meet at the British Coffee-House in King-Street, To-Morrow Evening, at Six o'Clock, to consult on proper Measures relating to our Trade, under its present Embarassments.—And it's desir'd every Person will attend this Meeting, at this critical Period. [1768]

In a Convention held at Sudbury, in the County of Middlesex, by a large Number of Delegates, &c. on January 5, 1775, the following Resolve passed, viz.

Whereas Isaac Jones of Weston is deemed an Enemy to his Country, and as it's not necessary he should keep a public House of Entertainment, there being two others kept near him on the same Road in Weston, by very worthy Persons, well accommodated therefor, who ought to have the Preference to sordid Enemies:—It is therefore Resolved, as the sense of this Body, That said Jones ought not to keep a public House.—And all Persons who will hereafter hold and carry on Connections with him, ought to be treated as Enemies to the Liberties of those British united Colonies in America. Signed by order of said Convention. *Attest.* JONATHAN WARD, Clerk.

CAMBRIDGE, June 1.

We are well informed, that a few Days after the Battle of Lexington, the Regular Troops stole away all the Cattle, Sheep, Hay, &c. from Governor's Island and Thompson's Island, in Boston Harbour.

NEW-LONDON, June 1.

Whereas the infamous Nathaniel Rogers, one of the Boston IMPORTERS, took a journey to New-York, and being arrived there, the Sons of Liberty had Intelligence of it, and assembling together carried his Effigy through the principal streets of that City, &c. Therefore he thinking it unsafe to abide there any longer, speedily made his Escape, and came to the East End of Long-Island, and being on Shelter-Island, the Sons of Liberty there having Intelligence by a Son of Liberty from New-York, who he was, and the reason of his precipitate Flight from thence—made his Effigy, which stood exposed to the Derision and Contempt of a Number of Spectators; they then fixed it upon a Pole, and carried it around by the principal Houses, (having this Label on its Breast in Capitals, NATHANIEL ROGERS, one of the infamous Boston Importers) and afterwards left it hanging by the Neck before the Gentleman's Door where he resided, as a monument of Shame and Disgrace to all betrayers of the Liberties of their Country: The next Day he got a Boat and embarked for Rhode-Island—and we hope he will be known when he arrives there, and be treated according to his Deserts. *Shelter-Island, May* 28, 1770.

BOSTON, March 14. [1768]

This is to inform the Publick, That the Hartford Post sets out on Thursday next, to perform the Stage from Boston to Hartford as usual; the Mail to be closed at 12 o'Clock.

BENJAMIN HART.

Hereby acquaints the Publick, That he has left Riding single Horse Post between Boston and Portsmouth, and now conveys Passengers from Boston to any Town between it and Portsmouth, and from thence to Boston in the same Post Stage, Curricle or Coach, lately improved by Mr. John Noble: He sets out from Boston every Friday Morning, and from Portsmouth Tuesday Mornings following: He will engage to reach Newbury the same Night as he leaves Boston, as he keeps fresh Horses at Ipswich for that Purpofe. He is to be fpoke with at Mr. Thomas Hubbart's, the Sign of Admiral Vernon, King-Street, from Wednefday Evenings, till early Friday Mornings, where all Baggage, Bundles, &c. will be receiv'd, and carefully deliver'd as directed. At Portfmouth Paffages, &c. may be engaged of him, or of Mr. John Stavers, Sign of the Earl of Halifax, where all Baggage, Bundles, &c. are deliver'd, and alfo receiv'd for Bofton—Half the Fare to be paid on engaging a Paffage, that no Perfons may be difappointed. The above Conveyance has been found very ufeful, and is now more fo, as there is another Curricle or Coach improv'd by Jos. S. Hart, which fets off from Portfmouth the fame Day this does from Bofton, by which an Opportunity offers for Travellers twice a Week from either Place. He therefore hopes for Encouragement from Gentlemen, Ladies, Travellers, &c. who may depend on Fidelity and Difpatch, and their Favours gratefully acknowledged by their humble Servant.

N. B. Enquiry may be made at Charleftown, at Mr. Jofeph Hopkins, near the Three Cranes. [1770]

Whereas many Perfons are fo unfortunate as to lofe their Fore-Teeth by Accident, and otherways, to their great Detriment, not only in Looks, but fpeaking both in Public and Private:—This is to inform all fuch, that they may have them re-placed with falfe Ones, that looks as well as the Natural, and anfwers the End of Speaking to all Intents, by PAUL REVERE, Goldfmith, near the Head of Dr. Clarke's Wharf, Bofton.

⁎ All Perfons who have had falfe Teeth fixt by Mr. John Baker, Surgeon-Dentift, and they have got loofe (as they will in Time) may have them faftened by the above, who learnt the Method of fixing them from Mr. Baker.   [1768]

ABRAHAM HUNT.

Takes this Method of informing the Public, that he undertakes to refine Wines in the moft effectual Manner, and in Cafe they fhould be upon the fret, to reftore them to their former quiet State; likewife to rack off and refine Cyders in the beft Manner, and (if defired) to preferve them in Cafks for drinking well through the prefent Year; Alfo, to Bottle both Wine and Cyders in the beft Manner.

N. B. Said Hunt may be fpoke with at the Dwelling-Houfe of Edmund Quincy, Efq; near the Poft-Office.   [1768]

STrayed away from Bofton Common, on Friday the 7th Inftant, a fmall Red Cow, with a fhort Tail, about 4 Years old, thin of Flefh. Whoever will return her to the Owner in Bofton, fhall be well rewarded for taking of her up. Enquire of Edes & Gill.

RAN-AWAY, this Day, a Servant Boy to the Subfcriber, named John Collins, about 18 Years of Age, a ftout, likely, fat, red-faced, well-looking fellow, blue Eyes, and brown Hair, dreffed in a brown Outfide Waiftcoat, with Pewter Buttons, a ftrip'd red blue and white under Waiftcoat, a Pair of large ftrip'd Woollen Trowfers, deep blue Stockings, and upon the outfide of his left Leg has a large Scar from a Wound lately healed. Any Perfon or Perfons who will be kind enough to apprehend faid Run-away, and fecure him in any of his Majefty's Goals, and give Notice thereof to Melatiah Bourn, Efq; of Bofton, or his Mafter, fhall receive Three Dollars as a Reward, and all neceffary Charges paid.

All Mafters of Veffels and others are hereby cautioned againft harbouring, concealing or carrying off faid Servant as they would avoid the Penalty of the Law.   SHUBAEL LOVELL.

N. B. If the faid John Collins is not immediately fecured on his being apprehended, he will again defert if poffible.

Barnftable, March 9, 1768.

DRUGS & MEDICINES.
JOHN LORING.

Has juft received from England, A General affortment of DRUGS and MEDICINES, of the beft Qualities, which he fells Wholefale or Retail, at his Shop fronting Cornhill, a little above the Market.— Alfo, BOERHAAVE'S CHYMICAL TINCTURE, prepared from an original Receipt, of which there is not perhaps any true Copy now extant.—It is a powerful Deobftruent, and an excellent Stomachic. It removes Diforders of the Kidneys, Liver and Mefentery. Is greatly ferviceable in Hectics, and with Caution may be ufed in the moft violent inflamatory Fevers. It is uncommonly efficacious in the Scurvy and Jaundice. As it is apt to increafe the Difcharge of Urine, it will not be advifeable to ufe it in Cafes where that Evacuation is too copius.—It is to be given in chronic Cafes Morning and Evening, to Adults from 40 to 60 Drops, to Children from 6 to 30, in Water or Wine, upon an empty ftomach.—In acute Cafes, it may be given once in 3 or 4 Hours as Occafion may require.

N. B. This Medicine has been ufed with the greateft Succefs, and has produced furprizing Effects in a great variety of Diforders; but as it is not known, at leaft not generally in this Country, and he defigns not to impofe on the Public, any Gentleman of the Faculty in the Town of Bofton, who fhall pleafe to make Trial of it, fhall be welcome to a Bottle; and he doubts not of the Approbation when they have experienced its Efficacy and Safety.—It will be fold at Two Piftareens a Bottle.   [1768]

NEW YORK DUTCH HOUSEHOLDS OF THE EIGHTEENTH CENTURY

As illustrated by the LIVING ROOM OF THE SCHENCK HOUSE now in the Brooklyn Museum in Brooklyn, New York

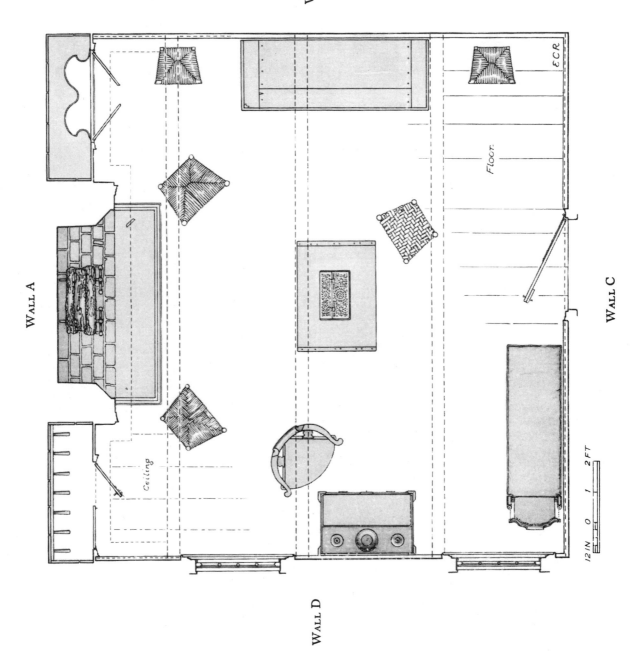

Wall A

Wall B

Wall C

Wall D

Ceiling

Floor.

ECR

12 IN   O   1   2 FT

Historical Note

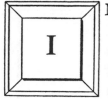I N reviewing the story of the founding of the Dutch colony of New Netherlands and its subsequent development it is enlightening to consider the essential difference in point of view of the Dutch colonists as compared with that of the New Englanders, or colonists to the south. Whereas most of the early settlers came to our shores to escape religious or political persecution as well as to satisfy a natural desire for greater liberty and freedom, the Dutch were primarily interested in setting up profitable trading relations with the Indians. In New Netherlands it was an individual enterprise; in New England a group enterprise led in most cases by a clergyman.

The English colonists came as a congregation and settled each village as a unit with well-founded civil and religious organization. Their purpose from the outset was to establish a permanent home. Their members were drawn from all social levels, and these differences persisted much as they had in England. Those families who belonged in England to the petty gentry tried in so far as circumstances permitted to maintain their old standards.

The Dutch colonists, on the other hand, were for the most part of the industrial class. They were accustomed to good living, but not much concerned with social distinctions until the advent of English colonists among them made them socially conscious, nor had they at first much community organization, in as much as trading was the primary interest. Holland during the seventeenth century had the highest standard of living of any country in Europe, due to her industrial and trading activities. This meant that a fairly large number of her mercantile class were tolerably well off, and as a result her early colonists were able to have more personal comforts than most of their neighbors. It must also be remembered that the Dutch had constant assistance from the parent country, whereas their neighbors to the north had to get along as best they could. Furthermore, the Dutch were even more thrifty than the other colonists. They held close family associations in high esteem, and cared little for social contacts with their neighbors. They were more interested in home comforts than the New Englanders and had greater knowledge of how to obtain them. China, pewter, and silver were commonly possessed by the majority of families in New Netherlands. In New England these were to be seen only in the homes of a few, and even then in small quantities. Many of the Dutch had been wealthy merchants at home, and were able to live over here on a scale commensurate with their former state. Since their lives were made fairly easy, they did not need to be so aggressive as the New Englanders. They made much of their homes and families, and took leisure to enjoy them as much as possible. The result was they advanced more slowly than New Englanders, so that by the mid-eighteenth century the standard of living of the two was about the same level. We may then

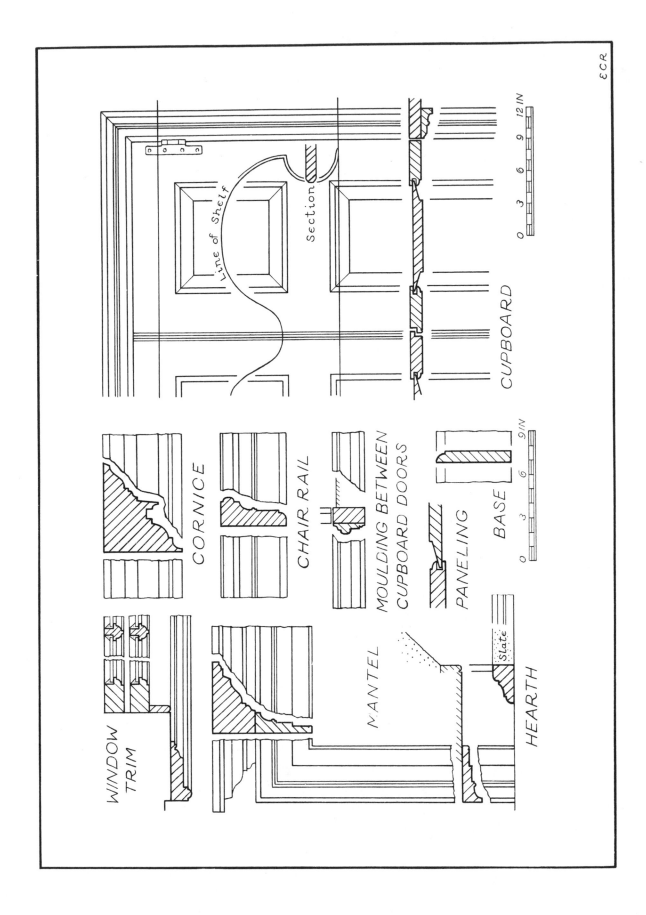

WINDOW TRIM

CORNICE

CHAIR RAIL

MANTEL

MOULDING BETWEEN
CUPBOARD DOORS

PANELING

BASE

HEARTH

Slate

Line of Shelf

Section

CUPBOARD

0 3 6 9 12 IN

0 3 6 9 IN

ECR

expect a prosperous farmer of Western Long Island to be living in a fairly large and well-equipped house of about the same condition as that of his neighbor in Connecticut. The difference lay in the fact that each followed in the tradition of his mother country. Even after 1665 New York was little changed from New Amsterdam except in name. The transfer of allegiance was probably not regretted by many as the Dutch were not politically minded. It was peacefully accomplished by Stuyvesant, who was not much blamed for failing to resist the English. The Dutch were left pretty much to themselves under the new regime, and continued to follow their old customs. Though they learned English, most of them spoke Dutch at home. Even after the Revolution the Dutch tongue persisted in many households, but this picturesque custom of using two languages had for some time been on the wane, as is eloquently shown by the appeal to Amsterdam in 1762 for a minister who could speak English.

The Dutch settlements on the western end of Long Island may be taken as characteristic. Here many families obtained grants of land varying in size from five hundred acres to several thousand. The earliest settlements were in Flatlands, the southeastern section of Kings County, in Gowanus, near the center of the present city of Brooklyn, and at Wallabout Bay, the site of the Brooklyn Navy Yard. Here they found open fields, admirably suited for building sites, with ample room for raising of crops without the necessity of clearing very much woodland. They came from a land of open fields, so did not relish the idea of blazing their way through virgin forests. In fact they had not the aptitude for this that the New Englanders had. The proximity to the harbor and New Amsterdam, the central trading town of the colony, made it comparatively easy for them to get their supplies from the mother country. Thus they were enabled to build comfortable houses a short time after arrival. Although most of the farmhouses were wooden, stone houses were far more common among the Dutch in the seventeenth century than elsewhere. Within the town limits of New York the majority of the dwellings were stone or brick. Kilns having been set up in the seventeenth century, bricks were easily available. Substantial aid from home in the way of tools and equipment, and sometimes of bricks themselves, simplified even more their building problems.

By the third quarter of the seventeenth century there were half a dozen small but thriving villages within the limits of what is now the city of Brooklyn; Midwout (Flatbush), New Utrecht, Breukelen, Flatlands, and New Lots being the most important. Scattered through these were an increasingly large number of story-and-a-half farmhouses with Dutch gambrel roofs and divided front doors. Within, the thrifty "huysvrows" pursued their manifold household duties with avidity. Among these were included spinning, weaving, soap and candlemaking, and a host of other items that each family had of necessity to perform. The farmhouses were undoubtedly better equipped than the average New England one. There were more

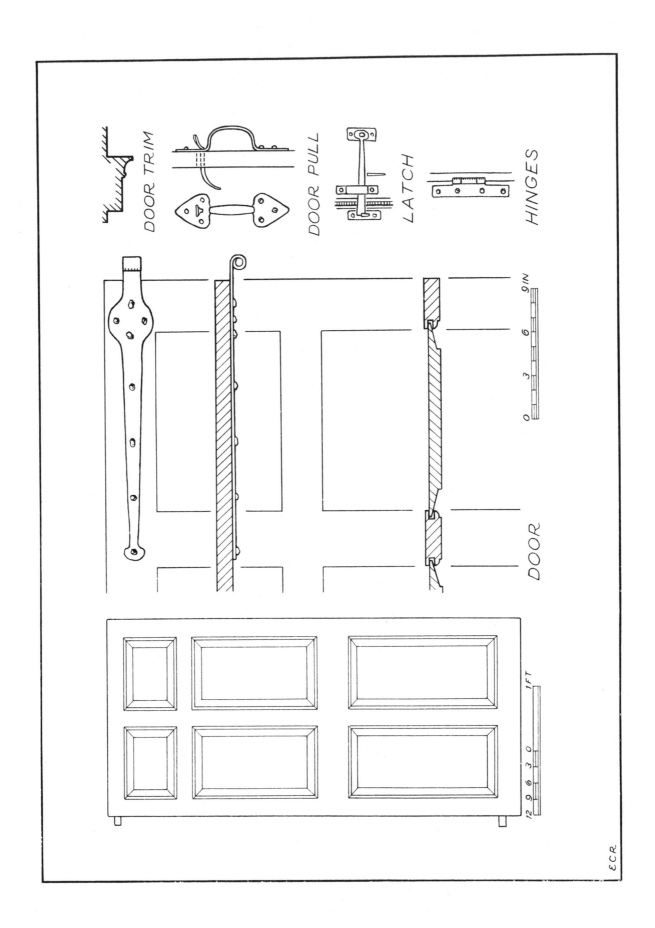

DOOR TRIM

DOOR PULL

LATCH

HINGES

DOOR

0   3   6   9 IN

12 9 6 3 0   1 FT

ECR

cooking utensils, a more liberal supply of linens, services of pewter, and a good showing of silver. These items meant more to the practical Dutch housewives than fine brocades and laces. Their taste was for dresses of plain material with little trimming, a neat cap with possibly a narrow band of simple bobbin lace. More finery than this would not have been in keeping with the somber long coat and breeches of their thrifty merchant husbands, who thought more of their long clay pipes and tankards than of brocaded waistcoats and lace frills.

Jutting out into Jamaica Bay is a point of land known as Flatlands Point, generally called Canarsie after the Indians who occupied it. Here, in 1654, Roelof Schenck, of patrician Dutch family, built a small wooden farmhouse. After being burned down it was replaced by a larger house shortly before 1760. This mid-eighteenth-century farmhouse, similar to dozens of others in the Hudson Valley, may be taken as a typical setting for a well-to-do Dutch family a quarter of a century or so before the Revolution.

New York Dutch Households of the Eighteenth Century

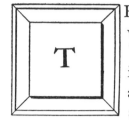

THE Schenck House is typical of the Dutch houses which have survived from the eighteenth century on Long Island and in the Valley of the Hudson. It was installed in the Brooklyn Museum in 1929 to save it from demolition. The original house was built around 1760 and remodelled in 1800. The tradition is that it stood on the site of an older house which went back a century, and it is possible that some of the timbers may have been taken from the older structure.

We gain a very good idea of what the older house must have been like from a contract drawn up in 1655 for the erection of a ferry house on Long Island:

We, Carpenters Jan Cornelisen, Abram Jacobsen, and Jan Hendricksen, have contracted to construct a house over at the ferry of Egbert Van Borsum, ferry-man, thirty feet long and eighteen feet wide, with an outlet of four feet, to place in it seven girders, with three transome windows and one door in the front, the front to be planed and grooved, and the rear front to have boards overlapped in order to be tight, with door and windows therein; and a floor and garret grooved and planed beneath [on the under side]; to saw the roof thereon, and moreover to set a window-frame with a glass light in the front side; to make a chimney mantel and to wainscot the fore-room below, and divide it in the centre across with a door in the partition; to set a window-frame with two glass lights therein; further to wainscot the east side the whole length of the house, and in the recess two bedsteads, one in the front room and one in the inside room, with a pantry at the end of the betste [bedstead]; a winding staircase in the fore-room. Furthermore, we, the carpenters, are bound to deliver all the square timber—to wit, beams, posts, and frame timber, with the pillar for the winding staircase, spars, and worm, and girders, and foundation timbers required for the work; also the spikes and nails for the interior work; also rails for the wainscot are to be delivered by us.

For which work Egbert Van Borsum is to pay five hundred and fifty guilders, one-third in beavers, one-third in good merchantable wampum, one-third in good silver coin, and free passage over the ferry so long as the work continues, and small beer to be drunk during work.

We have subsequently contracted with said Egbert Van Borsum to build a cellar-kitchen under said house, and to furnish the wood for it—to wit, beams and frame timber. There must be made two door-frames and two circular frames with windows therein, with a stairway to enter it, and to line the stairs in the cellar round about with boards, with a chimney mantel in the kitchen, and to groove and plane the ceiling. Egbert must excavate the cellar at his own expense. The carpenters must furnish the nails. For this work one hundred guilders are promised, together with one whole good otter skin. Moreover, Egbert must deliver all the flat wood-work required for the house, to wit, boards and wainscoting.

Dated 26th April, 1655, at New Amsterdam.*

The present Schenck House has many points of similarity to the older structure. Most of the Dutch country houses in New York State were framed of wood. A

*Translation from Volume I, Henry R. Stiles in *History of the City of Brooklyn.*

WALL A

HOLLAND DELFT DISHES
1st half 18th Century

SLAT-BACK ARMCHAIR
PAINTED RED
c. 1730

massive chimney was built into the house at one or both ends. Frequently the back of the chimney showed on the exterior as a panel of brick or stone. In the old Dutch houses, unlike their modern reproductions, chimneys were not built on the outside of the house, but on the inside. Records show that a few stone houses were built on Long Island and Manhattan in the seventeenth century. Dominie Selyns, of Brooklyn, wrote to friends in Amsterdam that his congregation was building him a large house, three stories high, "all of stone and based on a foundation of unmerited love." A brick kiln was established on Manhattan as early as 1660, and visitors to Amsterdam in the eighteenth century described the city houses as being all of brick. Country houses continued to be built of wood, with sometimes a front wall of brick or stone.

The most noticeable exterior characteristic of the Dutch frame house is the low-pitched gambrel roof. Invariably the upper plane of the roof was narrow and very flat in pitch. The lower plane was wide and generous and swept down over the side walls of the house with an overhang. This overhang seems to have been sufficient to shelter a comfortable bench or chair in early times, but in the nineteenth century the roof was usually lengthened along one side to provide for a porch across the entire front. There is a great deal of speculation as to the origin of the gambrel roof. It does not seem to have a Dutch source, and the probabilities are that it came from England, which would be natural, for from earliest times the Dutch made use of English carpentry. In 1642 two English carpenters from Stamford in the New Haven Colony framed and shingled the roof for the stone church built on the Island of Manhattan by William Kieft, director of the Dutch West India Company.

Roofs were commonly covered with shingles. Thatch seems to have been reserved for small out-buildings and sheds, although the counting house of the West India Company in 1626 was described as stone, thatched with reeds. There are records of roof tiles having been imported from Holland in the seventeenth century and used for buildings in New Amsterdam.

Shingles appear to have been the first covering for the outside wall. The favorite material for these in early times was good white oak split from heartwood in long lengths so that the surface exposed might be as much as from eight to twelve inches. According to de Vries, these oak shingles turned blue when they had weathered, and looked like the slate of the old country. Clapboards came into general usage during the latter half of the eighteenth century. Mouldings were used sparingly on the exterior and they were indistinguishable in type from those common in the simpler Georgian houses.

The Dutch door, which was divided laterally and opened in two parts, seems to have been of authentic Dutch origin. This ingenious invention was of the greatest practical value for it enabled the housewife to open up the house for ventilation, and at the same time to keep small children in and to shut out dogs, pigs, and chickens.

New York Dutch Households of the Eighteenth Century

Dutch frame houses impress us as modest cottages because of their one story or story-and-a-half height and their simple unpretentious design, but as we shall see, they were the homes of a well-to-do farmer and merchant class and frequently sheltered ample and even luxurious households. The Schenck House has a floor plan that is typical, not only of Dutch houses, but also of the English Georgian houses of the eighteenth century—a central hallway with two nearly square rooms on either side. A hall stairway leads to four similar rooms crowded under the low rafters of the roof. Frequently the kitchen would be a wing at one end of the house, as in the Dyckman House in New York City, or in a basement where sloping ground permitted this arrangement, or even in a small detached building. These homes had far more space than one would guess from the exterior. Under the roof of the Dyckman House were five bedrooms and an attic and four ground-floor rooms in addition to the kitchen and cellar.

During the eighteenth century specialization of rooms gradually developed in the colonial houses of America, though it was not until the days of the early Republic that the plans themselves began to show the development of this specialization. The most important room of the house was the kitchen-dining-living room, which opened off the central hall immediately to the right of the entrance. Opposite this, across the hall, was a large room which seems to have been in earlier times the master's bedroom, and the spinning, weaving, and sewing room. Later this developed into a sitting room and parlor. The two back rooms, often smaller in size, were used as bedrooms. Children and the household slaves slept in the low rooms under the roof. These attic rooms and the cellar were also used for storing provisions. In the cellar of the Schenck House was a fireplace, showing that this was used, as in many of the Dutch houses, for a winter kitchen.

Certain features of the interior were distinctly Dutch, though in most respects the interiors differed little from the Georgian homes of their English neighbors. The square joists of the ceiling were left exposed, as was the planed underside of the wide floor boards above. Apparently, in the early houses, these wooden ceilings were left to age a deep brown, but as the English houses came to have plastered ceilings early in the eighteenth century, the Dutch adopted the practice of white-washing their ceilings. The Dutch seem to have anticipated the space economies of the modern apartment for they made extensive use of built-in cupboard beds. One of these can be seen preserved in the back room of the Schenck House at the Brooklyn Museum. These beds took very little room as compared with the great canopied four-posters, and they could be curtained off by night for the privacy of the sleeper and by day for concealment. The round domical oven beside the wide fireplace is also credited to the settlers from Holland and is still known as the "Dutch oven." This oven may have been a Dutch invention, but we know it was in general use in the American homes of the English settlers in the seventeenth cen-

WALL B

KAS
MOSTLY OF CHERRY
AMERICAN. *c.* 1730

PAIR OF MAPLE SIDE CHAIRS
QUEEN ANNE STYLE
c. 1730

12   6   0   ·1 FT

tury. A final Dutch feature that may be mentioned is the gay picture tile decoration which covered the jambs of the fireplaces in the wealthier houses during the latter part of the eighteenth century.

The rural frame houses of the Dutch have no exact prototype in the old world. They were developed to meet the conditions of a different climate and to utilize the materials at hand, and the influence of English neighbors and artisans is apparent in them.

The city houses of New Amsterdam, however, suggested in appearance those of Dordrecht and Amsterdam that Vermeer liked to paint, and retained some of this character into the eighteenth century under English rule. A Swedish visitor, Professor Peter Kalm, thus described New York in 1742:

The streets do not run so straight as those in Philadelphia, and have sometimes considerable bendings; however, they are very spacious and well built and most of them are paved, except in high places where it has been found useless. In the chief streets trees are planted, which in summer give them a fine appearance and during the excessive heat of that time afford a cooling shade. I found it extremely pleasant to walk in the town, for it seemed quite like a garden. . . .

Most of the houses are built of bricks and are generally strong and neat, and several stories high. Some had, according to old architecture, turned the gable-end towards the streets; but the new houses were altered in this respect. Many of the houses had a balcony on the roof, on which the people used to sit in the evenings in the summer season; and from thence they had a pleasant view of a great part of the town and likewise part of the adjacent water, and of the opposite shore. The roofs are commonly covered with tiles or shingles; the latter of which are made of the white fir tree which grows higher up in the country. The inhabitants are of the opinion that a roof made of these shingles is as durable as one made in Pennsylvania of the white cedar. The walls were whitewashed within and I did not anywhere see hangings, with which the people of this country seem in general to be but little acquainted. The walls were quite covered with all sorts of drawings and pictures in small frames. On each side of the chimneys they had usually a sort of alcove and the wall under the windows was wainscotted and had benches placed near it. The alcove and all the woodwork were painted with a bluish grey color.*

A fair idea of the appearance of the interiors of eighteenth-century Dutch houses in New York may be reconstructed from studying the paintings of the Dutch masters of the seventeenth century. These masters delighted in depicting neat, well-appointed middle-class homes such as the early Dutch settlers left behind when they came out to New Netherlands. Many of the objects seen in these pictures were no doubt brought out to the new country in sailing ships and became the family heirlooms of the eighteenth century.

* From *Travels into North America* by Peter Kalm, Professor of Economy in the University of Abo in Swedish Finland. 2nd ed. London, 1772. Trans. by John Reinhold Forster, F.S.A. (Nov. 2, 1748.)

New York Dutch Households of the Eighteenth Century

An interior by Jan Steen shows a family at table. A white linen cloth has been spread over the Oriental carpet which covers the table. Tall wine glasses reflect the light from the casement window. Silver platters gleam and the lustre of china reflects the scene itself. Van Tilborg shows us large wainscoted rooms, the upper walls hung with paintings, the tables laden with silver and glass, the women dressed in shining satin, with the black and white of the men's costumes for background. Gerard Terborgh, Pieter de Hoogh, Jan Vermeer, G. Metsu, and Frans Hals give us as in a mirror the houses of Holland. They show great fireplaces faced with blue and white scripture tiles; four-poster beds with rich covers and curtains; velvet, brocade, or Oriental rugs on the tables; candlesticks of wrought silver; elaborate glass chandeliers, and the china and objets d'art brought from the East in Dutch ships. Maps vied with paintings on the walls, for every one took an interest in the trade routes traversed by Dutch ships.

This is the background of the Dutch colonists and, if we can judge from the articles imported by them in the seventeenth and eighteenth centuries, it was this life of the old world that they tried to reproduce in the new. No greater contrast can be imagined than that which existed between the attitude toward life of these Dutch settlers and the New England Puritans, who had for a time found shelter from religious persecution in Holland. The Dutch loved the good things of this world, especially the substantial satisfactions of a table heaped high with food and a house well appointed with good furnishings. The first poetry to be written in this country was composed by a Dutch genius who was inspired by the plentiful supply of fish and game. His poems are supposed to have been written, like Virgil's Georgics, as propaganda to induce settlers to take up the land. In one of them, he praises the air, water, earth, and ocean of New Netherlands and enumerates thirty kinds of fish and fourteen animals, besides birds, fruits, and herbs. In his "Spurring Verses" written in 1662 is this panegyric:

New Netherland's the flow'r, the noblest of all lands;
With richest blessings crowned, where milk and honey flow;
By the most High of all, with doubly lib'ral hands
Endowed; yea, filled up full, with what may thrive and grow,
The air, the earth, the sea, each pregnant with its gift,
The needy, without trouble, from distress to lift.

The birds obscure the sky, so numerous in their flight;
The animals roam wild, and flatten down the ground;
The fish swarm in the waters, and exclude the light;
The oysters there, than which none better can be found,
Are piled up, heap on heap, till islands they attain,
And vegetation clothes the forest, mead and plain.

JACOB STEENDAM, *Noch vaster.*

[102]

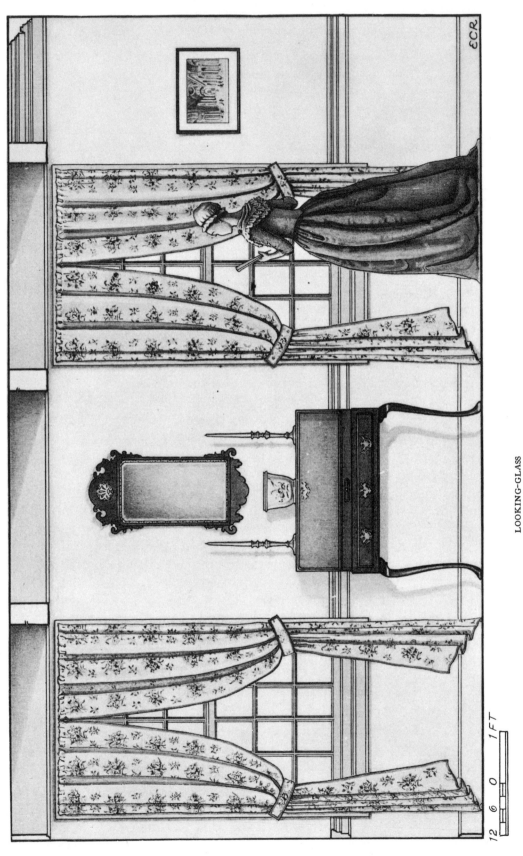

Wall D

12 6 0 1 FT

GLAZED CHINTZ
ENGLISH. c. 1750

LOOKING-GLASS
MAHOGANY VENEER
1750-1760

DESK
CHERRY. c. 1730

ECR.

New York Dutch Households of the Eighteenth Century

In a Dutch household the kitchen had a special importance as the place where food was prepared and eaten. The furnishings of the kitchen centered around the great fireplace, which commonly occupied almost the whole side of the room. Originally these fireplaces had no mantels, but later a narrow shelf was usually added. Often the wall above the fireplace on either side was panelled. Tables and chairs had a distinctly Dutch character even when they came from England or were made by English cabinetmakers, because England itself had adopted Flemish design and Hampton Court had become a veritable Dutch palace under William and Mary. The gate-legged dining table in Dutch kitchens had cabriole legs, terminating in a characteristic Dutch foot like an animal's paw. Usually these were uncarved, but in the finest examples they are actually shaped like an animal's foot. The chairs of the period show a great variety of form, but the characteristic Dutch type has the cabriole leg and Dutch foot and a high straight back with a wide vase-shaped center splat. Stretchers were often elaborately turned. The chairs sometimes had leather seats studded with brass nails or were upholstered in Turkey work or in the woven cane that had been introduced from the East.

A great many iron utensils testify to the activities of the kitchen. A wooden rack for spoons hung on the wall. Pewter and porcelain, much prized by the Dutch housewife, were kept in great Dutch cabinets. In the early inventories these are quaintly described as being made of nut wood. They were deep, wide cabinets with heavy panelled wooden doors, and they rested on squat legs, turned in the shape of huge flattened spheres of wood, often ten or twelve inches in diameter. Blue and white china vases and ornaments were placed along the top of the cabinet. From an early date the Dutch had a prosperous trade with the East and imported fine porcelain from China and Japan. By the latter half of the eighteenth century Eastern china had found its way into the Dutch colonies in such quantities as to supplant in part the earlier pewter ware. In careful inventories of householders we find ornamental figures or images of porcelain and china flower pots listed with the cups and saucers, tea jars, and teapots from the Far East and the blue Delft made in Holland.

In the better houses, the room across the central hall from the kitchen also had its fireplace set in a panelled wall. The fireplace opening was neatly trimmed by a bolection moulding. On either side were built-in cupboards containing more china and pewter. The chief articles of furniture were substantial chests, sometimes carved and sometimes covered with leather. In the cabinet or *kas*, which might be panelled, carved, or painted, was kept the family linen and clothing. Every housewife of means prided herself on the quantity of linen which she possessed, spun and woven by herself and her daughters. Although some cotton was grown on Long Island, very little of it was made into cloth. Painted or printed India calicoes were imported. These were used for dresses, for curtains, and for the narrow va-

lence which was often ruffled across the top of the fireplace opening. The windows
had checkered curtains or curtains of printed linen, usually in blue. The big Bible
with its heavy brass clasps was an item of furniture in itself. There were few other
books.

As in Holland, we find that Dutch citizens had a great liking for paintings,
prints, and maps. Apparently eighteenth-century America was already interested in
art of the sound, representative type. Many pictures were imported; a few were
the work of local artists. The first American portrait painter of whom we have a
record was the Dutchman, Jacobus Garritsen Strycker. He was a "limner" and also
a sheriff of the Dutch towns on Long Island. We get some idea of the subject matter of the paintings from old lists, such as the following:

> a great picture being a banquet with a black list
> one ditto something smaller
> one ditto a bunch of grapes with a pomegranate
> one with apricocks
> a small countrey
> a Break of Day
> a small Winter
> a cobler
> a portrait of my lord Speelman
> one Abraham and Hagar
> four small countreys
> one flower pot
> one countrey people frolick
> one sea-strand
> one portraiture
> a plucked cock torn
> two small countreys
> one flower pot small
> one small print broken
> thirteen East India prints pasted up on paper

Gradually the front downstairs bedroom was metamorphosed into a sitting
room. Tea seems to have been the agency that brought about this change. While
tea was rare at the end of the seventeenth century and one pound cost as much as
eight gallons of rum, this Oriental beverage had come into common use by the middle of the eighteenth century. It was drunk in the morning, and in the afternoon
between two and three o'clock. A whole new group of furnishings developed about
the tea ceremony. The small drop-leaf table, imported lacquer tea chests and trays,
or "teaboards," began to appear, and in the cupboards were to be found East India
cups and saucers, china teapots, silver milk pots, and bowls for sugar and silver

teaspoons. Many of the fine pieces of silver were made by New York silversmiths in the rich and rather heavy Dutch style.

It is pleasant to speculate as to whether we do not owe to the Dutch the admirable practice of drinking rum in tea. Certain it is we cannot imagine these hard-drinking Dutch citizens giving up their rum for the weaker beverage that had become the fashion, unless they were allowed to add a generous infusion of rum in their cups.

In the bedrooms, the four-poster came into fashion and gradually began to supplant the more compact but less comfortable built-in bed. These four-posters were high enough to permit a trundle bed for children to be rolled under them. We also find wooden cradles in which a restless baby could be rocked to sleep. During the seventeenth century the barn had been used frequently as an overflow for the boys and guests of the house, but by the eighteenth century there were comfortable beds indoors for every one. The custom was to sleep with windows and doors tightly bolted and the curtains of the built-in beds and four-posters tightly drawn, a practice that was supposed to keep out the unwholesome vapors which arose from the Long Island flats.

The Schenck House and its furnishings recall a tradition which does much to account for the realistic and material values which have always characterized New York. The city was founded by Dutch merchants, and its first trade grew as a result of their just and friendly dealings with the Indians, using wampum and beaver as a currency. In the eighteenth century the typical Dutch house was the comfortable home of a prosperous Dutch merchant who had access to world markets even in the comparative isolation of America. The home was the creation of a thoroughly democratic people who had a firmly rooted belief in this life and the pleasures of good and comfortable living.

CONTEMPORARY DOCUMENT

The Dutch Reform Congregations write to Holland begging that they be sent an English-speaking Minister to keep the Younger Generation in their Church.

Know therefore Gent.ᵐ That for fome Years paft the Inhabitants of our Province in General and the Citty of New York in Particular, Confifted by farr the Greateft part in Dutch People who Adhered to the Doctrine Conftituted by the National Synod of Dort. And they had formerly the greateft fhare (if not the whole) In the adminiftration of Government, and Even in our time have we had five of his Majefties Councill of this province Refideing in the Citty who frequented the worfhip of God performed in our Churches and were members in Communion with us. But fince their Death we have had none of our Members Raifed to that Dignity. . . . In Short our Influence in In Church and State Carried a fuperior fway in all the Counties of the province. But being an Englifh Coloney and all matters of Government, Courts of Juftice, and our trade and Traffick with foreigners Carried on in the Englifh Language has by the Lenght of time gradually undermined our Mother Tongue, in fo much that there is fcarce a principal family in this Citty and Even of our own Church whofe Children Clearly underftand the Dutch Language by means whereof we have Daily the Mortification to fee the Offfpring of the wealthieft members of our Congregation Leave our Divine worfhip, not being able to apprehend what is taught, And Join themfelves to different focieties that are amongft us, . . . Our Minifters, Elders & Deacons by and with the advice & Confent of the Great Confiftory or Kerkraad of our Church have thought it Expedient to call an Englifh minifter on the Aforefaid Eftablifhment not only to prevent a further Dimunition of our flock but Alfo to Receive into our Bofom again All fuch who have left us on Account of the Language only, And are defirous to Join our Communion again as foon as we get a Good Englifh Preacher. And whereas there are feveral Eminent Englifh Preachers in this Citty Belonging to Congregations who differ from us in worfhip, It Behooves us therefore in a peculiar manner to be provided with a perfon Every way Qualifyed not only to Edify ourfelves, But by his Piety Learning and Eloquence to draw others. . . .

> *Selections from a* Journal of the Proceedings of the Consistory of the Reformed Protestant Dutch Church of the City of New York. [New York Historical Society.]

Dated January 18, 1763.

THE
NEW-YORK MERCURY.

Selections from Issues between 1759-1765.

LONDON. May 6.

YESTERDAY morning, about nine o'clock the two Sheriffs went to the Tower, where they received Lord Ferrers. A mourning coach was provided by his friends to carry him to the place of execution ; but that at his particular requeſt, the Sheriffs permitted him to go in his own Landau, which waited for him within the Tower. He told Mr. Sheriff Vaillant, as they ſet in the Landau, that his dreſs, (light cloaths embroidered with ſilver) might ſeem odd, but that he had his reaſons for wearing them that day, which, however, he did not mention. The Landau was preceeded by Mr. Sheriff Errington in his chariot, and a party of horſe grenadiers and foot guards, and followed by a hearſe and ſix horſes. After taking notice of the innumerable multitude that crowded round him every foot of the way, he added, he ſuppoſed they came to ſee a LORD hanged : He had applied in vain to the King by letter that he might ſuffer in the Tower, where Eſſex, Queen Elizabeth's favourite, one of the anceſtors, was beheaded : He made this application with the more confidence as he had the honour he ſaid, to quarter part of his Majeſty's arms, and to be allied to him. To die at the place for executing common felons he tho't hard ; and obſerved that the appartus of death, and the being made a ſpectacle to ſuch multitudes, was worſe than death itſelf. The proceſſion from the Tower to Tyburn took up 2 hours and 3 quarters. His Lordſhip came up the ſtairs with great courage and reſolution, with his hat in his hand. The clergyman who attended him was the chaplain of the Tower, who had never ſeen him till that morning. This gentleman ſignifying to him that ſome account of his religious ſentiments would be expected, he made anſwer, that he did not think himſelf accountable for theſe to the public. That he had always adored *One God*, the maker of the world ; and for any peculiar notions of his own, he had never propagated them, or endeavoured to make proſelytes ; that he tho't it wrong to diſturb any national form of religion, as Lord Bolingbroke had done by the publication of his writings ; he added that the multitude of ſects and the many diſputes about religion had almoſt baniſhed morality. His ſhooting Mr. Johnſon, againſt whom he declared he had no malice, he aſcribed to his not knowing what he did, which diſorder was occaſioned, he ſaid, by many croſſes and vexations he met with at that particular time. He declined joining with the Chaplain in the prayers of the Church, but readily joined with him in the Lord's Prayer, which he ſaid he had always admired. After it was over he added with great energy, 'O Lord, forgive me all my 'errors, pardon all my ſins." When Jack Ketch's man came to tie his Lordſhip's hands, his Lordſhip miſtaking him for the executioner, gave him his purſe, which the executioner demanded of his man, and he refuſed to deliver it. This incident would have retarded the execution and greatly diſcompoſed his Lordſhip, had not Mr. Sheriff Vaillant interpoſed, and commanded them to proceed in their buſineſs, and end the diſpute : They then put on his white cap, and put on the haltar, which was a common one. He then ſtept up on the bulk in the middle of the ſcaffold, and after his cap being pulled over his eyes, Mr. Sheriff Vaillant gave the ſignal for ſinking the ſcaffold, which was done by knocking away a poſt from under it. His Lordſhip's body, after hanging one hour and five minutes, was cut down, and carried to Surgeon's Hall. From the time of his Lordſhip's aſcending the ſcaffold to his execution was about eight minutes.

The Rev. Mr. Whitefield, and one of his attendants were at the place of execution by nine, and had their coach drawn cloſe up to the ſcoffold, and the horſes taken off, but it being noticed to him, that his preſence was not neceſſary, he remained in his coach.

In the year 1752, his Lordſhip married his lady, who was the youngeſt daughter of Sir William Meredith : but ſhe has ſince been ſeparated from him, by an act of parliament, for cruel uſage.

NEW-YORK, July 14.

We hear that Colonel Young was taken priſoner, after the battle on the plains of Abraham, on the 28th of April laſt, in going ſo far in purſuit of the enemy, and by getting into a boggy piece of ground, he could not prevent himſelf from falling into their hands : His ſervant ſeeing the Indians coming towards him, ran to extricate his maſter out of his danger ; but was forbad, as it was impoſſible to aſſiſt him ; and very likely the Indians would kill the ſervant, tho' at the ſame time they might ſave his own life, being an officer of diſtinction.——As ſoon as the Indians had ſeized the Colonel, they began to ſtrip him, which they did all to his breeches, and were carrying him off to butcher him, when a French grenadier came up, who, with great difficulty (after making uſe of his arms and bayonet) prevented their putting their bloody deſign in execution, till a party of French ſoldiers came up, and reſcued him out of their hands.----As ſoon as the Colonel was relieved, he offered his purſe, wherein were ten guineas, which he had in his breeches pocket, to the grenadier for his behaviour, who generouſly refuſ'd the reward, thinking himſelf happy in relieving a gentleman, tho' an enemy, when in the hands of ſuch cruel ſavages :—The Colonel was then eſcorted to Monſ. Levy, the French General, and after informing him of the circumſtances of his being taken, and of the behaviour of the grenadier, requeſted that the 10 guineas might be delivered him ; which after great importunity, he accepted, tho' with reluctance, having done no more than his duty.--

From the London Gazette Extraordinary. Jan. 21, 1760.

WHITEHALL Octo. 17, Laſt night Colonel John Hale, and Captain James Douglas, late Commander of his Majeſty's Ship the Alcide, arrived from Quebec, with the following letters to the Right Hon. Mr. Secretary Pitt.

Copy of Letter from the Hon. General Monckton to the Right Hon. Mr. Secretary Pitt, dated River St. Laurence, Camp at Point Leon.

Sir,   Sept. 15, 1759.

I HAVE the Pleaſure to acquaint you, that on the 13th inſtant, his Majeſty's Troops gained a very ſignal victory over the French, a little above the Town of Quebec. General Wolfe, exerting himſelf on the Right of our Line received a Wound pretty early, of which he died ſoon after, and I had myſelf the great misfortune of receiving one in my right Breaſt by a Ball that went through part of my Lungs, (and which has been cut out under the Blade Bones of my Shoulder) juſt as the French were giving Wey, which obliged me to quit the Field. I have, therefore, Sir, deſired General Townſhend, who now commands the Troops before the Town (and of which I am in Hopes he will ſoon be in poſſeſion) to acquaint you with the particulars of that Day and of the Operations carrying on.
I have the honor to be, etc.   ROB. MONCKTON.

P. S. His Majeſty's Troops behaved with the greateſt Steadineſs and Bravery. As the Surgeons tell me that there is no Danger in my Wound, I am in Hopes that I ſhall ſoon be able to join the Army before the Town.

NEW YORK, Feb. 11, 1760.

Saturday laſt four Men were whipped round the City at the Cart's Tail, being convicted ſome days before of ſtealing ſeveral Things from different Perſons in this Place.

We are this week obliged to omit many Articles of News, on account of the Number of Advertiſements the Public has been pleaſed to favour the Printer of the Mercury with; but that Deficiency ſhall be made up the firſt opportunity.

WHEREAS Mary, the Wife of Chriſtian Clay, of this City, has eloped from his Bed: This is therefore to deſire all Perſons not to truſt the ſaid Mary, as no depts of her contracting will be paid from this date hereof, by Chriſtian Clay.

Now bound on a cruize againſt his Majeſty's Enemies,

The private Ship of War

T A R T A R,

THOMAS LAURANCE, Commander,

WILL ſail in four Weeks. All Gentlemen, ſailors and others that have a Mind to make their Fortunes, now is their Time. The Articles may be ſeen at the Rendezvous on the New-Dock.

WANTED (by the Society for Promoting Arts, etc.) 50 good Spinning Wheels. Any Perſon having it in their power to furniſh that number immediately is requeſted to apply to Meſſrs. Obadiah Wells, James Armſtrong, and John Lamb, who will agree with them for ſame.

New York, den 17 Juny, 1765.

GE drukt en te coop, by Sameel Brown, Boeck drukker; en by Dom. Haagoort, te Second River; Voor 4 Coopers. Een Bekent Muakinze Ontrent het drukken van een Seker Boek Genaamt Waarheyt en Vrede, etc. etc. etc. Met de Redenen daar toe Dienende voor alle de Kerken Raader en Gemeentens hier te lande, als ook deſſels condition, Nitgegere door.   GRHD HAARGOORT
Neder-Diuts Predicant, te Second River.

THE GRAND MANNER IN PHILADELPHIA

As illustrated by the DRAWING ROOM OF THE POWEL HOUSE

now in the Pennsylvania Museum of Art in Philadelphia

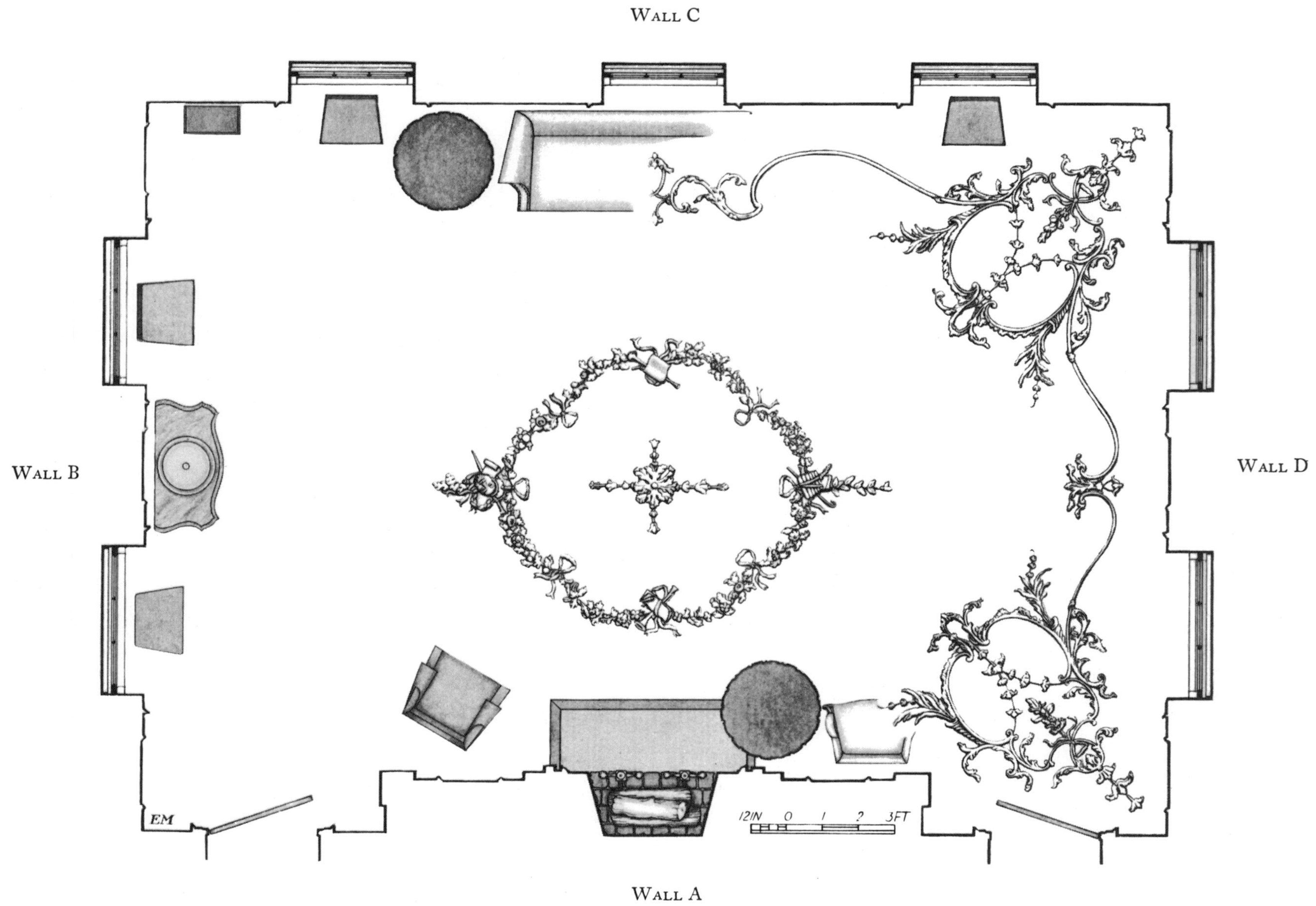

WALL D

WALL C

WALL A

WALL B

N.B. THIS AND THE FOLLOWING DRAWINGS SHOW THE ORIGINAL ARCHITECTURAL ARRANGEMENT

12IN 0 1 2 3FT

E.M.

Historical Note

SINCE the founding of Philadelphia, Penn's pious experiment, rapidly growing changes had taken place, until, with mid-eighteenth century, the city was grooming itself to be the metropolis of the Atlantic seaboard. World's People* were forging to the front in civic and social life, though the Quakers had not wholly lost their influence. The taste of one group naturally tended to make itself felt on the other, though the tendency was constantly toward a more florid opulence.

The French Wars, with the trade and privateering incidental, had, by the time of their close in 1763, brought an era of prosperity and money into the Delaware that gave the merchants an opportunity to exhibit their wealth in fine buildings and elegant domestic appointments. In the old city, the great residences, since pulled down, were designed with great ornamentation and elegance. The property from Spruce and Third Streets to Willing's Alley near Walnut Street was all occupied by members of the Willing family, while another member of the family, the Reverend Robert Blackwell, occupied a house of the same type on the property making the southeast corner of Third and Pine Streets. Charles Willing, founder of the family in America, had in 1746 built his house at the corner of Third Street and Willing's Alley. Coming from Somerset, England, he had an inborn affection for Bath and for the stone from which the houses there were built. So it was but natural that he should import the stone for his entrance trim. This was said to be the only doorway of stone in the city. His garden extended to the south, along Third Street. Colonel Byrd of "Westover," who married Mr. Willing's daughter Mary, built to the south of this the residence occupied by him at various times and later by Governor Penn and Chief Justice Benjamin Chew. This immediately adjoined the Powel House, the parlor of which is illustrated in this chapter. The Powel House also had its garden on the southern side, where it in turn adjoined William Bingham's superb mansion.

Samuel Powel, a member of the Carpenters' Company, son of a Quaker who had amassed considerable property, was under the tutelage of his eminently respected uncle, Captain Sammy Morris. He went abroad to make the Grand Tour before settling in the Third Street house. Captain Morris was a prominent member of the Gloucester Fox Hunting Club and the State in Schuylkill, two of the oldest social organizations in America.

Powel left Philadelphia the twenty-eighth of October, 1760, and wrote to his uncle a series of interesting letters during his travels. He tells us graphically how, on the first of November, the shores of Great Britain in sight, and everybody con-

* The Quakers called themselves "Friends," and those not of their ways but giving heed to the usages and ways of worldly affairs, "World's People."

[109]

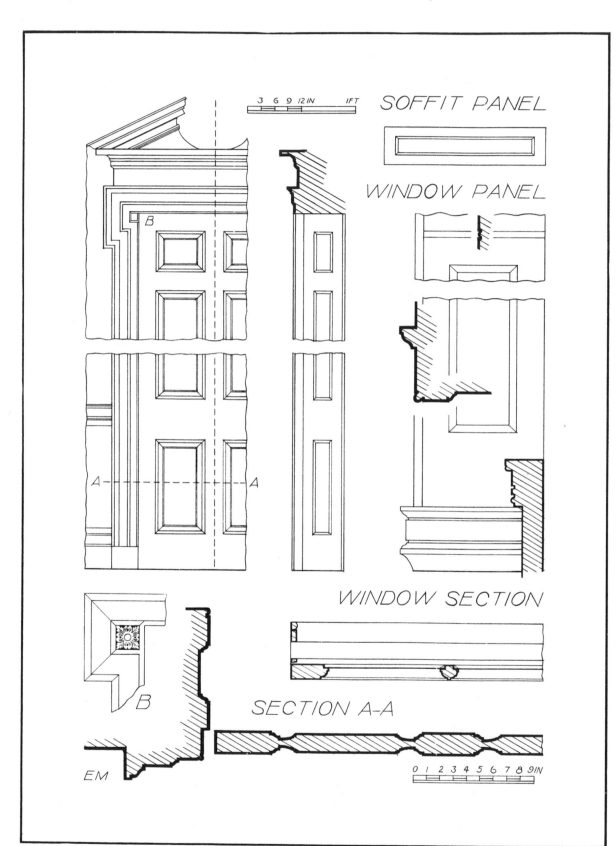

SOFFIT PANEL

WINDOW PANEL

3 6 9 12IN   IFT

WINDOW SECTION

SECTION A-A

B

A   A

B

EM

0 1 2 3 4 5 6 7 8 9IN

gratulating themselves on a speedy landing, all was quickly turned to fear as, abreast of Portland,

A Sail to windw'd and by her appearance unanimously concluded her to be a tender coming to press our people; in this belief we suffered her to approach, as without endeavor to fly; when to our great Astonishment, at about a Quarter of a Mile distance she fired a Shott and hoisted French colors; instantly followed by another Shott, both of which dropped alongside of our ship. Every means of safety seemed to be lost, unless we could outsail our antagonist, which did not appear at first probable. Entirely defenseless, at that Time, we could not resist, and the Wind was hardly strong enough to make us conjecture we could escape by sailing. Hurry and Confusion, among the Passengers, next ensued; every one endeavoring to secrete what they could, of their own, in order to a future Subsistence in France. Fear, had not however so strongly seized us but we made all the sail we could, and got what Guns we had (2 Swivels) over our stern & repaid the Compliment, standing in for the Shore at the same time & the Privateer after us. At length, upon doubling Peverell Point, we found we left the Privateer, & an English fort alarmed by our Guns blessed our Eyes with the Hopes of a speedy Relief. Observing our Signals of Distress they prepared to receive the Enemy, animating us by Signs and sending a Pilot to conduct us to an Harbour, who brought our Ship into Studland Bay, from whence we had the Mortification to see a Ship, about a League astern, taken and carried off by the Privateer. This Account may, to a Person not interested so much in the Affair, seem too prolix; but past Dangers are pleasant to relate, & past Deliverances shall ever be remembered by me with grateful Adoration to the Protector of helpless Man. . . .

I was yesterday at St. Jame's and had the Pleasure of seeing his Majesty going to Chappell. Addresses from all Quarters have been presented and amongst the rest from the Quakers. (London Decr. 8, 1760.)

News we have none material. Our expectations are . . . disappointed at the long Stay of our intended Queen. The People are Coronation Mad; & not the People of this Nation only. Foreigners of Distinction are daily crowding to London to see the Shew, which will be extremely magnificent. The Papers will inform you what Sums have been offered for Houses conveniently situated for the Sight. One Person has refused 550 for his House for the Day. (London 5th September 1761.) . . .

Yesterday the Coronation afforded as grand and Magnificent a sight as Britain ever beheld. I had the Happiness to get a good View of it. 'Tis said there were seats for fifty Thousand People within & without the Abbey estimated at 2 Guineas each on an Average. The numbers of People were almost incredible. Amidst the Multitudes who risqued their lives and Limbs on this Occasion, we do not hear of any accidents. Sitting up the whole Night before the Coronation and getting but little repose last Night I cannot be supposed in a Mood for writing a long letter. (London September 23, 1761.)

In Rome Samuel Powel was presented to His Royal Highness the Duke of York, and to the Pope, who he says received him "with great Courteousness and Affability asking many Questions concerning America. These circumstances I mention as I

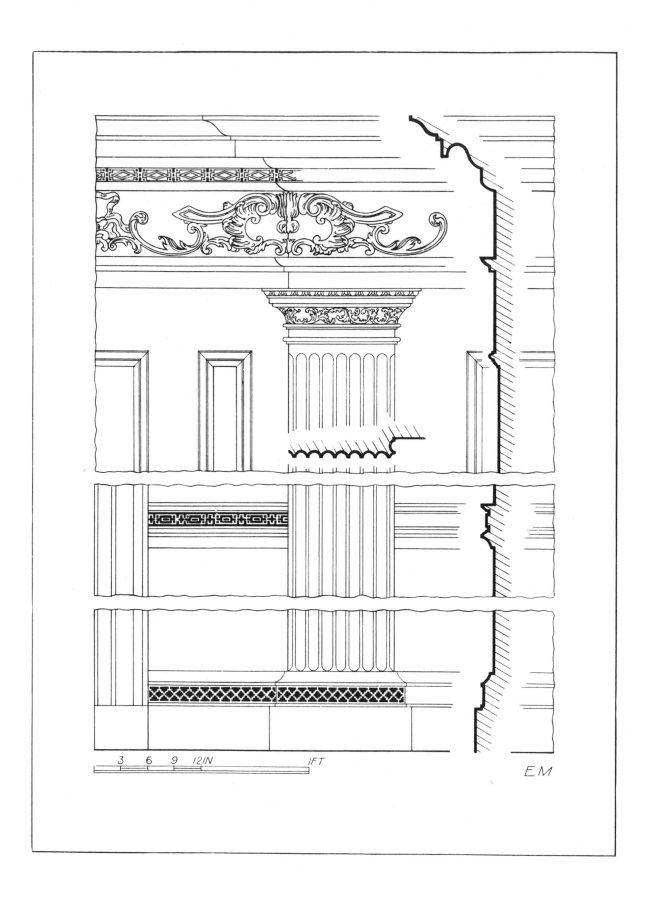

3   6   9   12IN   1FT

EM

flatter myself that you will participate of whatever affords me Pleasure, & not impute it to an Ostentatious Disposition."

While in Naples he purchased an "antique statue, some medals, a few pictures," which were shipped from Leghorn to Philadelphia. He cautions his uncle, "You will oblige me by ordering the Porters, who convey those Things from the Ship to your house, to be very careful least any Damage should happen to them."

One of these letters brings forth from Captain Morris a letter cautioning young Powel against the advisability of bringing house furnishings into the country. The Non-Importation Act had been signed, and feeling was running strongly against importations from abroad; and Captain Morris goes on to say that furniture "can be had as well and possibly more cheaply here than in London."

Before Samuel Powel returned to America, he was admitted to the Established Church, and when, in 1766, he took up his residence in Philadelphia, he was one of an ever-widening group who had become World's People. Whether or not his uncle's advice relating to the Non-Importation Agreement was having its effect, it is quite certain that the Third Street house was chiefly furnished by American craftsmen. Equally certain is the fact that the major portion of his plate he bought in London and brought with him. It would seem that this was the practice of Governor Penn, Mr. Willing, and others of a similar station in Philadelphia. Their homes were closely modelled on the metropolitan (London) taste, the woodwork being fashioned by the craftsmen here, though the lighter and more elegant appointments were imported. Life among the World's People followed the English traditions as closely as was possible in a new country.

Samuel Powel married Mr. Willing's daughter, became the last mayor of the city under the British rule and the first mayor under the congressional administration. His house in Third Street was a social center for World's People. Naturally, General Washington found this household the one in which he might be most at home during his residence in Philadelphia.

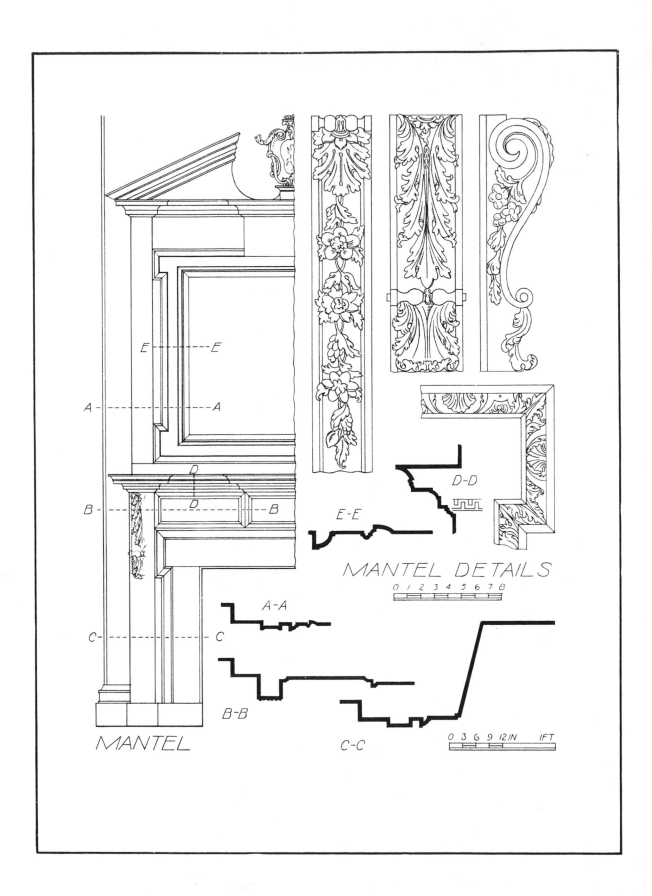

MANTEL

MANTEL DETAILS

0 1 2 3 4 5 6 7 8

E-E

A-A

B-B

C-C

D-D

0 3 6 9 12 IN   1 FT

WALL A

MAHOGANY WING CHAIR
CHIPPENDALE STYLE
PHILADELPHIA. *c.* 1770
ATTRIBUTED TO BENJAMIN RANDOLPH

PORTRAIT OF
MRS. MARGARET WILLING HARE
BY PEALE

PAIR OF CARVED AND GILDED MIRRORS
CHINESE CHIPPENDALE STYLE
ENGLISH. *c.* 1760

MAHOGANY WING CHAIR
CHIPPENDALE STYLE
PHILADELPHIA. *c.* 1770

TILT-TOP TABLE
CHIPPENDALE STYLE
PHILADELPHIA. 1760-1775

12 IN.   0   1   2 FT.

E. MELADY

The Grand Manner in Philadelphia

T HE Stedman-Powel House at 244 South Third Street, Philadelphia, was built in 1768 by Charles Stedman, a prosperous merchant, sea captain, and ironmaster. He had married Anne Graeme, whose grandmother became the wife of Sir William Keith (Governor of Pennsylvania from 1717 to 1726), and mistress of the stately country house, Fountain Low, in Horsham, seventeen miles from the city. That house, known to-day as Graeme Park, still retains its pristine appearance of two centuries ago.

The second owners of Charles and Anne Stedman's brick house in Third Street were Samuel Powel, lately returned home after six years spent in Europe, and his wife, Elizabeth Willing Powel. The wainscoting, carving, and plaster ornamentation of the house make it remembered among the brightest constellations in the firmament of pre-Revolutionary American architecture. Its two handsomest rooms on the second floor, long since in a state of sad disrepair and neglect, were salvaged and preserved by the Metropolitan Museum of Art and the Pennsylvania Museum of Art eighteen and ten years ago, respectively.

In 1785 the following record was made of Powel's house by "The Green Tree," officially "The Mutual Assurance Company for Insuring Houses for Loss by Fire."

Survey of a Three Story Dwelling House situate the west side third street between walnut Dimensions 31 feet by 45. Lower story back Room Mantle, Tabernacle frame. Two Pediments dintle Cornice round the Room Wainscoted surbase Windows cased with Architraves round Front room finished in the same stile second story back room the same as below front room wainscoted to the ceiling with fluted pilasters and highly Ornamented. Third story plain breasts surbase and wash boards windows cased and single cornice round the Room. Hall wainscoted surbase high and highly ornamented. Ramp't and twisted Mahogany stairs wainscoted with Mahogany two stories, two Mahogany Doors.

Back Buildings 66 feet by 14 two stories high nursery wainscoted surbase high cornice two rooms Kitchen finished in the best Manner one Cornice round the rest. Walls of back building 9 Inches; front House 14 Inches. Two small Trees before the Door and several in the Garden. Modillion Eaves.

The "front room wainscoted to the ceiling with fluted pilasters and highly Ornamented" in the foregoing brief survey of the Powels' house gives but a bare clue to the appearance of this drawing room that extended the width of the house on the second floor and overlooked the street. Here the unknown builder and carver lavished his skill from surbase to cornice and beyond, for one of the few plaster-ornamented ceilings of rocaille design in colonial America survives in this room.

As Fiske Kimball's searching investigations have shown, the basis of the decoration in the Stedman-Powel House—and in contemporary Philadelphia mansions also famous for their elegant interiors, Lansdowne, Mount Pleasant, and the Stamper-Blackwell House—was the engraved plates from the books of Abraham Swan, the English author of *Designs in Architecture* and *The British Architect or Builders Treasury of Staircases*, in various editions from 1745 to 1758. Reliance upon these books, as well as upon Isaac Ware's *Complete Body of Architecture*, is apparent in interior decoration executed between 1760 and the beginning of the Federal period. The usual treatment of rooms built just prior to the Revolution was to cover only the chimney breast and dado with wood, but in the drawing room of the Stedman-Powel House the walls were completely wainscoted and mouldings were applied to the plain surface to form panels. This procedure was in itself an innovation from the stile- and rail-fielded wainscot customarily employed in the first half of the eighteenth century.

The bands of frets carried around the base and dado of the room, no less than the elaborately rocaille carving applied to the frieze of the cornice, are derived from Swan's *Designs in Architecture*. Upon the mantel and overmantel is concentrated a wealth of ornament. From Swan's designs, also, are culled the leaf-covered consoles, festoons of flowers, and shell-studded architrave. On the block in the mantel's frieze Aesop's fable of the dog and his shadow is depicted amid reversed scrolls and foliation comparable in richness to surrounding ornamentation. As early as 1764 and 1770 editions of Aesop's and La Fontaine's fables illustrated by Gay, L'Estrange, and Dryden were catalogued by the Library Company of Philadelphia and thus were available for reference to Philadelphia wood carvers. (In the third edition of the *Director* Chippendale used several of Aesop's fables on mantel blocks in a manner similar to the treatment here.)

The overmantel, a restoration of the original, is crowned by a broken pediment which supports a cartouche bearing the arms of the Powel family. Originally, the six-panel mahogany doors flanked the chimney breast;* they are framed by eared architraves and topped by broken pediments, which echo the form of the one above the mantel. A glory scarcely equalled in any colonial house is the ceiling with its plaster relief ornament embodying the same graceful rocaille spirit as the carved woodwork below it. A mask, musical instruments, flowers, and bowknots incorporated into the pattern of the central oval serve as an appropriate indication of the room's festive purpose.

Nothing is known of the original furnishings of the drawing room during the occupancy of the Stedmans, but from Samuel Powel's letters, as well as from heirlooms now in the possession of his descendants, some idea of the appearance of the house in its heyday may be gleaned. From Venice under date of August 4, 1764, he wrote to his uncle, Samuel Morris, in Philadelphia:

* As they have been shown in the illustrations.

WALL B

SILK BROCADE CURTAINS

CONSOLE TABLE
MAHOGANY WITH MARBLE TOP
CHIPPENDALE STYLE
PHILADELPHIA. *c.* 1770

MAHOGANY SIDE CHAIR
WITH LABEL OF MAKER:
BENJAMIN RANDOLPH
PHILADELPHIA. *c.* 1775

MAHOGANY SIDE CHAIR
CHIPPENDALE STYLE
PHILADELPHIA. *c.* 1775
ATTRIBUTED TO BENJAMIN RANDOLPH

E. NEELADY

12IN   0   1   2FT

Whilst at Naples I purchased an antique Statue, some Medals, a few Pictures ec.ᵃ The Statue being prohibited to be sent out of the Kingdom, without an express Order from the King, & that being difficult to be obtained, has detained it with other Things so long that I began almost to despair of their ever being in a Way to see America.—This day however I have recd. from Naples which informs me of their being all shipped for Leghorn, from whence Mr. Rutherford has been kind enough to promise to forward them to Philad.ᵃ for me addressed to your care. I shall write to him by this Post & request that in Case he sends, the above mentioned Things by the Ship that is to sail for your Port, he will do me the Favor to inform you by Letter.—You will oblige me by ordering the Porters, who convey those Things from the Ship to your house, to be very careful least any Damage should happen to them. The Box with the Statue may as well remain unopened, unless you have a desire to see it's Contents. I shall be obliged to you to Open the Box where the Pictures are, & if they have taken no Damage by lying to return them to their Place. I believe I need make no Apology for not desiring any of my Friends to hang them up.

Several months later he again wrote his uncle, from London:

I have just now wrote to my Aunt D. informing her of my Intentions of selling my Furniture & Plate in Philadelphia, in Order to purchase new which I design to bring over with me. The Furniture was, by Will, equally divided between my Sisters & self. The Widow's Third I purchased, so that two Thirds of it are now my Property. If my Sister Sally should be desirous of taking it to herself, I shall be willing to let her have it for a less Sum than another Person would give. If it should not suit her to take it I should be glad you would dispose of it as soon as may be, reserving for me what I have mentioned to my Aunt and likewise the great Chest. Tho' I do not suppose it will bring any great Sum, yet I imagine the Money arising from the Sale will at least furnish me a dining Room, Parlour and Bed Chamber in an elegant & genteel Taste.

As to the Plate, what little of it falls to my Share, it is so old & bruised, that I think it best to supply its Place with new. I imagine old silver will yield as good a Profitt with you as here —if so 'twill be best to dispose of it in Philad.ᵃ As this is an Article of ready Sale at all Times, I shall be obliged to you to dispose of it & remit me the Money as soon as may be. I forget whether the Plate for the Tea Table is mentioned in the Will as bequeathed to my Sister S. if it is not mentioned I know it was designed for her & must be kept accordingly.

In speaking of Furniture I do not mean to include Linnen; which will be as useful as ever. Inclosed is my Aunt's Letter which I must beg you to deliver. With the compliments of the Season & every good Wish for my dear Uncle & Family I subscribe
Your most affect Nephew
London Dec.ʳ 26. 1764.
SAMUEL POWEL

The present furnishings of the drawing room comprise a number of handsomely carved examples of Philadelphia Chippendale furniture, which could hardly be surpassed for the quality of their workmanship or for their suitability to this background. A pair of side chairs formerly at Stenton, a pier table with a gray marble top, a pie-crusted tip table, and a folding card table, no less than the famous sample wing chair and side chair, exemplify in the elements of their ornamentation the best tradition of Philadelphia carving. The motifs most generally employed are finely serrated acanthus leaves, lambrequins, reverse scrolls, and dependent flowers, frequently displayed with diapered backgrounds and organized into patterns which the carver by his extraordinary skill and understanding has imbued with a vital spirit.

Although lacking the profuse enrichment of most of the furniture, several other pieces are highly distinguished. The tall mahogany case clock in the corner is branded with the name and marked with the engraved label of Edward James, a cabinetmaker active in Philadelphia until the close of the century; on the brass dial is inscribed the name of William Huston, another local craftsman. A side chair, unadorned by the carver save for the beading that outlines the back, is notable for the label of Benjamin Randolph, who engaged in furniture making as early as 1766. One of the handsomest sofas that remain from the pre-Revolutionary period stands beneath the windows. The long reversed curves of the back and boldly outsweeping arms find adequate balance in the strong, simply carved cabriole legs and claw feet. Though the piece lacks the enrichment of many contemporary sofas, its graceful and harmonious lines produce a triumph of design.

Over the mantel is a contemporary portrait of Mrs. Margaret Willing Hare, a sister of the hostess who presided over festivities that often brought Washington and other distinguished guests to this room. On the north wall hangs a three-quarter-length portrait of Washington, which is signed and dated: J. Wright 1784. This portrait was presented to Mr. and Mrs. Powel by Washington, who, after the evacuation of Philadelphia by the British, made his headquarters at the Powels' house and formed a friendship that lasted through life.

The three large windows are draped with short, festooned hangings after the fashion shown in Chippendale's *Director*. The fabric is a rare French silk brocade; the symmetrical disposition of the red, blue, and green floral sprays against the salmon colored ground proclaims a slightly earlier date than the room.

WALL C

TALL CASE CLOCK
CHIPPENDALE STYLE
PHILADELPHIA. c. 1775

PIE-CRUST TABLE
CHIPPENDALE STYLE
PHILADELPHIA. 1750-60

PAIR OF MAHOGANY SIDE CHAIRS
CHIPPENDALE STYLE
PHILADELPHIA. c. 1770

PAIR OF MIRRORS
HEPPLEWHITE STYLE
AMERICAN. c. 1790

SOFA. CHIPPENDALE STYLE
PHILADELPHIA. c. 1770

MAHOGANY CARD TABLE
CHIPPENDALE STYLE
PHILADELPHIA. *Dated* 1750

CONTEMPORARY DOCUMENT

In a Letter to Mrs. Hewson in England, Benjamin Franklin compares Pleasant Living in London with that in Philadelphia.

MY DEAR FRIEND.

Philadelphia, 6 May, 1786.

A long winter has paſt, and I have not had the pleaſure of a line from you, acquainting me with your and your children's welfare, ſince I left England. I ſuppoſe you have been in York-ſhire, out of the way and knowledge of opportunities; for I will not think that you have forgotten me. . . .

I have found my family here in health, good circumſtances, and well reſpeſted by their fellow citizens. The companions of my youth are indeed almoſt all departed, but I find an agree-able ſociety among their children and grandchildren. I have public buſineſs enough to preſerve me from *ennui*, and private amuſement beſides in converſation, books, my garden, and *cribbage*. Conſidering our well furniſhed, plentiful market as the beſt of gardens, I am turning mine, in the midſt of which my houſe ſtands, into graſs plots and gravel walks, with trees and flowering ſhrubs. Cards we ſometimes play here, in long winter evenings, but it is as they play at cheſs, not for money, but for honor, or the pleaſure of beating one another. This will not be quite a novelty to you, as you may remember we played together in that manner during the winter at Paſſy. I have indeed now and then a little compunſtion, in reflecting that I ſpend time ſo idly; but another reflection comes to relieve me, whiſpering, "*You know that the ſoul is immortal; why then ſhould you be ſuch a niggard of a little time, when you have a whole eternity before you?*" So, being eaſily convinced, and, like other reaſonable creatures, ſatiſfied with a ſmall reaſon, when it is in favor of doing what I have a mind to, I ſhuffle the cards again, and begin another game.

As to public amuſements, we have neither plays nor operas, but we had yeſterday a kind of oratorio, as you will ſee by the encloſed paper; and we have aſſemblies, balls, and concerts, be-ſides little parties at one another's houſes, in which there is ſometimes dancing, and frequently good muſic; ſo that we jog on in life as pleaſantly as you do in England; anywhere but in Lon-don, for there you have plays performed by good aſtors. That, however, is, I think, the only advantage London has over Philadelphia.

Temple has turned his thoughts to agriculture, which he purſues ardently, being in poſſeſſion of a fine farm, that his father lately conveyed to him. Ben is finiſhing his ſtudies at college, and continues to behave as well as when you knew him, ſo that I think he will make you a good ſon. His younger brothers and ſiſters are alſo promiſing, appearing to have good tempers and diſpo-ſitions, as well as good conſtitutions. As to myſelf, I think my general health and ſpirits rather better, than when you ſaw me. The particular malady I then complained of continues tolerable.

With ſincere and very great eſteem, I am ever, my dear friend,

Yours moſt affectionately,

B. FRANKLIN.

CONTEMPORARY DOCUMENT

The Philadelphia Ladies of 1760 *favorably impress an English Minister.*

The women are exceedingly handfome and polite ; they are naturally fprightly and fond of pleafure ; and, upon the whole, are much more agreeable and accomplifhed than the men. Since their intercourfe with the Englifh officers, they are greatly improved ; and, without flattery, many of them would not make bad figures even in the firft affemblies in Europe. Their amufements are chiefly, dancing in the winter ; and, in the fummer, forming parties of pleafure upon the Schuilkill, and in the country. There is a fociety of fixteen ladies, and as many gentlemen, called the fifhing company, which meet once a fortnight upon the Schuilkill. They have a very pleaf-ant room erected in a romantic fituation upon the banks of that river, where they generally dine and drink tea. There are feveral pretty walks about it, and fome wild and rugged rocks, which, together with the water and fine groves that adorn the banks, form a moft beautiful and pictur-efque fcene. There are boats and fifhing tackle of all forts, and the company divert themfelves with walking, fifhing, going upon the water, dancing, finging, converfing, or juft as they pleafe. The ladies wear an uniform, and appear with great eafe and advantage from the neatnefs and fim-plicity of it. The firft and moft diftinguifhed people of the colony are of this fociety ; and it is very advantageous to a ftranger to be introduced to it, as he hereby gets acquainted with the beft and moft refpectable company in Philadelphia. In the winter, when there is fnow upon the ground, it is ufual to make what they call fleighing parties, or to go upon it in fledges ; but as this is a practice well known in Europe, it is needlefs to defcribe it.

> *Selections from* Travels through the Middle Settlements in North America in the Years 1759 and 1760, *by the Rev. Andrew Burnaby.*

The PENNSYLVANIA *GAZETTE*.

Selections from Issues during 1768.

JUNIATA, Jan. 22, 1768.

BROTHERS of the Six Nations, Delawares, and other Inhabitants of the West Branch of Susquehanna, hear what I have to say to you. With a Heart swelled with Grief I have to inform you, that Frederick Stump and John Ironcutter, hath, unadvisedly murdered Ten of our Friend Indians near Fort Augusta.--The Inhabitants of the Province of Pennsylvania do disapprove of the said Stump and Ironcutter's conduct: and as Proof thereof I have taken them Prisoners, and will deliver them into the Custody of Officers, that will keep them ironed in Prison for Trial: and I make no Doubt, as many of them as are guilty, will be condemned, and die for the offence.

"Brothers, I being truly sensible of the Injury done you, I only add these few words, with my Heart's Wish, that you may not rashly let go the fast Hold of our chain of Friendship, for the ill conduct of one of our bad Men. Believe me, Brothers, we Englishmen continue the same Love for you, that hath usually subsisted between our Grandfathers, and I desire you to call at Fort Augusta, to trade with our People there, for the Necessaries you stand in Need of. I pledge you my Word, that no white Man there shall molest any of you, while you behave as Friends. I shall not rest Night or Day, until I receive your Answer.

Your Friend and Brother,

W. PATTERSON.

The following is the Extract of a letter, which came by Express on Saturday last, from a Chief of the Indians, living at the Great Island, in the West Branch of the Susquehanna, in Answer to the Message sent them by Captain William Patterson, published in No. 2041, of this Paper.

Loving Brother   February 17, 1768.

I received your Speech by Gersham Hicks, and have sent one of my Relations to you with a String of Wampum, and the following answer. Loving Brother

I am glad to hear from you.---- I understand that you are very much grieved, and that Tears run from your Eyes.---with both my Hands I now wipe away those Tears; and as I don't doubt but your Heart is disturbed, I remove all the Sorrow from it, and make it easy as it was before. I will now fit down, and smoke my Pipe.---I have taken fast Hold of the Chain of Friendship: and when I give it a Pull, if I find my Brothers, the English, have let it go, it will then be time for me to let go, too, and take care of my Family.----There are four of my Relations murdered by Stump; and all I desire is, that he may suffer for his wicked action; I shall then think that your People have the same Goodness in their Hearts as formerly and intend to keep it there. As it was the Evil Spirit who caused Stump to commit this bad Action, I blame none of my Brothers the English but him.

I desire that the People on Juniata may fit still on their Places and not put themselves to any Hardships, by leaving their Habitations; whenever danger is coming, they shall know it before it comes on them.

I am   Your loving Brother,

To Capt. William Patterson.   SHAWANA BEN.

On Friday morning last, a number of Armed Men (about 80, it is said) went to the Gaol of Carlisle, which they entered by Force, and carried off the abovementioned Frederick Stump and John Ironcutter, notwithstanding the Opposition and Persuasions of the Majestrates, and others, to the contrary.

Notice is hereby given, that the Subscriber, Silk Spinner, from Charles-Town, in South Carolina, and living in an Alley, in Front-street, near the Sign of the Queen of Hungary, would be glad to serve those who have cocoons to spin; and all persons who have an Inclination to see the Curiosity of spinning of Silk, will be shown the same, by their humble servant.   ELIZABETH TASERNER.

Since our last embarked on board the Snow Penn, for Bristol, on his way to Sweden the Reverend Doctor *Charles Magnus Wrangel*, late Rector of the Swedish Churches in America.

PROVIDENCE, Dec. 19.

"A number of young ladies, of as good families as any in town, from the laudable motive of shewing their willingness to submit to frugality, and encourage industry, had yesterday a spinning entertainment at the home of Captain Esek Hopkins in this town; when 18 of them spun 40 skaines of fine linen yarn, as a proof of their industry and drank only *Labrador Tea*, and coffee, in testimony of their frugality.---They concluded the evening with innocent mirth, such as might neither counteract the work of the day, or blemish the character, of sober and virtuous young ladies.---An example of industry this to the young men.

"We can assure the Public that Mr. Eknezer Hurd, of Connecticut, who has rode Post for 40 years between this City and Seybrook, had made in his own Family, this present Year, by only his Wife and Children, no less than 500 Yards of Linen and Woolen, the whole of the Wooll and Flax of his own Raising."

NEW HAVEN, Feb. 26.

Last Friday, pursuant to the sentence of the Superior Court then sitting at Fairfield, Archibald Tippenny, Lewis Bennet, John Mallett, and Nathaniel Bunnell, were cropt and branded with the letter C on their foreheads, for counterfeiting the lawful money bills of this colony, New York bills, dollars, etc.

LONDON.

March 19.   Yesterday, at four o'clock in the afternoon, died the Rev. Mr. Stern, author of Tristram-Shandy, some volumes of Sermons, and the Sentimental Journey.

Alas, poor Yorick! I knew him well,
A fellow of infinite jest, most excellent fancy, &
Wit, humour, genius, hadst thow all agree
One grain of wisdom had been worth the three.

July 22.   Six more of our ships are ordered for Boston as fast as possible, who are to take more troops on board; government being now determined that the laws passed in England, respecting America, shall be observed and enforced, and their officers protected, at all events.

PHILADELPHIA, November 24.

Letters from London mention that Dr. Franklin is indefatigable in his endeavours to convince the Ministry of the Loyalty of the Colonies, and that a tender and motherly Behaviour on the Part of Britain, would go further to support her Authority with her American Children, than all her Forces by Sea and Land.

Doctor *Benjamin Franklin* is chosen one of the Council of the Royal Society for the present year.

Letters from Paris say, "Mr. Franklin, celebrated for the experiments and discoveries in electricity, which he made in America, and carried to the utmost degree of perfection, was lately in this city, when the learned and ingenious flocked to see and to converse with him."

In the year 1745, when Cape-Breton was reduced (chiefly by the people of New-England) a calculation was then made what numbers were fitting to bear arms, in case of non-success in that famous enterprize, it was found 100,000 men, from 18 to 60, could be mustered in 24 hours, with arms and provisions for six days each man, in or near Boston. It is well known the militia of New-England and New-Hampshire exceed 200,000 men, capable of bearing arms; notwithstanding those people are at present (to serve, no doubt, sinister views) represented as a disloyal and disaffected community; the judicious answer is, Great-Britain itself cannot produce loyaller nor better subjects, than those despised misrepresented colonies are looked on at this time.

LONDON, September 22.

Extract of a letter from a Gentleman at Erfurt, August 28.

" In the Church of the Peterſbourg Benedictines, here, is ſhown the Tomb of Louis, Count Gleichen, of the illuſtrious Houſe of Swartzbourg, which had given an Emperor to Germany. The Count was made Priſoner in an Engagement againſt the Saracens, and ſuffered a long and ſevere Captivity. As he was at work one Day in the Gardens of the Sultan, he was accoſted and aſked ſome Queſtions by his Maſter's Daughter, who was walking there. The agreeable Perſon of the Count, and his addreſs in working ſo pleaſed the Princeſs, that ſhe promiſed to ſet him free, and go off with him, provided he would marry her. ' I have a Wife and Children ' anſwered he, - - - ' That ſignifies nothing ' ſays ſhe, ' the Cuſtom of my Country allows a Man to have ſeveral Wives.' The Count was not obſtinate, he acquieſced to this Reaſon, and gave her his Promiſe. The Princeſs made uſe of ſuch Speed and Addreſs to releaſe him from his Captivity that they were ſoon ready to embark on board a ſhip. They arrived ſafely at Venice. The Count there found one of his Domeſtics, who had been travelling about to gain Intelligence of him, and was informed by this Servant, that his Wife and children were well. He haſtened immediately to Rome, and after having ingenuouſly related what had happened, he obtained of the Pope a ſolemn Permiſſion to keep both his Wives. This happened in The Year 1240, and in the Pontificate of Gregory XI. If the Holy Father ſhewed himſelf indulgent, the Count's wife was not leſs complaiſant ; for ſhe greatly careſſed the Saracen Lady ; who had been the cauſe of her recovering her dear Huſband ; and conceived for her Rival a peculiar Tenderneſs. The Saracen Princeſs made a ſuitable return to all her Civilities ; and being herſelf ſterile, ſhe tenderly loved the great number of children the Counteſs bore. - - - At Gleichen is ſtill ſhewn the Bed whereon the Count and his two Wives lay. After their Death, they were all three buried in the ſame tomb, as appears by the following Epitaph : ' Here lie the Bodies of two rival Wives, who with unparallelled Affection loved each other as Siſters, and me extremely. The one fled from Mahomet to follow her Huſband ; the other was willing to embrace the ſpouſe ſhe had recovered. United by the Ties of matrimonial Love, we had, when living, but one matrimonial Bed, and in our Death only one Marble covers us.' "

Private letters by the Jenny, Captain Orr, who is juſt arrived from Boſton, ſay, that the principal merchants and traders of that place have reſolved not to receive any Britiſh manufactures, from the 1ſt of January 1769, to the 1ſt of January 1770.

Meſſieurs HALL and SELLERS

The following Tranſlation of Bourne's little Poem, which he calls " Decor Inemptus ", by a Gentleman of this Town, lately come to my Hands ; and as it contains ſo juſt a Compliment to many of my fair countrywomen, your inſerting it in your next Gazette will oblige
Your Friend
T. C.

* " Decor Inemptus "

The fair Quaker Maiden, neat, elegant, plain,
With juſtice the Praiſe of the World ſhall obtain,
Content with the Beauty by Nature beſtow'd
Unpractiſ'd the Licence by Cuſtom allow'd ;
Regardleſs of Faſhions, ſhe thinks herſelf dreſt,
Without-tort'ring her Hair, or expoſing her Breaſt.
But the modeſt Reluctance that faintly reveals,
Enhances each Charm, which it ſhews or conceals,
The Girls who have borrow'd gay Burdens from *Art*,
And are of *Themſelves* ſo *little* a Part,
With Envy ſhall view e'ery ſweet native Grace,
That Breathes in her Form, or that Blooms in her Face ;
With Envy ſhall Sigh, while their Hearts muſt confeſs,
That Lovely Simplicity's Beauty's beſt Dreſs.

* Native Beauty.
D.

On Wedneſday next the Anniverſary Commencement of the New-Jerſey COLLEGE will be held in the Church at Prince-town. The Exerciſes of the Day will begin at Ten o'clock.

THE FREEMEN of the City and County of Philadelphia, are deſired to attend at the State Houſe, on Saturday next, at Two o'clock in the Afternoon, to conſider proper Inſtructions to be given to our REPRESENTATIVES, on the preſent alarming and critical Situation of theſe Colonies.

" Thoſe who would give up *eſſential Liberty*, to purchaſe a little *temporary Safety*, DESERVE neither *Liberty* nor *Safety*.

AN ASSEMBLY ROOM OF WASHINGTON'S TIME

As illustrated by that from the GADSBY TAVERN, *Alexandria*
Virginia, now in the Metropolitan Museum of Art in New York City

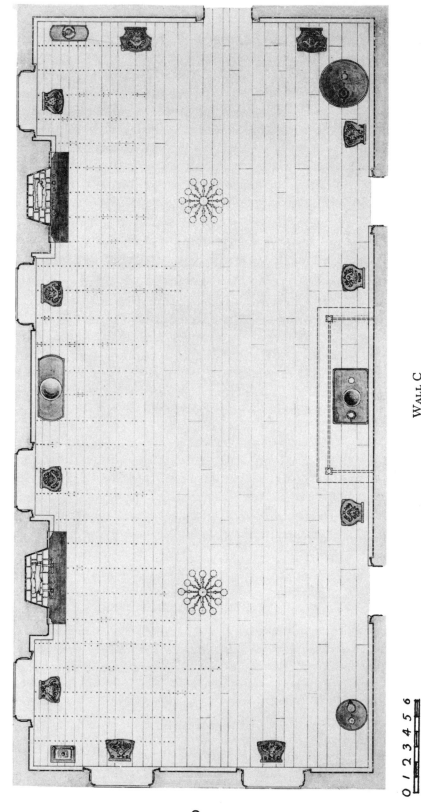

WALL A

WALL B

WALL C

WALL D

0 1 2 3 4 5 6

Historical Note

IN the early 1790's Alexandria was the principal commercial city of the region lying between Richmond and Baltimore, and a favorite stopping place on the main route between the South and the national capital at Philadelphia. As such, it was decidedly a good hotel town, and John Wise was justified in expecting a wide patronage for his new venture, when in 1793, he announced the opening of

his new and elegant Three-Story brick-House, fronting the West-end of the Market House which was built for a tavern, and has twenty commodious well-furnished Rooms in it, where he has laid in a stock of good old Liquors.

The tavern* was leased to John Gadsby who, in partnership with the proprietors of the Spread Eagle Inn at Philadelphia and the Swan Inn at Lancaster, Pennsylvania (at that time the largest inland city in the country), owned and operated a line of stagecoaches running south and west out of Philadelphia.

Virginia has long been noted for its elegant assemblies, and pains were taken to insure that the assembly or ballroom of the new tavern should be found worthy of the patronage of the élite of the country. While half the town must have waited on tiptoes for its grand opening, this event undoubtedly furnished a very particular excitement and delight to the Negroes of the community. What with the pastries to be made and tasted by the cooks in the tavern's great kitchen; the moguls from the neighboring plantations to be helped from their lumbering chariots; the wine, brandy, and punch to be gleaned from the discarded glasses; the racy gossip to pass on to black friends from the country of the doings of their white folks at the ball —this must have been a night of nights for them, and supremely so for the three or four Negro fiddlers who were able to display themselves and their musicianship in the conspicuous musicians' galleries for hours on end, while earning a dazzling dollar in the bargain! †

Considering the strenuous duties they would be called upon to perform at the ball, the gentlemen qualified to purchase tickets of admission were perhaps the least enthusiastic of those awaiting the opening of the new room. The waltz, though known to certain European circles, had not yet reached the United States; the minuet had lost its vogue; and the swinging of one's partners through the vigorous and interminable Roger de Coverleys and gavottes that stretched deep into the night must have taxed the endurance of even the strongest and most ardent of the male dancers.

* Known equally well as the City Tavern and as the Gadsby Tavern.

† Advertisements of the time offering Negroes for sale or promising a reward for the return of runaways speak of their ability to play the French horn, "banger," guitar, or flute, as well as the fiddle; though orchestras were usually composed of violins.

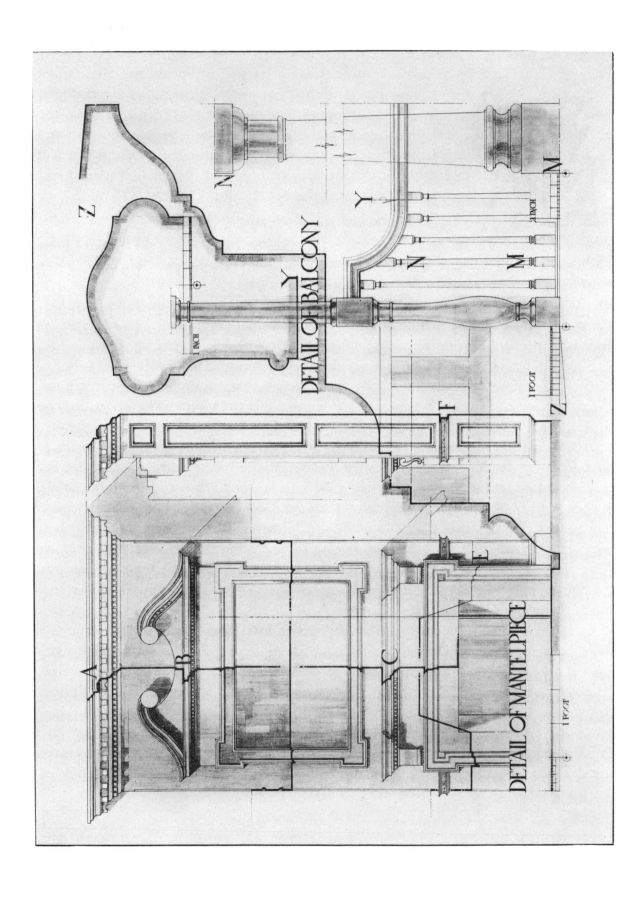

DETAIL OF BALCONY

DETAIL OF MANTELPIECE

Historical Note

A sketch of the historical background of the Gadsby Tavern would be incomplete without at least a passing reference to its patronage by Washington, whose plantation at Mount Vernon was only eight miles away. We know from the memoirs of his adopted son, Washington Parke Custis, that the last ball which he attended was one at the tavern in 1798. Moreover, almost the last of his letters was a response to an invitation from the Washington Society of Alexandria to join the Society's projected assemblies at the tavern for the winter of 1799-1800, in which he said:

Mount Vernon, 12 Nov., 1799.

Gentlemen:

Mrs. Washington and I have been honored with your polite invitation to the assemblies in Alexandria this winter, thank you for this mark of your attention. But alas! our dancing days are no more. We wish, however, all those who relish so agreeable and innocent an amusement all the pleasure the season will afford them.

Your most obedient and obliged humble servant,

Go. Washington.

An overnight visitor, interested in the furnishings of the ballroom, would have been struck by the fact that but few of the exquisite chairs, sofas, and other pieces of furniture were of local workmanship. Most, perhaps all, would have borne the name or mark of some English workman or that of one of the cabinetmakers of the North. At a time when the homes and public buildings of Pennsylvania, New England, and New York were being embellished with pieces of exquisite local workmanship by Phyfe, McIntire, Savery, Goddard, or one of the less well known Pennsylvania Dutch cabinetmakers, Virginia, the largest and most opulent of all the states, had developed almost no cabinet work of outstanding merit. The social conditions which attracted the skilled artisans from Europe and developed the latent craftsmanship of the cabinetmakers of the North, had no counterpart in the South.

Perhaps, to a visitor, an even more striking feature of the evening would have been the number of Scotch burrs which he encountered in the course of the evening. The great tobacco trade of Glasgow, Greenoch, Dumfries, and other parts of southwest Scotland brought hundreds of Scottish merchants to Virginia in colonial days; and Alexandria, as one of the most important ports of the state, had its full share of these foreign traders. During the Revolution they remained loyal to Great Britain (were, indeed, almost the only avowed Loyalists in the colony), and in consequence suffered heavy losses. But within a decade after the close of the war they had picked up many of the threads of their extensive American business enterprises, and the marked Scotch character of the architecture of the tavern, described by Mr. Waterman in the chapter which follows, was doubtless attributable to their influence.

[125]

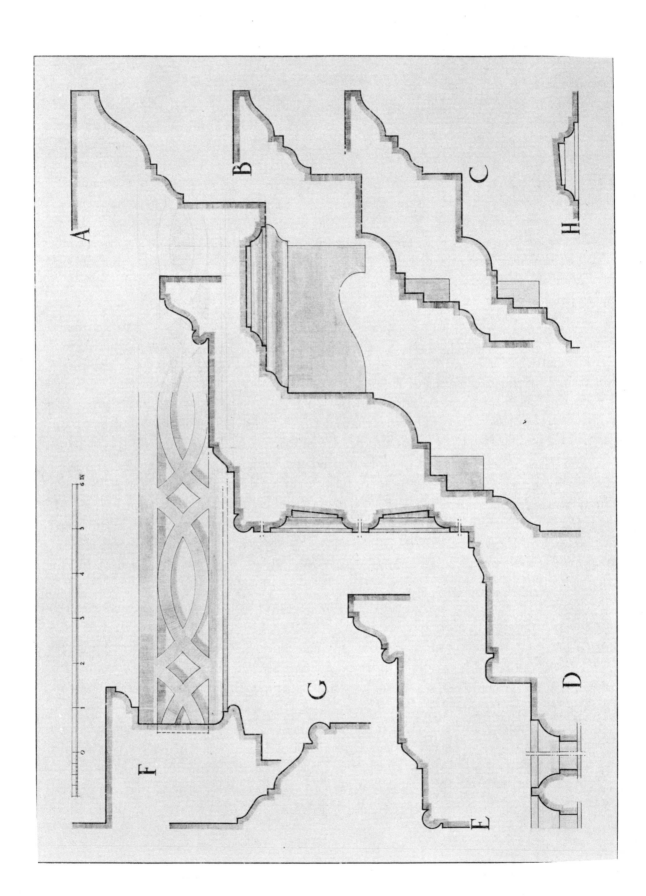

WALL A

PORTRAIT OF GEORGE WASHINGTON
BY CHARLES WILLSON PEALE
AMERICAN SCHOOL. 1741-1827

DROP-LEAF TABLE
WALNUT
AMERICAN
2nd quarter 18th Century

PORTRAIT OF
CADWALLADER COLDEN
BY JOHN WOLLASTON
AMERICAN SCHOOL
(active 1751-1769)

PORTRAIT OF
MRS. ALICE CHRISTIE COLDEN
BY JOHN WOLLASTON
AMERICAN SCHOOL
(active 1751-1769)

SIDE CHAIRS
WALNUT
PHILADELPHIA
2nd quarter, 18th Century

0 1 2 3 4 5 6

An Assembly Room of Washington's Time

THE conservatism and independence of the Scotch character are well shown by the architecture of Alexandria. Politically, it was one with the rest of Virginia, but architecturally, completely divorced from other parts of the colony except for Dumfries, a town now virtually disappeared, twenty-five miles to the south. Both of these towns were settled by Scotsmen and the bond between them and the mother country was jealously maintained. For example, William Ramsay of Alexandria returned to his native Dumfries in Scotland in 1765 and was signally honored by having the freedom of the city bestowed upon him; and Defoe wrote of the important trade that existed between that city and the English colonies.*

Just how close the architectural parallel is between the colonial architecture of Alexandria and its environs and Scotch contemporary architecture, it is difficult to say. Neither has been carefully enough analyzed by architectural writers to make this possible. The difference between Alexandria building, as exemplified by Gadsby's Tavern, and other Virginia architecture is obvious. The most elementary characteristic of the latter is verticality of the window void — that is, the sash opening of the windows, inside the staff beads. The ordinary Virginia proportion is about two and a half squares high, ranging to over three as an extreme at Rosewell, in Gloucester County. In Alexandria, however, the openings are definitely less vertical and seldom reach two squares in height. Also, the usual Virginia sash is three lights wide, but in Alexandria the early sash is almost without exception four lights wide. These variations give the buildings a definitely different character. Design of wood, stone, and brick detail in the two localities is equally differentiated.

Aside from the Scotch versus English influence, there was also the conflict going on in Virginia, in the last quarter of the eighteenth century, among three schools of architectural thought: i.e., the conservative Georgian, the fashionable Adamesque, and the intellectual classic revival, the last fostered by Jefferson. Of these three the Gadsby Ballroom easily falls within the first, but the chasm that existed between it and the other post-Revolutionary Virginia work of the same type is shown by the crisp beauty of the mantel and door designs, the work of a designer thoroughly at home in his style as contrasted with the same features in the great room at Elmwood, in Essex County (some years earlier), which are clumsy and incompletely understood renderings of the same school.

There are not many rooms in Virginia comparable with the Gadsby Ballroom, but perhaps it is illuminating to consider the Mount Vernon Ballroom which was finished in 1785 and was built only a few miles distant. The whole background of

* Daniel Defoe, *A Tour Through the Whole Island of Great Britain*, Volume II, page 122. London, 1769.

[127]

the house is English colonial, and while Washington used full Georgian motives, such as the Palladian window and the imported marble mantel, yet he managed to give it the flavor of Adamesque work, then the fashion in England, by the use of a graceful coved ceiling with rich stucco ornament in that style. The Barton Meyers house containing the outstanding examples of Virginia rooms in this style was built in Norfolk in 1795, and these interiors are innocent of any lingering Georgian character or detail. Norfolk was the other important Virginia port, but its commerce was essentially with London and Bristol instead of with North British ports.

The elementary qualities of the Gadsby Ballroom are spaciousness, agreeable proportions, and skillful architectural design, all of which make one think of Carlyle's observation regarding Wren's design of Chelsea Hospital, that it was the "work of a Gentleman." This air of good breeding is strongly felt in the ballroom, and one can sense that it was built as an assembly room for gentlefolk. The dexterity of the designer is shown by the adaptability of the room, for as a public meeting place it would have many uses, for sober as well as gay occasions, and for none would it be an inappropriate background. The woodwork, though fairly elaborate in its general scheme, is simple and restrained in detail and imparts to the room a quiet gravity. For the splendid balls given in the room this background was a perfect foil, and the brilliant costumes of the women of Oriental, Lyons, or Spitalfields silk in the incoming French style must have been splendidly displayed against it. Fortunate in the distribution of its elements (except for the unavoidable wall pier on the center of the short axis), the room is equally fortunate in the quality of its architectural detail. This is consistently and correctly in the style of the mid-Georgian period of Sir William Chambers.

In its original position in Alexandria in Gadsby's Tavern, the ballroom was lighted by windows on three sides, while on the remaining side were two doors, as at present, leading from the hall, with centered between them the musicians' gallery. These doors are on axes with the two fireplaces, making the latter the definite focuses of the design. The mantels, of the frontispiece type, are applied to sheathed chimney breasts and are tied to the rest of the room by a fine panelled dado below a plastered wall, and by a vigorous cornice, enriched with modillions and dentils. The dado, being identical in height with the window stool, runs uninterruptedly around the room except at the doors and mantels. The other element in the room is the musicians' gallery, which from its position alone is hopelessly unrelatable to the rest of the woodwork, except in scale and character. Its position against the entrance wall is fortunate as it does not take its place in the composition until the rest of the room has been seen.

The fireplaces are faced with marble, a modern replacement, and are framed with a fully moulded architrave, which is extended laterally at the top to form "ears" or crossetts. At the head, this architrave forms the lower member of a full

WALL C

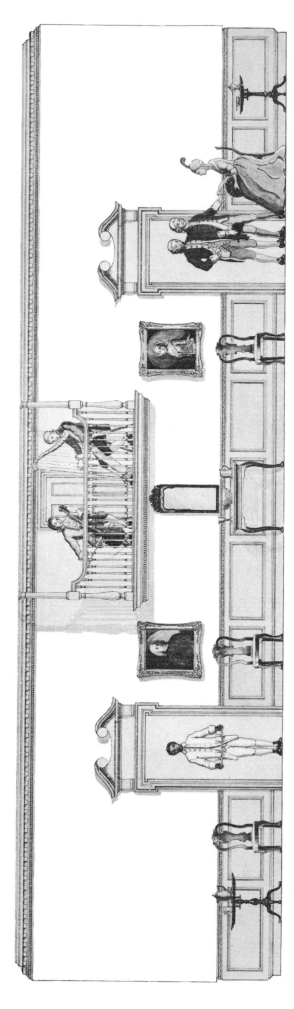

TIP-TOP TABLE
WALNUT
AMERICAN
2nd quarter
18th Century

PORTRAIT OF
GABRIEL MANIGAULT
BY JEREMIAH THEUS
(?-1774)

SIDE CHAIRS
WALNUT
PHILADELPHIA
2nd quarter 18th Century

LOOKING-GLASS
LACQUERED ON DEAL
ENGLISH. *c.* 1725

PIER-TABLE
MAHOGANY
AMERICAN
c. 1720

PORTRAIT OF
MRS. GABRIEL MANIGAULT
BY JEREMIAH THEUS
(?-1774)

TIP-TOP TABLE
APPLEWOOD
AMERICAN
3rd quarter
18th century

0 1 2 3 4 5 6

classic entablature, the denticulated cornice becoming the mantel shelf. This is supported on scrolled consoles, boldly pierced in side elevation, around which the cornice makes a slight break. The consoles rest on a row of guttae. Carrying out the scheme of the fireplace surround, the overmantel panel is formed by a simplified architrave which breaks out in crossetts at each corner. The shape of these panels is horizontal and they may well have been meant to contain scenes painted on the wood or on canvas to fit the shape, as in the northwest room at Mount Vernon. This overmantel panel is capped by a very charming scrolled pediment above a plain frieze. The ogee of the scroll is adroitly worked out, and the moulding it carries is stopped against uncarved rosettes with scrolled sides. The pediment mouldings are enriched with a dentil band. On account of the unusually lofty ceiling height of the room these full frontispiece mantels are agreeably contained on the chimney breast below the cornice. (In the Carlyle House near by, however, where the ceilings are lower, the entire pediment has had to be omitted and the resulting relationship is very poor.)* The doorway echoes the mantel treatment, the architrave breaking out at the lintel into crossetts, the plain frieze containing consoles which support diminutive scrolled pediments.

The Georgian flavor was retained in Alexandria building until the second decade of the nineteenth century, by which time the town was fairly well built up, with the result that the late eighteenth-century air has been preserved even up to the present.

The furniture, authenticated as of early Alexandria, and now to be seen there, is much like that generally found in Virginia: some fine imported pieces in the style of Chippendale; some simpler homemade interpretations of the same, domestic Sheratonesque, and Empire. Of these two latter groups, some was made in Alexandria, but most of the better pieces are assigned to Philadelphia by their present owners, many of whom are descendants of the original purchasers. One of the most individual pieces is a secretary, owned by William Ramsay, and now the property of a descendant. It is of mahogany, with a simple slant-front base; the feet are ogee brackets, and the drawers shut flush, without a lip, but are beaded. The corners are treated with quadrant Doric colonettes, after the fashion of a tall clock, but without flutes. These also occur on the bookcase above. The latter has panelled doors, the panel being raised by a delicate bolection moulding. The whole is surmounted by an ogee broken pediment, with denticulated cornice, and in the center is featured an elaborate but archaic cartouche, carved with a mask. The cabinet is elaborate, the drawers setting back in scrolled blockings. There are seven concealed drawers; all the drawers are lined with oak. While patently British, the writer would attribute the piece to Scotland without hesitation. It is probable that William Ramsay purchased it on his trip in 1765. He refers to it in his will of 1789.

* Holden and Coffin, *Brick Architecture of Maryland and Virginia*. (Illustration, plate 107.)

Some silver was made in Alexandria in the eighteenth and early nineteenth centuries, but, by and large, the fine pieces are English or "Philadelphia." From the seventeenth century on, silver was ordered from England by the Virginians. In 1688, William Fitzhugh of Bedford, in King George County, wrote his factors in London and ordered large quantities of silver.* There are numberless records of silver ordered from England, and many fine examples of English silver remaining in Virginia.

Mr. Okie, in his *American Silver and Old Sheffield Plate*, enumerates ten silversmiths working in Virginia before 1800. He begins with Pierre Harache of Williamsburg, dating him at 1691, when Jamestown was still the capital, and Williamsburg was still Middle Plantation. Also of Williamsburg, he lists Samuel Galt (1749), James Craig (1750), and James Getty (1772). Later in the century, he gives silversmiths as working in Petersburg, Norfolk, and Alexandria. Described as of the last city are Charles Burnette (1793) and Adam Lynn (1796).

In the Clearwater Collection is a fine helmet-shaped creamer mounted on a turned stem and square base. This has a beading at lip and stem and is six and three-eighths inches high.† This is the work of J. Adam, a silversmith who worked in Alexandria about 1800. This classic type of design was much used in the city at that time, if unidentified pieces still remaining in the hands of old residents are really indigenous. There are several examples of urn-shaped comports and sugarbowls, and helmet-shaped creamers, upon most of which delicate bands of beading are found. Some pieces are attributed to a Mordecai Miller of Alexandria, who is said to have worked about 1800. All of the early silver seen in Alexandria, however, was English, of Georgian design.

The last fifty years of the eighteenth century and the opening ones of the nineteenth, up to the development of the railroad and diversion of trade to Baltimore, were great ones for Alexandria. In no American city was the grace of living more appreciated and practiced. Its citizenry was distinguished, wealthy, and cosmopolitan, and the legacy of beauty it left us is a great one. At its finest it is to be seen in the Ballroom of Gadsby's Tavern. Nowhere can better be appreciated the vitality of design of the architecture of the early Republic, nowhere more faithfully mirrored the sturdiness and elegance of our ancestors, fresh from the achievement of a great ideal, and still undismayed by the mechanized civilization whose working was to plunge their grandchildren into the chaos of a civil war.

* William Fitzhugh's *Letterbook*, 1679-99 (photostat copy), page 157. Library of Congress.

† C. Louise Avery, *Clearwater Collection, Based on the American Silver of the XVII and XVIII Centuries*, page 119. New York, 1920.

WALL D

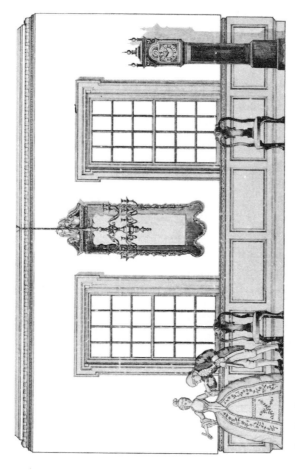

SIDE CHAIRS
WALNUT
PHILADELPHIA
2nd quarter 18th Century

0 1 2 3 4 5 6

BRASS CHANDELIER
ENGLISH
2nd half 18th Century

LOOKING-GLASS
MAHOGANY, CARVED AND GILDED
AMERICAN. *Middle of 18th Century*

TALL CLOCK
WALNUT VENEER ON
PINE CASE. *c.* 1725

CONTEMPORARY DOCUMENT

Philip Vickers Fithian, just out of Princeton, describes a Ball in Eighteenth-Century Virginia.

We fet away from Mr. Carters at two; Mrs. *Carter* & the young Ladies in the Chariot, Mrs. Lane in a Chair, & myfelf on Horfeback — As foon as I had handed the Ladies out, I was faluted by Parfon *Smith*; I was introduced into a fmall Room where a number of Gentlemen were playing Cards (the firft game I have feen fince I left Home) to lay off my Boots Riding-Coat &c. — Next I was directed into the Dining-Room to fee young Mr. *Lee*; He introduced me to his Father — With them I converfed til Dinner, which came in at half after four. The Ladies dined firft, when fome Good Order was preferved; when they rofe, each nimbleft Fellow dined firft — The Dinner was as elegant as could be well expected when fo great an Affembly were to be kept for fo long a time. — For Drink, there was feveral forts of Wine, good Lemon Punch, Toddy, Cyder, Porter &c. — About Seven the Ladies & Gentlemen begun to dance in the Ball-Room. — firft Minuets one Round; Second Giggs; third Reels; And laft of All Country-Dances; tho' they ftruck feveral Marches occafionally — The Mufic was a French-Horn and two Violins — The Ladies were Dreffed Gay, and fplendid, & when dancing, their Skirts & Brocades ruftled and trailed behind them! — But all did not join in the Dance for there were parties in Rooms made up, fome at Cards; fome drinking for Pleafure; fome toafting the Sons of america; fome finging "Liberty Songs" as they call'd them, in which fix, eight, ten or more would put their Heads near together and roar, & for the moft part as unharmonious as an affronted * — Among the firft of the Vociferators was a young Scotch-Man, Mr. *Jack Cunningham*; he was nimis bibendo appotus; noify, droll, waggifh, yet civil in his way & wholly inoffenfive — I was folicited to dance by feveral, Captain Chelton, Colonel Lee, Harry Lee, and others; But George Lee, with great Rudenefs as tho' half drunk, afked me why I would come to the Ball & neither dance nor play Cards? I anfwered him fhortly, (for his Impudence moved my refentment) that my Invitation to the Ball would Juftify my Prefence; & that he was ill qualified to direct my Behaviour who made fo indifferent a Figure himfelf —

Dated Jan. 18, 1774.

Selection from Philip Vickers Fithian, Journal and Letters, 1767-1774. *Edited by J. R. Williams, Princeton*, 1900. *By permission of the Princeton University Library.*

*This word is left blank in the original copy.

CITY - TAVERN,

Sign of the Bunch of Grapes.

THE Subſcriber informs his cuſtomers, and the Public in general, that he has removed from the old houſe, where he has kept Tavern for four years paſt, to his new and elegant Three-Story Brick-Houſe, fronting the Weſt-end of the Market-Houſe, which was built for a Tavern, and has twenty commodious, well-finiſhed Rooms in it, where he has laid in a large ſtock of good old Liquors, and hopes he will be able to give ſatisfaction to all who may pleaſe to favour him with their cuſtom.

JOHN WISE.

Alexandria, Feb. 20, 1793.   3m.

JOHN SMITH, Dancing-Maſter.

INTENDS to open a Dancing-School at the houſe of Mr. William Wilson, Carpenter, in Water-ſtreet, on *Saturday* the 20th inſtant. He will teach in the moſt faſhionable modes at preſent: each ſcholar to pay *Four Dollars* per quarter—one half to be paid on entrance, and the other half to be paid at the expiration of the quarter.

The Subſcriber has juſt opened

A Houſe of Entertainment,

IN that noted and commodious dwelling, lately occupied by Mr. John Wise. He has ſupplied himſelf with a moſt excellent Cook, who was for many years employed as ſuch by the President of the United States; has engaged two very complete Waiters; two active and ſmart Oſtlers; has been very particular in the choice of his Liquors, and ſelecting his Proviſions of every kind; and as he is determined to pay the ſtricteſt attention to his buſineſs, he flatters himſelf, that thoſe who may be pleaſed to favour him with their cuſtom, will not find themſelves diſappointed at the uſage they ſhall meet with.

Alexandria, Jan. 18, 1793.   JOHN ABERT.

MR. WILLIAMS,

PORTRAIT PAINTER.

(Late from Fredericksburg.)

INTENDS to ſtay a few weeks in this town. Should any Ladies or Gentlemen be deſirous of having their Likeneſs taken, their obliging demands will be attended to, by application being made to him at Doctor *Lang's*, in Duke-Street, where a few ſpecimens of his performances may be ſeen.

His prices depend on the manner and ſtyle of Painting—half price is expected at the firſt ſitting.

Alexandria, May 14, 1793.

☞An APPRENTICE wanted by the Printer's hereof.

FOREIGN INTELLIGENCE.

NATIONAL CONVENTION OF FRANCE.

Monday, *January* 21.

REPORT upon the DEATH of LOUIS XVI.
made to the Commons.

JACQUES ROUZ, (Prieſt and Preacher of the Sans Culottes, one of the Commiſſioners named by the Commons to aſſiſt at the execution of Louis) ſpeaks:

"We come to give you an account of the miſſion with which we were charged. We went to the temple where we announced to the tyrant that the hour for his execution was arrived.

"He deſired ſome minutes alone with his Confeſſor. He wanted to give us a parcel for you; but we obſerved we were only charged to conduct him to the ſcaffold. He anſwered, 'that is true,' and gave the packet to our colleague. He recommended his family, and requeſted that Clery, his valet de chambre, ſhould be that of the Queen, and then haſtily ſaid of his Wife. He further requeſted that his old ſervants at Verſaillies, ſhould not be forgotten. He ſaid to Santerre—Marchons—let us go on.— He walked through one court and got into the carriage in the ſecond. The moſt profound ſilence reigned during the whole proceſſion. Nothing happened. We never loſt ſight of Capet, till we arrived at the Guillotine. He arrived there at ten minutes after ten—he was three minutes getting out of the carriage—he wiſhed to harrangue the people—Santerre oppoſed it. His head was ſevered from his body. The citizens dipped their pikes and handkerchiefs in his blood!"

Santerre.—"You have heard an exact account of all that paſſed. Louis wanted to ſpeak of mercy to the people, but I would not let him."

Extract of a letter from Bridgetown, Barbadoes, dated the 29th inſt.

"Many inhabitants of this town aſſembled, and had the effigy of Thomas Paine, with his "Rights of man," carried about the town; and afterwards burnt him on the parade, in the green, juſt above the Cage, while the band played God ſave the king." [In the true ſpirit of ſwine, who are known to be ſo enamoured of the mire and filth of their incloſure, as frequently to lacerate the hand that lets down the fence for their deliverance.]

Feb. 15. Capt. Bligh could gain no intelligence of the mutineer Chriſtian, and his accomplices, who were on board the Bounty. When they returned to Otaheite, after executing their infernal project, the natives, ſuſpecting ſome miſchief from the non-appearance of the commander and the gentlemen with him, laid a plan to ſeize the veſſel and crew, but a favorite female of Chriſtian's betrayed the deſign of her countrymen; he put to ſea in the night, and the next morning the ſhip was nearly out of ſight.

BY THE PRESIDENT OF THE UNITED STATES.

A PROCLAMATION.

WHEREAS it appears that a ftate of war exifts between Auftria, Pruffia, Sardinia, Great Britain, and the United Netherlands, of the one part; and France on the other—and the duty and intereft of the United States require, that they fhould with fincerity and good faith adopt and purfue a conduct friendly and impartial towards the belligerent powers·

I HAVE therefore thought fit by thefe prefents, to declare the difpofition of the United States to obferve the conduct aforefaid towards thefe powers refpectively; and to exhort and warn the citizens of the United States carefully to avoid all acts and proceedings whatfoever, which may in any manner tend to contravene fuch difpofition.

AND I DO hereby alfo make known, that whofoever of the citizens of the United States fhall render himfelf liable to punifhment or forfeiture under the law of nations, by committing, aiding or abetting hoftilities againft any of the faid powers, or by carrying to any of them, thofe articles which are deemed contraband by the *modern* ufage of nations, will not receive the protection of the United States againft fuch punifhment or forfeiture; and further, that I have given all inftructions to thofe officers, to whom it belongs, to caufe profecutions to be inftituted againft all perfons, who fhall, within the cognizance of the Courts of the United States, violate the laws of nations, with refpect to the powers at war, or any of them.

IN TESTIMONY whereof, I have caufed the feal of the United States of America to be affixed to thefe prefents, and figned the fame with my hand.—Done at the City of Philadelphia, the twenty-fecond day of April, one thoufand feven hundred and ninety-three, and of the Independence of the United States of America the feventeenth.

By the President   G. WASHINGTON.
THOS. JEFFERSON.

ALEXANDRIA, Dec. 22, 1795.

Extract of a letter from a gentleman in South Carolina to his friend in Virginia, dated Oct. 6, 1795.

" Our newfpapers of this date give us an account of a moft extraordinary fweepftakes at Leed's town for 600 guineas on the 15th September, won by M. L. Wafhington's mare in 8 minutes 31 feconds. The gentlemen of the turf here think it no running; neither is it to be compared to the running of our nags. I tell them that fuch is the refpect that I always retain for Virginia, that the miftake is in the printer. I believe that there are five horfes in this ftate would beat Mr. Wafhington's mare, two I am fure of—that if you Virginians would run for 5000 guineas inftead of 500 lbs in a centrical part, fuch as Fayetteville, North Carolina, it would be immediately accepted by the South Carolinians."

ALEXANDRIA, Feb. 9.

At a meeting of a number of gentleman at the houfe of JOHN WISE, on Monday the 8th of February, to make arrangements for the ball to be held on the 11th in commemoration of the birth of the PRESIDENT of the UNITED STATES, it was agreed—that the ball be held at the houfe of John Wife, and that the gentlemen be admitted by tickets only; the price of which fhall be three dollars and twenty five cents each—*John Fitzgerald, E. C. Dick, William Herbert, R. Conway, James Watfon,* and *Auguftus S. Smith* were appointed managers for the night, and the rules eftablifhed for the regular affemblies are to govern them. If any perfon attempts to enter without a ticket, the door keeper fhall inform the managers, who are bound to prevent fuch intrufion.

N.B. Tickets to be had at the rooms adjoining the bar, and gentlemen are earneftly requefted to provide themfelves previoufly to the night of the ball.

NOTICE TO THE CAVALRY.

THE members of the Alexandria Troop of Cavalry are hereby requefted to attend on parade on the 11th inft. precifely at 11 o'clock, at the Court Houfe, completely equipped in celebration of the birthday of our illuftrious and beloved Prefident.

     E. C. DICK, Captain.

W. TONKIN.

Joiner, Cabinet Maker and Glozier, Begs leave to inform the public of his having commenced bufinefs in the back part of the houfe lately occupied by Mr. Sweeney, in King ftreet, and flatters himfelf that by an indefatigable attention he will merit the favors of thofe who may be pleafed to honor him with their commands.

Alexandria, Jan. 11, 1796.

☞THE LADY Who was kind enough to borrow a light coloured *Broad Cloth Cloak*, at the conclufion of the Ball on the night of the 24th inft. will be obliging enough (if fhe has done with it) to fend it to the ftore of Samuel Craig, where the owner will apply for it.

Alexandria, March 26.

WANTED TO HIRE.

A NEGRO Woman who underftands houfe work. She muft be well recommended for honefty and fobriety. Enquire of the printers.

N.B. She muft be without hufband or child, and neither take fnuff, chew nor fmoke tobacco.

A COOK wanted for a Tavern.

MR. PRICE,

The advertifement which appeared in your laft paper refpecting a cloak, is by many confidered of fo extraordinary a nature as to require the attention of the managers. Coming from a lady, and applicable to all the ladies who attended, it is certainly a violation of every rule of decency and good breeding, and it is fubmitted to the managers whether the writer of the advertifement is entitled to attend the affemblies in future.

     A SUBSCRIBER.

Alexandria, March 29.

SQUARE-RIGGER PROSPERITY

As illustrated by the DINING ROOM FROM "OAK HILL," *Peabody*

Massachusetts, now in the Museum of Fine Arts in Boston

WALL A

WALL D

WALL C

WALL B

Floor Plan

SCALE OF FEET

window
here
originally

Historical Note

WHEN we look with admiration at the examples of Georgian architecture which remain to us in and about Salem, and which are only surpassed in this country by some of the mansions in Maryland and Virginia, we cannot help wondering how it happened that hardly a century after the colonists first landed in our wilderness, such prosperity could arise as to make possible these creations.

The first settlers of Salem arrived in 1626 and for years they struggled with bitter adversity in the form of the weather, the wilderness, and the Indians, many of the natives being hostile. They were obliged to build rush huts for their first shelters, clear the ground for tillage, scour the sea for fish, and hunt wild animals for food and peltry, so that little time could be spent by them on creature comforts, the necessities being paramount in their lives.

How could the descendants of those first men, leading the roughest kind of existence, build in three or four generations such beautiful and luxurious homes as those that we see to-day? Philip English was perhaps the first man to build a house comparable to the ones with which we are familiar. His house, that stood for one hundred and fifty years, was erected before 1700 on Essex Street in Salem. Later homes, such as the ones built by Richard Derby in 1750 and Benjamin Perkins in 1756, followed, with many others, until the series reached its height in the creations of McIntire and Bulfinch at the end of the eighteenth century.

When we ask ourselves how this great flowering was possible in so short a time, it is evident that the answer is found in the rapid rise of trade and the immense profits of sea-borne traffic directed by shrewd and daring navigators and merchants, the two being frequently synonymous at that time. These men, touching with their trade all the then known parts of the world, had an opportunity to see at first-hand the various civilizations of the East and West. This learning they added to their knowledge of English culture, and strove to implant in their colonial existence the comforts and luxuries of cultivated life. Increasing wealth enabled them to have what they thought the best and to pass on to their colonial neighbors the desire to emulate them.

Thus, in an incredibly short time, we see many of the colonists, not only in Salem but throughout the Atlantic seaboard, becoming wealthy and enjoying maritime prosperity in their own lives, and indirectly helping others to imitate their standards.

Let us look for a moment at the situation in the beginning and rapidly trace the rise of this prosperity which enabled so fitting an expression, and which has left such beautiful and enduring monuments and associations for us.

When the early colonists left England and landed on our shores, their ships' companies were composed mostly of yeoman stock, seeking either freedom for religious expression, better living conditions or, frankly, adventure. Naturally they sought a haven for their boats and settled along the shores, harbors, or rivers, since water was the only highway in those days and they could not stray far inland without danger. Fish must have composed a large part of their diet until land was cleared and crops planted. After simple houses had been built and towns had begun to grow, maritime pursuits contributed largely to their livelihood. They sent out fishing vessels, and as their catches were more than enough for immediate needs, fish became a current item for barter. Furs, which they not only could secure themselves, but also could obtain from the Indians in exchange for metal, arms, powder and ball, became the second important medium of trade.

The commodities available to them were useful for trade, and could very profitably be exchanged either in the neighboring colonies or later in the West Indies for much that they needed.

The ships that brought the colonists over the sea were also used to take their surplus goods to England to be exchanged there for necessary articles. In this way foreign trade was begun and, continuing with varying results, eventually brought much wealth to the colonies. The vessels at first were very small and even those used until the Revolutionary War and for some time after were incredibly little. Most of the first boats built at Salem were open and used for fishing; later they were decked when captains essayed longer voyages. As late as 1700 by far the largest number of vessels out of Salem were ketches of from 20 to 40 tons, with only 4 to 6 men for crew.

Most of Philip English's vessels were two-masted ketches, with square sails on the foremast and fore-and-aft rig on the mainmast, the latter being shorter than the former, a rig that would certainly be laughable to-day, yet these little vessels traded with the West Indies and even went as far as the Azores and occasionally to London. The schooner-rig did not come into existence until about 1720. While England had fairly large vessels, the colonists could not afford to build them, and as their first boat of any considerable size happened to be unsuccessful commercially, they thought it safer to use smaller vessels, so the advent of large ships was put off until a considerably later day.

In looking over the ventures in trade which the people of Salem undertook, the growth may roughly be classified as follows:

1629-1640   Fish trade flourished about the North Shore from Boston to Gloucester, and then at greater distances along the coast.

1643   Trade first began with the West Indies.

1640-1670   Trading at Virginia, Bermuda, Antigua, and even to England occasionally.

1670-1700 Trading with other parts of Europe, including Spain, France, and Holland, as well as the West Indies, Azores, and Madeira.

1700-1775 Sharply expanding trade with varying periods of depression due to the French and Indian War, but with an increasing number of distant ports.

1775-1784 Trade, which was almost wiped out by the Revolution, for some years after made a steady growth.

1784 Derby's "Light Horse" first opened the Russian trade.

1785 "Grand Turk's" voyage to China as the first Salem ship.

1788 First American flag flown in the East India waters by one of Hasket Derby's ships at Calcutta.

1791 First vessel sent by Salem direct to Sumatra.

1796 Opening of trade with Batavia and Manila—in both ports by Salem vessels.

1798 Hasket Derby opens the Mocha and Siam trades.

To get an idea of the cargoes, the report of the hated Randolph to the Committee for Trade and Plantations in 1676 may be referred to. Briefly he said, relating to what the colony had to offer:

All there is needed for shipping and naval furniture as excellent oake, elme, firre, birch, pines for masts, the best in the world, pitch, tarre, hemp, iron, clapboards, pipe staves, plankes and deal boards. It abounds with horses, beefes, sheep, hogs and goats with a mighty number of wild beasts whose skins produce great profit yearly. Also great plenty of wheat, rye, barley, oats and peese and fruits of most kinds. Fish of all sorts, especially cod, mackerel and herring. These are staple commodities and are exported.

The commodities imported are tobacco, sugar, indigo, cotton, wool, ginger, log wood, fustiks, cocao and rume, the which are again exported to other parts.

The trade is carried on to most parts of Europe as England, Scotland, Ireland, Spain, France, Portugall, Holland, Canaries and the Hans Townes. Some ships are sent to Guinea, Madagascar and those coasts, and some to Scanderoon, laden with masts and yards.

With reference to Scanderoon, to which Randolph refers and which means the port of Alexandretta in Syria, Phillips in his *Salem of the 17th Century* expresses doubt if any vessels from that port went to Syria for he found no record of them.

We also wonder why Randolph mentioned hemp and iron as native products, since the former must have been imported and the latter was not mined to any extent at that time. Fustics were also grown in the West Indies.

At this time, 1680, Phillips estimates the vessels of Salem as follows:

5 Ships over 100 tons.

70-80 Brigs & Ketches from 30-100 tons.

50-60 Sloops or Smacks of small size.

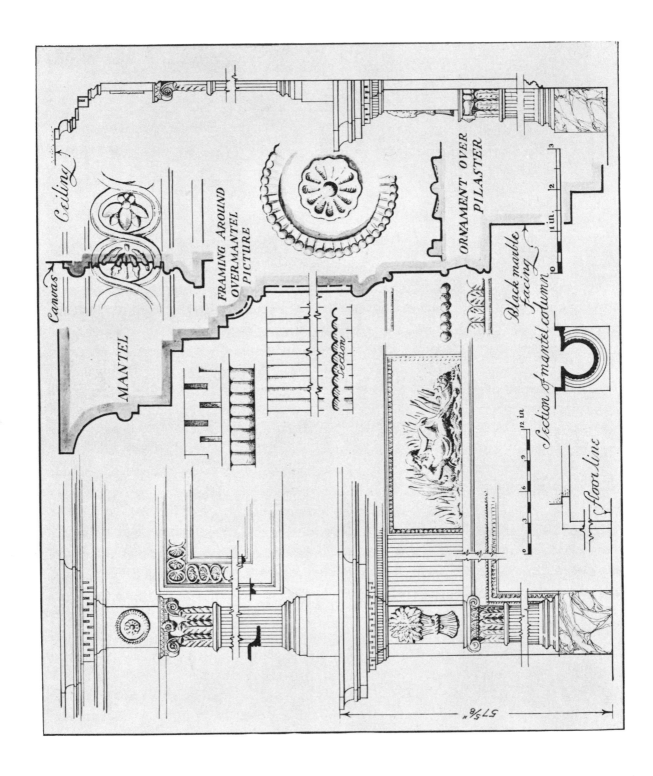

Ceiling

Canvas

MANTEL

FRAMING AROUND
OVERMANTEL
PICTURE

Section

ORNAMENT OVER
PILASTER

Black marble
facing

Section of mantel column

1 in.

12 in

floor line

57⅝"

A good deal of building material was imported during the rise of the early foreign trade. The houses and buildings were at first very simple. With chimneys made of wattles daubed with thick clay, and paper coated with linseed oil in the windows, they did not satisfy the growing needs of the settlers. Glass and lead for window frames were imported between 1630 and 1640 for use in casement windows. Sliding sashes were not adopted until shortly after 1700.

While clay was first used on some of the walls, lime and plaster were imported quite early, for in 1641 we find lime and hair mentioned among the imports, as well as glass and lye. Lime was often used in a thin coat to finish a clay wall and of course for mortar in masonry work about the fireplaces. Frequent fires and consequent destruction of property led to the use of brick, first in chimneys and later for walls.

It is curious that the first brick house was built in Salem in 1707 but was pulled down because it was thought to be too damp. This prejudice postponed the building of masonry and brick houses for some time. In Boston there were so many disastrous fires that the selectmen decreed in 1760 that no houses should be built in a stipulated area except of brick or stone with a tile or slate roof. Though only applicable to Boston, yet this made quite a difference in the architecture of the buildings throughout the whole Bay Colony.

Thus the ground was laid for the eventual erection of the beautiful Georgian houses, when the prejudice against their dampness disappeared, their durability and fire-resisting qualities began to be appreciated, and wealth came to enable their construction.

Few of these improvements could have taken place had not the people been successful in trade, because they would not have had the means to gratify any taste for better living. It must not be supposed, however, that trading and business did not have, even in the early days, their ups and downs, with attendant prosperity and depression. There were many such occurrences. The physical dangers of the sea were always present and the losses by storm were heavy, due to the small size of the vessels, which could not withstand the buffeting of the seas. No accurate charts were available, the coasts were not well known, the knowledge of navigation was very elementary, and all these things contributed to loss of vessels and lives.

It would seem to us to-day the height of folly to venture in such small boats in uncharted seas without instruments to determine one's position, and yet it was the customary thing to do so for a great many years. Any one of these handicaps would be enough to-day to deter a mariner from leaving port; in fact, one could hardly imagine taking such risks. One's amazement is aroused when it is remembered that they had no chronometer, were ignorant of the use of the quadrant, and could not possibly determine their position except by dead reckoning and the log. Though the science of navigation began to be understood in the eighteenth century, it was

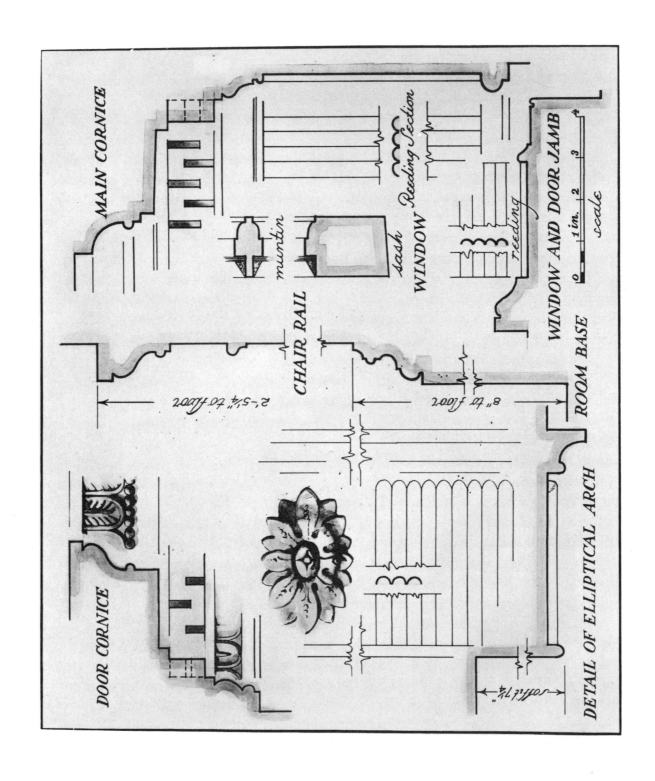

MAIN CORNICE

DOOR CORNICE

CHAIR RAIL

2'-5½" to floor

muntin

sash

WINDOW Reeding Section

reeding

WINDOW AND DOOR JAMB

8" to floor

ROOM BASE

soffit 7¼"

DETAIL OF ELLIPTICAL ARCH

0   1 in.   2   3   4
scale

not until Bowditch of Salem published his *American Practical Navigator* in 1801 that real accuracy began. Even in 1784 when Derby's "Grank Turk" sailed to Canton and was the first Salem ship to reach that port, all she had for navigation aids were a few erroneous charts, a sextant, and a glorified but inaccurate book of geography called *Guthrie's Grammar*! And this famous boat was only 300 tons burden, was less than 100 feet long, and carried a very small crew. This was more than one hundred and fifty years after the Salem trade began, so that the risks taken by the earlier ships were still greater even though their voyages were shorter.

Besides the danger of the seas and the perils due to the ignorance of navigation, there was the ever-present risk of pirates. Trouble with Indians was another menace, for at times the natives attacked even the vessels, and during the French and Indian War, which raged so many years, ships were captured by Frenchmen, and the losses to the traders were very heavy. It is not to be supposed, however, that the settlers took these insults lying down, for they armed their ships heavily and often fought their way through, even capturing many of the enemy traders with valuable cargoes.

The Barbary Pirates began their depredations on our commerce as early as 1660 and made many captures of vessels and men, who were usually held for ransom and sometimes kept in slavery. In fact, this menace was not removed until our successful war against the Barbary States in 1816, when the danger of pirates was practically eliminated by Decatur. During more than one hundred and fifty years, however, they did an immense amount of damage to Salem and its merchants.

Another difficulty against which the merchants struggled constantly was the hampering of trade put upon the colonists by England's regulative acts. The natural handicaps and the very high insurance premiums were serious enough, but the unfavorable conditions imposed by the home government were much worse. These were designed not only to raise taxes for the Crown but to keep the control of business in the hands of the English merchants at the expense of the colonists. These decrees, against which most active opposition was aroused, caused such great and increasing feeling of resentment that it may be said the Revolution was largely brought on by the situation thus stupidly created.

Before matters reached this critical stage, however, the colonists resorted to many subterfuges to get around the regulations and duties. A favorite one was to register a vessel in France, Holland, or some Continental country, and under another flag evade the English laws and continue their lucrative trade. In spite of many setbacks and often fighting for existence, so much so that occasionally the results were on the wrong side of the ledger, trade grew with the increase of population and the mounting wants of the people, so that after the French and Indian War, wealth, which had begun slowly to accumulate, flowed in much more rapidly.

As risks were great, so were the profits, and by glancing at a few of the voyages of our ships, we can appreciate how it was that successful merchants finally obtained so much money that they could express their longings for comfort and luxury by erecting such splendid houses and furnishing them with such beautiful objects that they are highly prized to-day.

Before this time, however, Salem, and other ports, had built shipping yards, sail and rigging lofts, and created a large chandlering business, so that a great fleet of ships could be built, outfitted, and repaired at reasonable expense in a short time. Thus the stage was set for the voyages which brought such rich results to the merchants. A few of these will be cited.

Elias Hasket Derby's venture in the "Mount Vernon," which was only 100 feet long and 400 tons burden, taking a cargo of sugar to the East and returning with silks and wines, netted a profit of $100,000.00 on an investment of $43,000.00, or about 250 per cent.

Though the first China voyage of the "Empress of China" earned only 25 per cent, the "Experiment," an eight-ton sloop which followed the "Empress," netted 72 per cent on her original venture in seventeen months. But these figures are as nothing compared with a single voyage of the "Rajah" under Captain Carnes for the Salem merchant, Peele. This little vessel of only 130 tons, on that particular trip to Sumatra, loaded wild pepper in bulk for a return cargo, and netted 700 per cent profit above the cost of the ship and cargo! This voyage alone made a small fortune for the owner.

It was such voyages that laid the foundations for many a fortune in Salem and enabled the successful merchants to own great fleets of vessels, which equalized their risks by opening many channels to trade, so that if it were poor in one direction, or if one ship were lost, they would recover for the setback in other seas with different vessels.

A glance at a few of these many prosperous traders will be of interest in this connection.

Philip English, who has already been mentioned as perhaps the first of a long line of successful men, came to Salem in mid-seventeenth century and went to sea, becoming a captain before 1670 and in command of his own vessel. By 1686 he became so wealthy that he built the Essex Street house known as English's Great House, previously referred to, which stood so long, but which was of quite a different type of architecture from the Georgian type of house that we admire in Salem to-day, being built with an overhanging second story and several gables. In 1692 English was probably the richest man in the colony, owning twenty-five vessels and trading with Barbados, Bilbao, St. Kitt's, Jersey, and France.

Both English and his wife suffered greatly in the witchcraft delusion. She was first accused as a witch and then he was denounced, and to save their lives they had to flee to New York where they resided until the frenzy passed. In spite of their unjust treatment, when they heard that Salem was suffering and many were in want, due to the depression at that time, English sent a vessel laden with wheat for distribution to the poor. When later they were enabled to return, they were received with great rejoicing by the town.

The Derby family was one of the most successful in foreign trade for several generations, and Richard, born in 1679, grandson of that Richard Derby of Devonshire who founded the family in Salem, went to sea early and commanded as well as owned a vessel while still a very young man. He was later the owner of several vessels, and not content with his profit on this side of the Atlantic, he established the East India trade in New England. His son of the same name, born in 1712, inherited his father's ability as well as part of his fortune, and at the age of twenty-two was master of the "Ranger" and was trading on his own account with Cadiz and Malaga. He commanded other vessels of his own, but in 1753 he retired from the sea and devoted himself to increasing his fleet and trading with numerous ports. During the French and Indian War he armed his vessels and protected his ships and cargoes by fighting when necessary. It was his cannon, by the way, that Gage tried to capture when he sent Colonel Leslie to Salem in 1775.

Elias Hasket Derby, the son of this merchant, became eventually the richest man in New England. He was well trained for the position he was later to fill. Graduating from Harvard, he was sent to England and the Continent, where he mastered several languages and made a study of foreign trade. He returned while still a young man to enter his father's counting house at Salem, having charge of his accounts and later engaging extensively in trade. In 1775, at the age of thirty-six, he had seven vessels engaged in foreign trade alone, and later he owned a considerably larger fleet. Though he faced ruin in the approaching war with England, he did not desert his countrymen, as did so many of the colonists, but clung to the patriots' cause on account of his indignation at the oppressive acts of England in hindrance of commerce. He did his share in arming a considerable number of privateers sent out by Salem men during the Revolution, which in all totalled one hundred and fifty from this one port.

After the great business depression caused by the Revolution began to abate, Salem, due to its intrepid and persevering merchants, opened a new area of trade, which has been referred to in a previous table, and prosperity began, which refilled the almost empty coffers of many of Salem's hitherto successful merchants.

Thus arose the fortunes, princely for those days, which caused the fame of the Derbys, Pingrees, Perkinses, Nicholses, Peabodys, Grays, Shreves, Silsbees, Wests, and others whose names can be linked with the noble family residences they left to their descendants.

After this rapid glance at the growth of maritime prosperity, it only remains to mention the house in Peabody, known as "Oak Hill," concerning which Mr. Hip-kiss' interesting and scholarly monograph is to deal. This house was built by Captain Nathaniel West for himself and his bride, who was the daughter of Elias Hasket Derby, from whom she inherited the land on which the house still stands. While some of the Derby profits paid for the land, West, who was very successful, probably provided the house, and a glance at his career will be of much interest.

He was born in Salem in 1756 and lived to the great age of ninety-five, being a most active man until almost the end of his career. He possessed great energy and enterprise, went early to sea, and at the age of nineteen was in command of a merchant vessel in the West Indies trade, where he was captured in 1775 by a British frigate, whose commander fortunately recognized him as the son of an old friend. He caused West to serve as a midshipman, and treated him kindly; but it can be imagined that this position galled young West considerably. When in London he was sent ashore from the British 74, on which he was serving, and placed in command of a press gang. Seizing this opportunity he made his escape, reached Lisbon, and boarded the Salem privateer "Oliver Cromwell," which took him home after an exciting chase by a British frigate that continued for three days. As the wind was very light at this time and as West knew his fate if captured as a British deserter, he encouraged the crew by every means, even tugging at the sweeps himself, and he was a great help in saving the ship from capture. Later he commanded this very vessel and made several voyages in her.

During the Revolution he was master of the "Black Prince," taking several prizes, and at one time boldly entering the harbor of Cork and actually cutting out and carrying off a vessel as a prize. After the war he enlisted in commerce and amassed a large fortune in trade with China, India, and even the Northwest Coast. It was his vessel "The Patty," which his brother Edward commanded, that was the first American ship to visit Batavia in 1792. His ship the "Minerva" was the first Salem vessel to sail around the world, and no doubt some of the profits of that very voyage went into "Oak Hill," because it was during its construction that she returned.

He united personal frugality, economy, and untiring industry, and he is said to have remarked that without these attributes no man could be rich and with them few could be poor. It is the exercise of these qualities by Salem men, particularly in the field of foreign trade, that explains the erection of such mansions as "Oak Hill" and other noble Salem houses that remain to us.

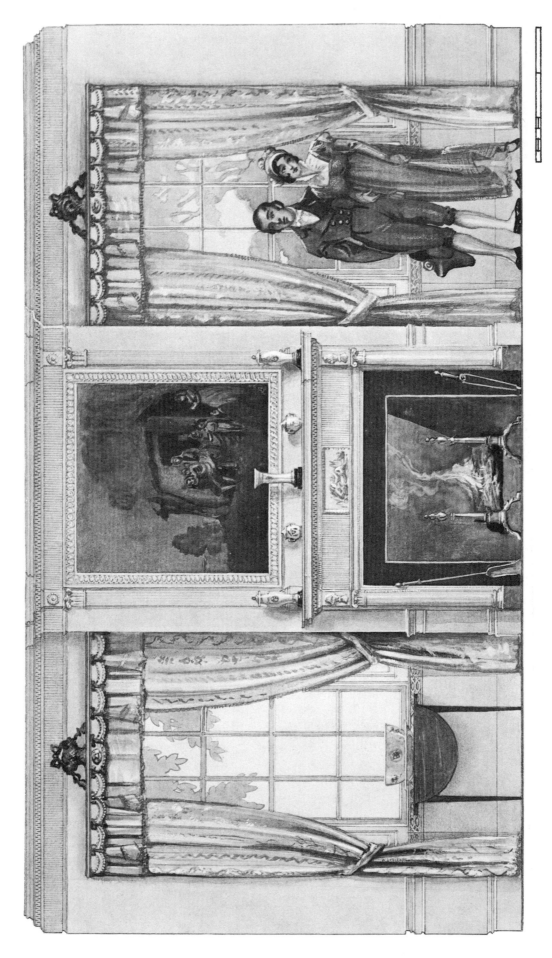

WALL A

CHINESE LOWESTOFT MANTEL ORNAMENTS

PORCELAIN BOWL
CHINESE LOWESTOFT

PEMBROKE DROP-LEAF TABLE
MAHOGANY
HEPPLEWHITE STYLE. *c.* 1790

Square-Rigger Prosperity

THE building of the house at Peabody, Massachusetts, from whence this room came, was made possible in 1801 by wealth acquired in a remarkable period of maritime enterprise at Salem, and this was doubly true, for the owner was the daughter of Salem's great merchant, Elias Hasket Derby, and the wife of a very successful one—Nathaniel West.

In a part of present-day Peabody which was then "South Danvers" Mr. Derby established his country place with fine gardens and a greenhouse which contained, among other horticultural rarities, lemons and oranges, all under the care of his Alsatian gardener, Mr. Heussler. Mr. Derby had bought land aggregating 188 acres, and it was known collectively as "The Farms." To his eldest daughter, Elizabeth, he bequeathed part of this land—one of the farms—which had been in his possession from 1789 to 1799, by coincidence, a decade when American ship-owners more than trebled their share in the cargoes which made up the exports and imports of the nation. On her land, about 90 acres, she built her house.

Two fine examples of domestic architecture built for members of the same family and designed by the same architect offer interesting comparisons. One, Elizabeth Crowninshield Derby's Mansion at Salem, was completed in 1799, and the other, Elizabeth Derby West's country house, was first occupied in 1801. The first stood but sixteen years, the second, later known as "Oak Hill," still stands (1936), although a good deal modified and lacking its three principal rooms, which were removed to the Museum of Fine Arts at Boston in 1922.

It has been said that nothing gave Mr. Derby more pleasure on Sunday afternoon than to ride with Mrs. Derby in their coach to The Farms, accompanied by other members of his family on horseback. It was his place in "South Danvers" rather than the Mansion in the city that pleased him especially; the Mansion was, to his mind, "Mrs. Derby's." Her fine house, and that of her daughter, built after her father's death, had that grace and refinement characteristic of works of the late eighteenth century, and moreover they actually expressed the desires of these two women.

In December, 1798, Derby, the active man of affairs, wrote to his agent in London with reference to a letter of credit: "Mrs. Derby wants something to complete her house; she will write you. It is a business I know nothing of. I have given her an order for £120; you will do as she may direct with it."

In October, 1801, the Reverend William Bentley wrote in his diary: "Through the great pasture we passed to the house erected by Mr. West & executed in the taste and under the direction of his wife, eldest daughter of the late E. H. Derby."

Upon these two admirable, perhaps ambitious, undertakings fell sunshine and shadow. The Derbys had but a few months in which to share their new house, for they both died in 1799, the year of its completion; and to the Wests at "South Danvers" came unhappiness and divorce in 1806.

It is known that Samuel McIntire served as architect for the Derbys, since his original drawings are preserved in the Essex Institute at Salem, and although we have no documentary evidence that he also designed the house for the Wests such proof is hardly required. Among his drawings is one showing a plan and four elevations of the Derbys' "North-west Chamber." The design, at first glance, might easily be mistaken for a room built for the Wests. Then, too, we have an original bill showing that the architect's son, Samuel Field McIntire, supplied Madam West with a small number of supplementary ornaments, thus continuing the McIntire service, it seems, after his father's death. The bill is dated May 29, 1813, and Samuel McIntire died February 6, 1811.

The three rooms at the Museum of Fine Arts are the parlor, the parlor chamber, and the dining room. They are exhibited with authentic objects and materials of the period placed as nearly as the practice of the time can be determined through careful research. Trustworthy and fascinating sources of study are the recorded inventories made in both the Derby Mansion and the West country house, and in the former each room is named, with its contents itemized down to the hearth brush and the entry mat.

The room illustrated herein is the dining room which stands as an exemplar of American style at the end of the eighteenth century. A quarter of a century earlier we find a more masculine vigor in design and a quarter of a century later the heavy-handed manner of the "Greek Revival."

Samuel McIntire, the admirable craftsman-architect, was self-taught and his activities with but few exceptions were confined to Salem itself. Among his books were but half a dozen volumes on architecture, such as Ware's, Langley's, Pain's, and one of *Palladio's Architecture*. Then, too, he owed something to Charles Bulfinch, ten years his junior. Bulfinch, who was wholly professional in his practice, had sailed in 1785 to Europe for a two years' stay "gratifying my curiosity for the sight of building, etc.," to quote his own words, and he had, obviously, looked long, even longingly, upon the works of Robert Adam. Bulfinch made some of the original studies for the Derby Mansion, as Fiske Kimball has demonstrated in his small volume *The Elias Hasket Derby Mansion in Salem*, and it is shown that McIntire had personal knowledge of or data concerning admired features of two houses designed by Bulfinch—the Barrell and Russell houses in Charlestown.

McIntire was, nevertheless, a designer in his own right, and the room selected for this monograph illustrates his ability to work in an accepted manner and yet with a personal handling. The scale relations and disposition of ornament are admirable and his marked use of reeding as a surface motif gives the room its individ-

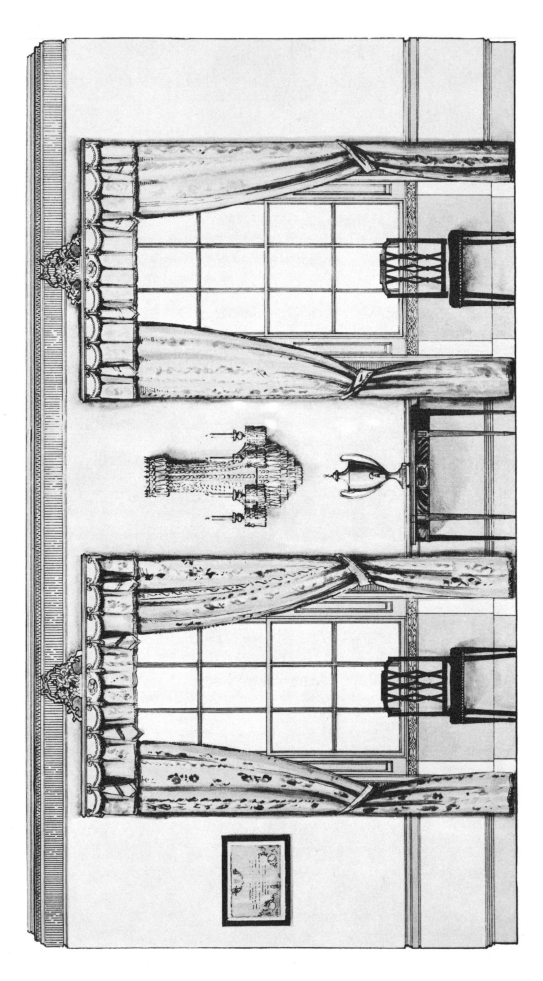

WALL B

ORMOLU AND CRYSTAL WALL LIGHT
ENGLISH. *Late 18th Century*

WINDOW HANGINGS OF
FRENCH LAMPAS
LOUIS XVI

MAHOGANY SIDE CHAIRS
SHERATON STYLE
AMERICAN. *c.* 1790

CARD TABLE
HEPPLEWHITE STYLE
MAHOGANY WITH INLAY
AMERICAN. 1785-1795

MEMBERSHIP CERTIFICATE
SOCIETY OF THE CINCINNATI
FOR SAMUEL WHITWELL
SIGNED BY GEORGE WASHINGTON
1784

uality. Ornamental items, such as capitals, rosettes, enriched mouldings, floral pendants, and panels of bas-relief, were not carved, as one might have expected them from the skillful McIntire; they were cast in "French putty" and fixed in position. This was a concession to the practice of the time and further evidence of the indirect influence of the brothers Adam in England. Although the ornamental parts simulating carving were more or less stock forms cast in moulds, their placing demonstrates McIntire's ability as a designer. The mouldings in wood, on the other hand, were still cut in the traditional method of the eighteenth century, and bases, chair rails, mantelpiece, door heads, and room cornice were designed and shaped in accordance with the ability to work good white pine with moulding planes in the hands of knowing and patient craftsmen. Forty-six of these planes were listed in the inventory of McIntire's possessions.

The house itself was treated with a simple charm. It was entirely of wooden construction, two stories high, with a four-room plan divided by a middle stair-hall; a service wing extended westward. Open porches flanked the façade at the northern and southern ends. The entrance doorway was one with a semi-elliptical arch, glazed over the panelled door, with glazed side panels.

The Reverend William Bentley summed up his impressions of the house when he visited it on October 24, 1801. He wrote in his diary:

Its front eastward commands a most extensive prospect. The house in front is of two stories with four equal rooms. The apartments are furnished in as good order as any I have ever seen. The furniture was rich but never violated the chastity of correct taste. The family of Esqr. Collins joined us to enjoy the rich beauties which multiplied around us. The pictures were excellent. The paper & linen hangings were superb. The movable furniture, rich, uniform, but simple. The Mirrors were large & gave full view of everyone who passed, & were intended for the house in Town but were exchanged as those for this Seat were too large. The markee Bed was preferred to the full bed for its simplicity. It was surmounted by a golden eagle. The work of the room was finished by the needle of Mrs. West. The back part of the house combines every convenience belonging to the farm house or the elegant Country seat. We could not enumerate the beauties we saw. All we could not see, as they were not glaring, but asked our search, & long attention . . . .

Through rare good fortune, twenty-five objects formerly owned by Mrs. West have come back to these rooms of hers at the Museum of Fine Arts. Among them are examples of American chair and cabinetmaking of the first order, examples that place the designer-craftsmen of Salem among the best of Philadelphia, Boston, and Newport. Chairs with carved backs, card tables, a carved fire screen, a secretary, a sofa, are of the finest of their kind. One chair has a carved and pierced splat following almost identically a sketch preserved at the Essex Institute in Salem which was drawn by Samuel McIntire, and, in fact, signed by him. McIntire has much to his credit as an architect and it is well to remember that he had rivals in the field of cabinetmaking and carving. His friend William Bentley, the diarist, wrote of him on October 8, 1802: "In architecture he excells any person in our country, & in his executions as a Carpenter, or Cabinet maker. His brother executes the work at Allen's farm." This brother was probably Joseph.

We have discovered, however, that during McIntire's working years, say from 1780 to 1811, there are records of no less than sixty-five cabinetmakers in Salem and in addition five chairmakers and two turners. John and Charles Lemon, William Hook, Nehemiah Adams, Joseph True, Nathaniel Appleton, and Thomas Needham were some of the men who were masters of their craft.

Thomas Needham, with John Osgood, merchant, and Jabez Baldwin, jeweller, served as appraisers of Mrs. West's estate, and the items of their inventory indicate the fine furnishings in the house. A long list of furniture, carpets, pictures, tableware, hangings, and all the appurtenances of a country seat, includes silver plate valued at $1,318.92.

As the dining room is furnished in its museum setting every object dates from the end of the eighteenth century. The Ushak carpet is of a kind known to have been imported by the merchants of the period. The fireplace linings of soapstone, the facings and hearth of black slate are original and unrestored. The Chinese-Lowestoft porcelain on the mantelshelf awaits improvement, for it was customary to have two beakers and three covered vases to make the usual garniture. The painting over the mantelpiece in oil-color represents "Saturday Night," a subject based on a popular picture by an English painter, William Redmore Bigg, R.A., whose works were presented in black and white by engravers of the time. It is a tradition in Salem that this and its companion piece "Sunday Morning" in the West's parlor were painted by Michele Felice Corné, the Italian painter who came to Salem in 1799 from Naples in Mr. Derby's "Mount Vernon," the ship which made one of those extremely profitable voyages mentioned by Mr. Hollis French in his Historical Note.

The woodwork of the room is painted in a color which duplicates, we believe, that first used. It was found by uncovering portions of each successive layer of paint.

The three rooms at the Museum of Fine Arts, Boston, exemplify the ability of American craftsmen, and the taste of well-to-do men and women, at about the year 1800, who owned ships that made their way through every sea to all the ports of the world.

WALL D

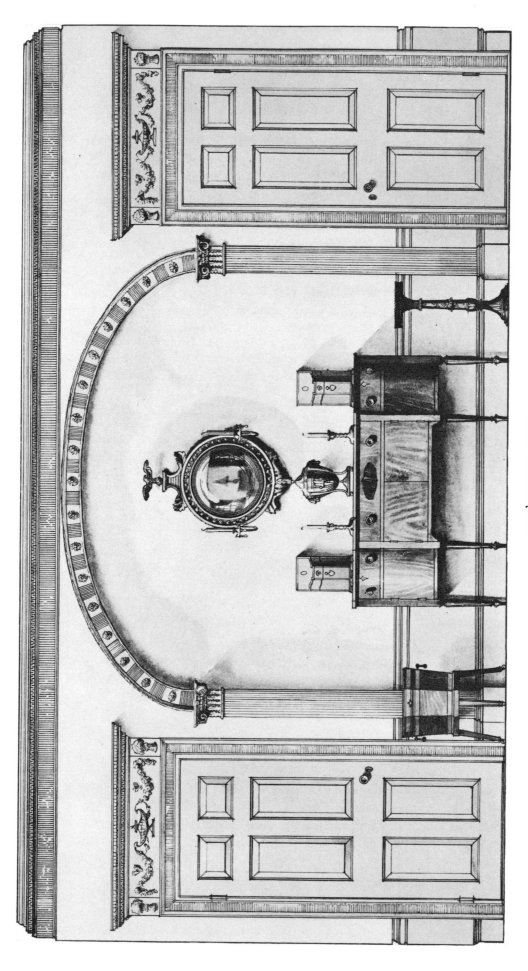

WINE COOLER
MAHOGANY WITH
BRASS FITTINGS
AMERICAN
c. 1790

BULL'S EYE GIRANDOLE
c. 1800

SHEFFIELD URN
ENGLISH. c. 1800

PAIR OF KNIFE-BOXES
MAHOGANY. ENGLISH. 1780

SIDEBOARD. MAHOGANY WITH INLAY
SHERATON STYLE. AMERICAN. c. 1800

TURNED
MAHOGANY STAND
ATTRIBUTED TO
MCINTIRE. c. 1800

CONTEMPORARY DOCUMENT

The Letter of Instructions from the Joint Owners of a Merchant Ship to the Captain of their Vessel about to sail.

Salem, June 16th 1809.

CAPT. JONATHAN P. FELT,
  Sir,

  You being master of the Ship Monk, now ready for sea, & bound on her 5th voyage, have our instructions to embrace the first favourable opportunity of wind, & weather, & proceed to Civita Vecchia, in the Pope's Dominions, & there sell our cargo, if you think it for our interest to have it sold there; but if not, you have our advice to take it to some other port, where you are permitted by the Belligerents, without running any risque by a breach of Blockade Laws, Orders in Council, or the decrees of the Emperor of the French; in short, endeavour to find a good market, & make use of prudent measures in doing it.

  After having disposed of said cargo, as afore mentioned, you may take a cargo for the north, or the United States, or to any other ports where permitted as above. But in all your undertakings, we caution you against breaking any of the laws & decrees above mentioned, as thereby serious consequences may arise.

  The cases & baskets of Sweet Oil, are articles good to import to this country. Spanish Brandy has leſsened in esteem here. The Red Claret, in 58 to 60 gallon casks, always saleable with us for the West India market. If at Smyrna Opium & Fruit make good return articles, or a cargo for some port in Europe. But we do'nt expect the present cargo will go far up the Streights for sale; how far must be left to your good judgment, & discretion, while on the spot, as to the risk you may have to run.

  The exceſs of our stock, after purchasing another cargo, is to be placed into the hands of Samuel Williams Esq. Finsbury Square, London, for acct. of William Orne, seven eighths, & Charles Henry Orne, one eighth; the present owners thereof. After the above advice, we submit the whole to your prudence, & discretion, not doubting your best endeavours to promote the interest of the voyage.

  We expect to allow you a commiſson of two pr. Ⅎ. on the net sales of the present cargo; & one per. cent. on the net cost of the homeward cargo; & should you, while abroad take in any cargo, & proceed for a port in Europe, or elsewhere you are to charge one prct. on the nt. cost, & one pr. Ⅎ. on nt. sales thereof: which, with your wages & privilege, as per Shipping Articles, are in full for your services for the voyage.

  Recommending you to Almighty protection, & wishing you a safe & prosperous voyage, we remain your friends.

WILLIAM ORNE
CHARLES HENRY ORNE.

Selection from Ships Papers, *Volume II, Essex Institute, Salem, Massachusetts.*

JOSEPH GARDNER,

Bridge-Street,

BEGS leave to inform his Friends and the Public in general, that he has a complete ſet of the much admired, and univerſally celebrated

Wooden Horſes;

where Gentlemen and Ladies may ride in private; having a perfect CIRCUS built for the purpoſe. —This truly pleaſing and innocent amuſement is in the higheſt eſtimation in the principal European countries, and in America—eſpecially in Philadelphia, Newyork, Baltimore, Boſton, etc. etc.—Giving the greateſt ſatisfaction being highly recommended by the firſt phyſicians, as the moſt operative for the circulation of the blood.

The CIRCUS opens for Ladies and Gentlemen every morning, Sundays excepted, from 4 until 7 o'clock —and for Gentlemen and Ladies every Wedneſday and Saturday afternoon from 2 till 8 o'clock.

SALEM, June 30.

WANTED, November 18, 1800.

A BOY from the country, about 14 years of age, as an apprentice to the Cabinet Making Buſineſs. Inquire of the Printer.

AMERICAN GALLANTRY.

Extract of a Letter from Capt. WHITNEY, *of the ſhip* Hiram *to a gentleman of this town, dated,* "*Fort Royal, (Martinique) November* 18.

"I arrived here the 13th inſt. after being twice taken and re-taken; and one hundred and two days at ſea. I left Liverpool, the 2d of Auguſt, and on the 13th September, being in longitude 55, and latitude 29, I was taken by a French ſloop of war, and all my people taken out, except HARRY,[†] one man, and a boy of twelve years of age, an aprentice of mine; and manned with ten French men, and ordered for Cayenne.—I being determined on an attempt to re-take my ſhip, on firſt diſcovering her to be French, loaded my piſtols and hid them in a crate of ware, which had I not done, I ſhould have loſt them, for no leſs than three different times were my trunks ſearched for them, as was the cabin and all parts of the ſhip, which they could come at; they found my ammunition, but my piſtols were ſecure, and ſuch was their extreme caution, that they would not allow any man to be off deck; but eat, drank, and ſlept on deck.

Finding that I could not obtain any advantage of them, by getting them below, I determined to attack them openly by day light. Therefore at about four o'clock on the fourth day after being taken, I ſecured my piſtols in my waiſtband, having previouſly told HARRY and my man, my determination, and directed them to have a couple of handſpikes where they could claſp their hands upon them in an inſtant, and when they ſaw me begin, to come to my aſſiſtance.

The Prize Maſter was now aſleep on the weather hencoop, his mate at the wheel, and the crew on different parts of the main deck, Under theſe circumſtances I made the attempt by firſt knocking down the mate at the wheel; the maſter ſtarted up ſo quick, that I could get but a very ſlight ſtroke at him; upon which he drew his dirk upon me—but I cloſed in with him, ſallied him out of the quarter rail, and threw him overboard. But he caught by the main chains, and ſo eſcaped going into the water. By this time I had the remaining eight upon me, 2 of whom I knocked backwards off the quarter deck, and Harry and my man, coming aft at this time with handſpikes, played their parts ſo well among them, that I ſoon got relieved. I then drew a piſtol, and ſhot a black fellow in the head, who was coming at me with a broad-axe; the ball only cut him to the bone, and then glanced—but it had an excellent effect, by letting the reſt know that I had piſtols, of which they had no idea. By this time the mate, whom I firſt knocked down, had recovered, and run down to his trunk, and got a piſtol, which he fired directly at my man's face, but the ball miſſed him.

The Prize Maſter, whom I hove over the quarter, got in again, and ſtabbed Harry in the ſide, but not ſo bad as to oblige him to give out till we had conquered. In this ſituation we had it *pell mell* for about a quarter of an hour, when we got them a running, and followed them on, knocking down the hindmoſt, two or three times round the deck, when a part of them eſcaped below, and the reſt begged for mercy, which we granted on there delivering up their weapons, which conſiſted of a diſcharged piſtol, a midſhipman's dirk, a broad-axe, and a hand ſaw, &c. We then marched them aft into the cabin, and brought them up, one at a time, after ſtrictly ſearching them, and confined them down forward."

Ten days after this daring action, Capt. W. was again captured by a privateer ſchr. from Guadaloupe, who plundered his ſhip of 8 or 10,000l. ſterling, put on board a crew of 15 French, and ordered her for Guadaloupe. After being in their hands 46 days, he was retaken by an Engliſh frigate & ſent into Martinique.

† Second Mate, a brother of Capt. W. aged 17 years.

IMPORTANT CAPTURE.

On Saturday anchored in *Nantaſket Roads*, the United States frigate *Boſton*, George Little, Eſq. commander, with her prize, the French national corvette *Le Berceau*, commanded by citizen Louis Andre Senes, captured on the 12th October, in lat. 22, 50, N. long. 51, W: after an action of one hour and forty minutes. *Le Berceau* mounts 22 French nine, and 2 twelve pounders on one deck; and had on board at the commencement of the action 230 men.—Her loſs was 35 killed, and a number wounded. The force of the *Boſton*, is 24 twelve and 8 nine pounders, and 230 men. . . . The *Prize* loſt all three of her maſts, and was very much diſabled. The *Boſton* is much injured in her maſts, ſpars, rigging, and ſails, which obliged *Capt. Little* to return from his cruiſe to refit. We are informed, *Captain Little* has expreſſed in ſtrong terms his approbation of the conduct of his officers and crew, during the action; and conſidered that it would be injuſtice to the commander of *Le Berceau*, not to ſtate that he gallantly defended his ſhip as long as ſhe was capable of making a defence.

MANUFACTURE OF PAPER.

In England a mode has been diſcoved of manufacturing paper from *Straw*. It is of ſtrong conſiſtence, and though it retains the colour of the material from which it is made, will ſerve for packing parcels, printing handbills, poſting bills, and ſuch other ordinary purpoſes. It is hoped, therefore, that the invention will be likely to reduce the preſent advanced prices of rags and paper, and deſtroy a moſt infamous monopoly.

HUMANITY.

We are informed that the Abolition Society of Pennſylvania, at their ſpecial meeting on the 7th inſt. appointed a ſpecial committee to watch over the ſituation of the Black People already brought, or which ſhall hereafter be brought into this port under the acts of Congreſs againſt the Slave Trade, to afford them ſuch neceſſary aſſiſtance and protection, as may be in their power, and to provide ſituations for ſuch of them as ſhall be found to be free.

ELECTIONEERING.

KNOW all men by theſe Preſents, That on Monday the 6th day of April next, every *genuine* republican federaliſt, every friend to the Conſtitution, and every lover of his Country, will *turn out*, and beſtow his vote on
ELBRIDGE GERRY, Eſq.
for Governor—and
WILLIAM HEATH, Eſq.
for Lieut. Governor.
Neither of theſe Gentlemen have ever ſigned away the ſacred Elective Rights of THE PEOPLE.

Female Electors.

Single Females in the State of New-Jerſey, poſſeſſed of a certain property, and having paid taxes, are entitled to vote at elections. We underſtand that at the late election, there were many exerciſed their priviledge.

The Riches of the Sea.

The ſchooner Two Siſters, David Fornis, jun. maſter, lately arrived at Beverly from the Grand Bank, with a fare of 500 quintals of fiſh. This veſſel has performed three fiſhing voyages this ſeaſon, in the ſhort ſpace of ſix months and an half, and landed, at leaſt, 1700 quintals—a very rare inſtance of induſtry and ſucceſs.

EDUCATION.

Mr. BIGLOW informs his friends, that he has taken the commodious building, in Marlborough Street, lately erected by the Rev. Dr. Barnard's Society, where he continues by the aſſiſtance of Mr. Maxcy, to qualify boys for College, for the Counting room, and for Sea. Mr. Biglow will open a ſecond School

For Young Ladies only,

on the 1ſt of April next, from 11 till 1 o'clock, for Reading, Writing and Arithmetic; and from 5 till 7, for Engliſh Grammar, Geography, Aſtronomy, &c.

A Young Married Woman, whoſe huſband has been impreſſed on board an Engliſh Man of War, and ſhe by this cruel deed deprived of a livelihood, wiſhes to take a Child to Nurſe, in order to obtain a bare ſubſiſtence.
Inquire of the Printer.

For *Wilmington*, N. C.

The SCHOONER

J O H N,

HENRY SAUNDERS, *Maſter;*—will ſail in 8 or 10 days. For freight or paſſage, apply to the maſter on board, at Mr. Peirce's wharf.

Who has for Sale,

100 barrels of T A R; 20 barrels
ROSIN, a few barrels

F L O U R.

Salem, Dec. 29.

F O R   S A L E,

THE Schooner Bloom, 20 tons burthen, fit for the Fiſhing buſineſs, in which ſhe has been employed—is well found, and will be ſold at a bargain. She now is at the Lower Wharf in Beverly. For particulars, apply to CHARLES ADAMS.
Beverly, Jan. 1, 1801.

THE EMPIRE STYLE IN AMERICA

As illustrated by the PARLOR FROM IRVINGTON, NEW JERSEY

now in the Brooklyn Museum in Brooklyn, New York

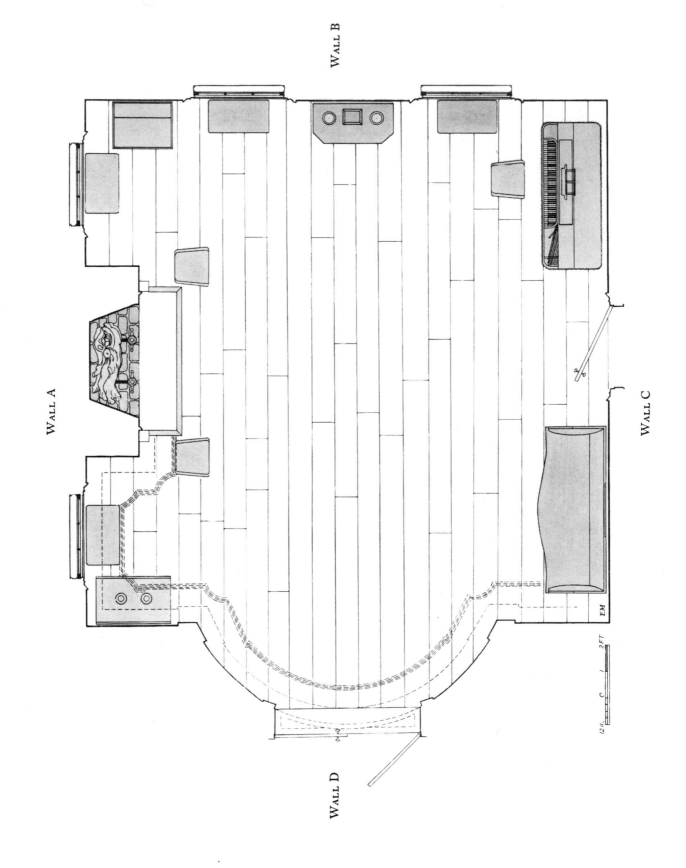

WALL A

WALL B

WALL C

WALL D

12 IN.   0   2 FT

Historical Note

BEING situated between New York and Philadelphia, New Jersey had the advantage of an especially favorable location. Not only was she the link between these two important centers, but also the main tie between the North and the South. For this reason the Jersey colonists, in particular those living on the main stagecoach routes, must have been in closer touch with general colonial activities than any other single colony. Another unique feature was the cosmopolitan character of the populus. East Jersey formed part of the Hudson Valley Dutch settlement, whereas West Jersey was developed partly by the English and to some extent by the Swedes. Though all Jersey became English territory in 1663, the minor factions continued to assert themselves, at least locally. From 1713 to the close of the French and Indian War in 1763 most of the immigration was German and Scotch-Irish, so that by the time of the Revolution the population was more mixed than that of any other colony. This mingling of traditions and frequent contact with the outside world would naturally tend to prevent the forming of peculiarly localized customs. The Dutch of East Jersey lost their individuality much sooner than their compatriots isolated on Western Long Island.

In dealing with the early nineteenth-century New Jersey, a town such as Irvington, then known as Camptown, cannot be singled out for its peculiar attributes, but must rather be regarded as representing a characteristic town of the middle states. The point of view of the people was perhaps a little more liberal than that of the New Englanders, but less grandiose than that of the great plantation owners of the South. The tone of the community was set by New York, which was first of all a commercial center. Philadelphia was unquestionably the social center of the country, with Boston, in a less ostentatious way, a close second. From an intellectual point of view, too, these two cities were probably a little ahead of New York at the time.

By the first quarter of the nineteenth century towns on the eastern seaboard were thriving and active. The favorable outcome of the War of 1812 and the promulgation of the Monroe Doctrine in 1823 served quite justly to stimulate the pride of the young Republic. The tendency now was to turn to internal affairs. Ever-increasing trade in the Far East and the opening up of Western lands was proving extremely profitable, with the result that an increasingly large number of merchants found themselves in a position of being able to build houses of ample proportions in the currently fashionable Greek Classical style. Characteristic of this type was the house under consideration, built in Camptown (Irvington), New Jersey, about 1820. Although at the time it was considered a country house on the outskirts of

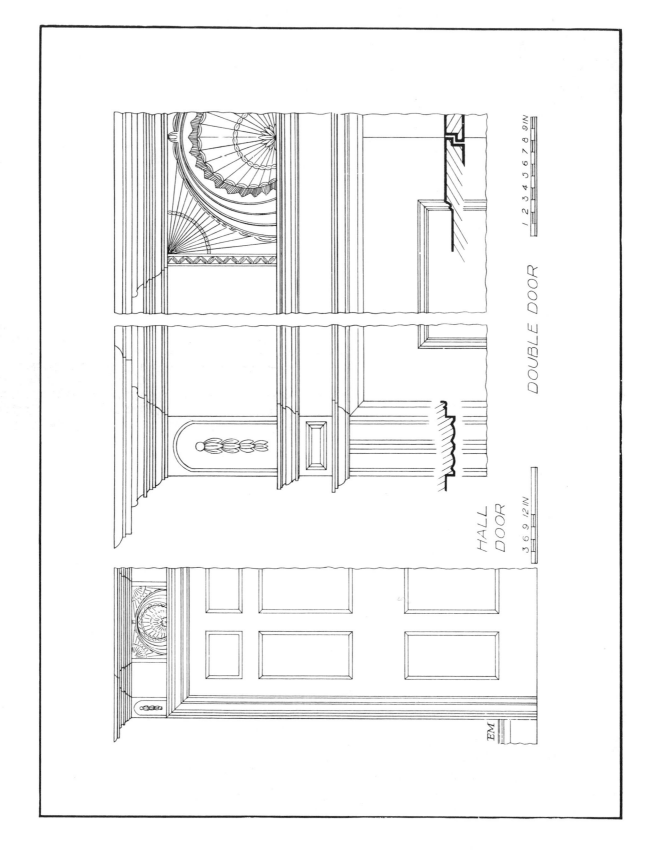

DOUBLE DOOR

1 2 3 4 5 6 7 8 9IN

HALL
DOOR

3 6 9 12IN

EM

Newark, it was, nevertheless, easily accessible from New York. The Newark-to-Hoboken stage connected with the new steam ferry opened in 1811 across to Barclay Street, New York. An alternative route was Newark to the Paulus Hook (Jersey City) ferry. The city markets and shops proved tempting to the Jersey inhabitants and enabled them to keep their households quite up to the standard of a city establishment. Every country place had its well-stocked kitchen garden and fruit orchard as well as its own dairy farm. Game was plentiful in the woods near by, and fish easily obtainable. European wines were imported in large quantities—especially Canary and Madeira. It is no wonder, then, that the tables of the period were set with a great variety and an appalling quantity of food and drink. Lavish entertaining which had subsided during the Revolution was revived and continued to be the practice in large houses both in town and country. Dancing and gaming were popular as well as chamber music. Simpler entertainment, such as quilting parties, spelling bees, and donation parties for the parson, played a prominent part in the life of the day. The latest fashion in dress was a matter of great concern with the men as much as with the women. Blue was still a favorite color for men's coats. This appeared with white or fawn-colored nankeen trousers ankle length, though breeches were still worn with formal dress. Dresses were a little fuller than during the Empire period and not quite so high-waisted. Worn ankle length, they were made to stand out around the bottom. Sleeves were beginning to be full toward the shoulders. Hair was worn higher than it had been and false curls added. High-crowned bonnets with plumes came into vogue, and the ever-present white muslin of the Empire period was replaced by colored silks, or black, which was introduced for the first time in 1820. London was still the dictator of styles, though Paris during the Empire period and later exerted a greater and greater influence. The presence of foreign diplomats in Washington served to give a more authentic version of European manners and dress, and the latest word from the capital was eagerly sought.

During the second decade of the nineteenth century America was just becoming literary conscious. The *North American Review* started in 1815. Irving's *Sketch Book* appeared in 1819 and Bryant's first volume of poems in 1820. Just after this Cooper's novels came out in quick succession.

The 1820's were altogether peaceful and prosperous. Difficulties of governmental organization following the Revolution were fairly well smoothed out and the problems of slavery and states rights leading to the Civil War were not yet acute. Internal problems were now of paramount importance. The Louisiana Purchase in 1803 and the acquisition of Florida in 1819 turned the attention of the country to the infinite possibilities of developing these new lands, and the great influx of immigrants after the Napoleonic War furnished the necessary men for pioneering.

Newark and the near-by villages owed their prosperity largely to the commer-

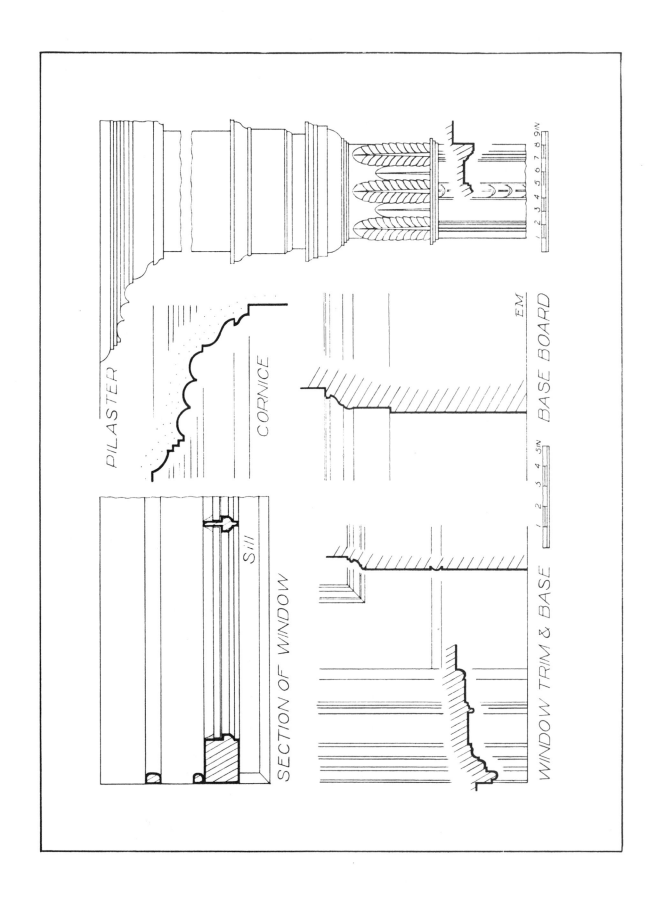

PILASTER

CORNICE

BASE BOARD

EM

SECTION OF WINDOW

Sill

WINDOW TRIM & BASE

1 2 3 4 5 6 7 8 9 IN

1 2 3 4 5 IN

cial traffic on the Passaic River. Messrs. Stephens, Condit and Cox operated a line of freight boats, and their associates Messrs. Stephens, Condit and Wright conducted a profitable business in outfitting whaling vessels and in the manufacture of casks used for sperm oil. Transportation facilities improved greatly after the Revolution, so that even without the railroad, which was soon to be introduced, communities were in far closer touch with each other than during the previous century. This enabled manufacturers to disperse their goods to ready markets, making it profitable to establish glass and china factories, mills, and tanneries, thus relieving the dependence on Europe for manufactured articles. Glassmaking, though started in the seventeenth century, came into prominence in South Jersey during the second quarter of the eighteenth century. After being temporarily suspended during the Revolution, the industry was revived toward the end of the century. Isaac Thorne and the Harmony Glass Works were among those active in Glassboro in the 1820's, while there were other factories at Clementon, Millville, and Malaga. Earthenware took the place of pewter soon after 1800, though no great amount was manufactured in New Jersey until after 1830. Shipbuilding was one of the main activities of the coast, and sawmills and iron foundries were kept busy furnishing materials for the shipyards. John Stevens of Hoboken built in 1809 the "Phoenix," the first seagoing steamboat, and in 1818 the Vail works at Speedwell produced machinery for the "Savannah," the first steamboat to cross the Atlantic. Bog iron, discovered in Jersey swamps as early as 1666, was until well into the nineteenth century the main source of material for cannon balls, rails, and other building equipment.

It is apparent that there were many sources of wealth in the opening years of the nineteenth century in New Jersey. The well-to-do citizen quite naturally created living conditions to suit his means. An amply proportioned house gave the necessary setting for gracious living as well as indulgence in the whims and fancies of the age, not only in architectural design and furnishings, but in the manner of entertaining, food, dress, and amusements. The Irvington rooms afford us an opportunity to picture the home of a prosperous Jersey merchant-farmer in the 1820's.

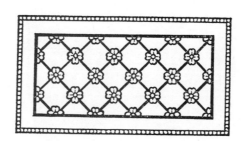

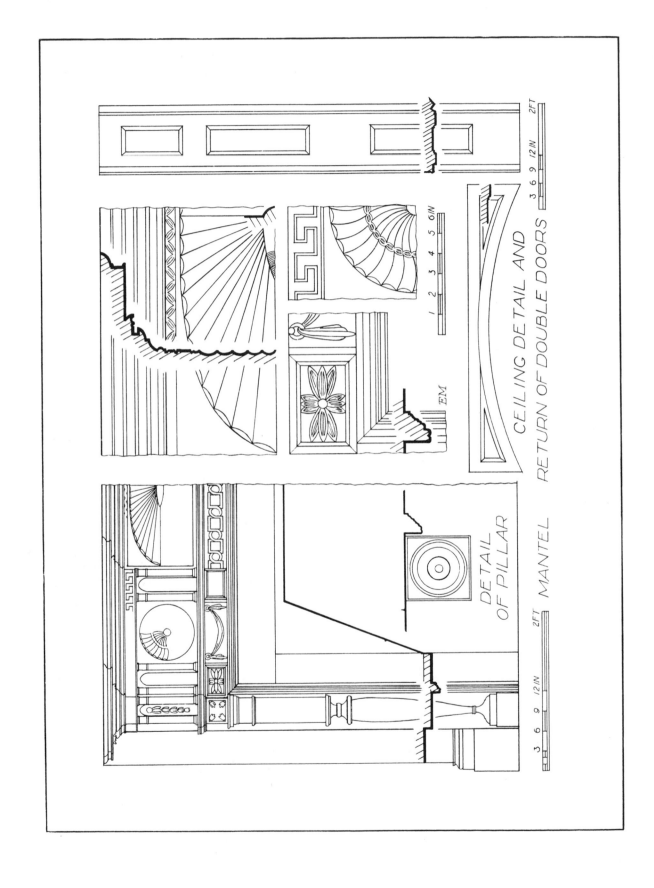

CEILING DETAIL AND
RETURN OF DOUBLE DOORS

DETAIL
OF PILLAR

MANTEL

WALL A

MAHOGANY STOOLS IN
STYLE OF DUNCAN PHYFE
c. 1810

MANTEL GLASS AND ORNAMENTS
EMPIRE STYLE

MAHOGANY SIDE CHAIRS
STYLE OF DUNCAN PHYFE
c. 1820

DAMASK CURTAINS
1st quarter of
19th Century

The Empire Style in America

C HARACTERIZED by Thomas Jefferson as "rude, misshapen piles," buildings in the various colonial styles quickly lost favor in the larger cities of the young Republic. Thus a new architectural style, based on the monuments of ancient Greece and Rome, was inaugurated by a bloodless revolution of fashion. Among the American protagonists of the classical revival were Jefferson and his pupil Robert Mills, Charles Bulfinch, Samuel McIntire, and John McComb; and from Europe came James Hoban, Henry Latrobe, and Pierre Charles L'Enfant to design important public buildings.

The classic style had been introduced into England in 1758 by the brothers Adam, and two books which had contributed largely to its formation there were also known to the able group of amateur and professional architects working in America in the late eighteenth century and the early nineteenth. These were Major's *Ruins of Paestum* and Stuart and Revett's *Classical Antiquities of Athens*. In circulation among both urban and rural builders were the works of the sixteenth-century Italian architect Palladio; the American editions of the *Practical House Carpenter*, by James and William Pain, and the *Builder's Pocket Treasure*; and the native *Country Builder's Assistant* and *American Builder's Companion* issued by Asher Benjamin in 1796 and 1806, respectively.

Spaciousness, privacy, and convenience were taken into consideration for the first time in America in houses of the Republican period. As many surviving floor plans and elevations and, fortunately, innumerable actual buildings indicate, the exponents of the classic style in America designed high-ceiled, well-fenestrated rooms and ingeniously contrived secret passages, additional staircases, and dumbwaiters for service. The flexibility of the new principles permitted many innovations in the arrangement of interiors, notably in the privacy of the chambers on the upper floors and in the novelty of the geometric contours given to the principal apartments. Rooms were frequently oval, round, or curved at one end; the window architraves, doorways, and mantels followed the lines of the shaped walls.

The new vocabulary of ornament demanded as a foil pale-tinted plaster walls simulating the Graeco-Roman backgrounds of marble and stucco. As the eighteenth century waned wood panelling was no longer used to finish entire rooms. It was sometimes used upon the chimney breast for the mantel, and, less frequently, for the overmantel; and still served as the material for the dado rail, bases, and the architraves of windows and doors.

With the lightening of the architectural mass as a whole and the delicate treatment of mouldings, the ornament applied to mantel and doorway, more often cast in composition than carved in wood, thoroughly accorded in scale and character

[159]

with the structural background. Mythological compositions and draped figures representing the Muses, the Virtues, or the Seasons, augmented by festoons of husks, paterae, sheaves of wheat, and similar details culled from the dictionary of antique design, were the stock in trade of McIntire, Welford, and countless others working throughout the Atlantic seaboard. Country carpenters and foreign-trained craftsmen alike lent their personal interpretations to the classic style. Carved geometric motifs upon woodwork seem generally to post date both composition and carved Adam ornament.

The facts are fugitive concerning the house at Irvington (formerly Camptown), New Jersey, from which this parlor was taken. It has long since been demolished, and we know only that it stood on the crest of a hill and was approached by a long avenue bordered by hawthorn; that it faced a park shaded by linden and magnolia trees and adorned with flowering shrubs; that it was flat-roofed; and that its rear windows looked out upon a circular fountain and an octagonal summer house several stories high. This is fragmentary, indeed, but gives us a suggestion of a country house of some elegance, commensurate with the handsome interior woodwork. The flat roof indicates the temple form of domestic architecture which was introduced by Jefferson and which in the second quarter of the nineteenth century became a national style, as the works of Martin Thompson, Ithiel Towne, Alexander J. Davis, Nicholas Biddle, and J. R. Brady bear witness. In northern New Jersey stone houses of the so-called Dutch colonial type, with sweeping roof lines and clapboarded gable ends, continued to be built during the early nineteenth century, particularly along the banks of the Hackensack River in Bergen County. Our house, in adjacent Essex County, carried a more metropolitan stamp, reflecting the current taste of its day.

As one enters the parlor the boldly conceived and executed mantel on the opposite wall presents the main feature of the room. In the tapering columns supporting the entablature and in the oval and round swirls of gouged work carved upon the frieze with six pairs of smaller intercepting columns, it is readily apparent that the builder has relied upon light and shade and contrasting scale to achieve a successful design. In view of the fact that Irvington was easily accessible by water from New York, it is not surprising that almost identical mantels are frequently found in houses on Long Island and in the Hudson Valley, particularly in Dutchess County houses prior to 1825. One in a house built by James Given about 1811 has all the elements of the Irvington mantel; another from the Mesier house in the same locality also relies upon a combination of columns and gouged fans for its decoration.

Flanking the chimney breast are two windows with six-paned narrow muntined sashes typical of the early nineteenth century; two similar windows break the west wall. Opposite the latter, in a semicircular alcove, a double doorway gives a vista of

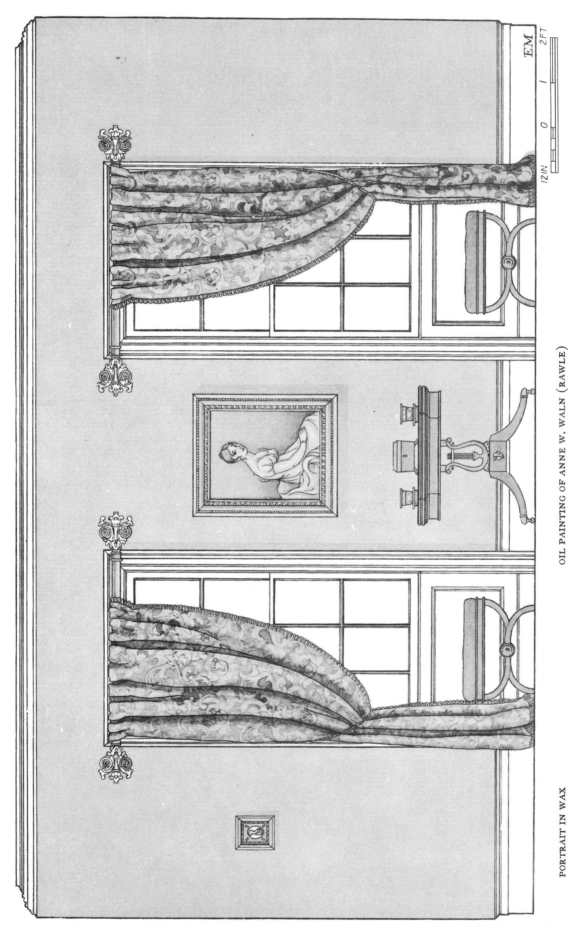

WALL B

PORTRAIT IN WAX

OIL PAINTING OF ANNE W. WALN (RAWLE)
BY THOMAS SULLY

LYRE TABLE
STYLE OF DUNCAN PHYFE
c. 1810

PAIR (OF SET OF FOUR) STOOLS
STYLE OF DUNCAN PHYFE
c. 1810

the dining room beyond. The entablature of the doorway is an elongation of that of the entrance; the same quarter-fan and sunburst motifs fill the center of the frieze, and pendent husks are carved upon the end blocks. An added refinement is the convexed shaping of the center of the entablature to correspond with that of the mantel. The doors, composed of shallow sunken panels, are mounted with oval brass knobs. At the sides of the alcove are double pilasters which support capitals embellished by three vertical water leaves separated by smaller leaves of similar form. An overlapping-scale motif is carried down the center of each pilaster.

Hepplewhite's *Guide*, published in 1788, and Sheraton's *Drawing Book*, issued in 1791, were books of furniture design almost universally known by American craftsmen at the close of the eighteenth century. The engraved plates were interpreted with considerable freedom and understanding by skilled cabinetmakers throughout the Union. The classic manner was manifested in the severity of structural outline, tapered supports, and occasional compromises with geometric curves. Profuse carving was abandoned in large measure in favor of handsome veneered surfaces and delicate patterns inlaid with satinwood, bird's-eye maple, stained holly, and other exotic woods. About 1820 the Empire style was inaugurated by a literal borrowing of antique forms in the shape of concaved supports, lion masks, and realistic paw feet. Proportions were massive, and the larger pieces of furniture were truly monumental.

The furnishings of our parlor cover a period of some three decades, beginning about 1795. The earliest piece is a New York sofa of pleasing Hepplewhite design. The four front legs are tapered and enriched with satinwood husks, set close together in a typically Knickerbocker manner; the narrow, moulded frame of the rectangular back culminates in a slightly raised, reeded panel at the center of the top rail. Two pieces are of Sheraton design. One is a Pembroke table with clover-shaped drop leaves and the "balloon-shaped" foot and fillets at the top of the leg, refinements which are found on some of Phyfe's documented work. The second example is a small desk having the appearance of a box standing upon four reeded legs; half of the upper part falls forward, revealing the fittings of a writing desk.

The rest of the furniture is in the Empire style. Perhaps the most important piece is a rosewood piano mounted with ormolu and further decorated with gold stencilling along the keyboard, which bears the inscription: "Made by John Kearsing from London for John J. Rickers, 187 Broad Way, N. York." The base of the piano is typical of the work of the New York cabinetmaker Michael Allison. It is of the pedestal type, resting upon four hairy paws overlaid with gilded acanthus leaves, and in turn, supporting four carved and gilded columns. Under the windows are four small benches covered in haircloth and similar to engraved designs of tête-à-tête seats, dated 1804, and signed, J. Taylor, London; a card table with a double-lyre pedestal and brass mounts; and three side chairs. The design of the chairs might represent Phyfe's work of 1820—the plain, sabre-shaped legs, the sunken panel of the top rail, and the pierced splat of carved leaves and spirals being features of furniture owned by that master at the time of his death.

A large overmantel looking-glass, contemporary in date with the sofa, is of generous proportions but does not give an impression of massiveness because of the delicacy of the reeded, palm-capped columns entwined with leaves and the latticed cornice backed by robin's-egg blue.

Three portraits in oil are noteworthy examples of early nineteenth-century painting. At the right and left of the entrance door are likenesses of Mrs. James Bogert and her son, James Bogert, Jr., painted by Samuel Waldo and William Jewett in the second quarter of the century. Between the windows Thomas Sully's masterly portrait of Anne W. Waln depicts the fresh loveliness of young womanhood.

The accessories of the room complement the background and furniture. The double-branched Sheffield silver candlesticks upon the mantel, the blue and white creamware flowerpots upon the table, and the mahogany tea caddy on the desk all betray the classical influence at work in their form and embellishment.

Against the cream-colored plaster walls and the white woodwork, the rich crimson damask draperies, boldly festooned from gilt poles carved with Empire finials, provide the strength and accent required by the austerity of the setting.

In New Jersey the names of Robert Rhea, a joiner of Monmouth County, Maskell Ware, a chairmaker of Cumberland County, and Matthew Egerton, a cabinetmaker of New Brunswick, span the years from the close of the seventeenth century to the early years of the nineteenth century. To mention the stately wainscot chair joined by Robert Rhea and carved with his initials and those of his wife Jeanette, together with the date 1696; the comely five-arched slat-back chairs of maple made by Maskell Ware nearly a hundred years later; and the sophisticated mahogany and satinwood case pieces fashioned in the Hepplewhite style by Matthew Egerton and his son, is to suggest in the briefest possible way the history of furniture-making in New Jersey during the century and a quarter that preceded the building of this room.

WALL D

GILT LOOKING-GLASS
c. 1810

MAHOGANY TABLE
DUNCAN PHYFE STYLE
c. 1810

12IN   0   1   2FT

CRAYON PORTRAIT

HORSEHAIR COVERED SOFA
MAHOGANY WITH INLAY
SHERATON STYLE
c. 1800

CONTEMPORARY DOCUMENT

Excerpts of the Official Record of John C. Calhoun's Speech in Congress, Feb. 4, 1817, in which he declares the Need of Roads and Canals for the Welfare and Development of the Country.

. . . At peace with all the world, abounding in pecuniary means, and, what was of the most importance, and at what he rejoiced, as most favorable to the country, party and sectional feelings immerged in a liberal and enlightened regard to the general concerns of the nation—such, said he, are the favorable circumstances under which we are now deliberating. Thus situated, to what can we direct our resources and attention more important than internal improvements? . . . In fact, if we look into the nature of wealth, we will find that nothing can be more favorable to its growth than good roads and canals. . . . If we were only to consider the pecuniary advantages of a good system of roads and canals, it might indeed admit of some doubt whether they ought not to be left wholly to individual exertions; but when we come to consider how intimately the strength and political prosperity of the Republic are connected with this subject, we find the most urgent reasons why we should apply our resources to them. . . . We occupy a surface prodigiously great in proportion to our numbers. The common strength is brought to bear with great difficulty on the point that may be menaced by an enemy. It is our duty, then, as far as in the nature of things it can be effected, to counteract this weakness. Good roads and canals judiciously laid out, are the proper remedy. In the recent war, how much did we suffer for want of them! Besides the tardiness and the consequential inefficacy of our military movements, to what an increased expense was the country put for the article of transportation alone! In the event of another war, the saving in this particular would go far towards indemnifying us for the expense of constructing the means of transportation. . . .

But on this subject of national power, what, said Mr. C., can be more important than a perfect unity in every part, in feelings and sentiments? And what can tend more powerfully to produce it, than overcoming the effects of distance? No country, enjoying freedom, ever occupied anything like as great an extent of country as this Republic . . . and, what is most remarkable, such is the happy mould of our Government, so well are the State and general powers blended, that much of our political happiness draws its origin from the extent of our Republic. . . . Let it not, however, be forgotten, let it, said he, be forever kept in mind, that it exposes us to the greatest of all calamities, next to the loss of liberty, and even to that in its consequence—*disunion*. We are great, and rapidly—he was about to say fearfully—growing. This, said he, is our pride and danger—our weakness and our strength. Little, said Mr. C., does he deserve to be intrusted with the liberties of this people, who does not raise his mind to these truths. We are under the most imperious obligation to counteract every tendency to disunion. The strongest of all cements is, undoubtedly, the wisdom, justice, and, above all, the moderation of this House; yet the great subject on which we are now deliberating, in this respect, deserves the most serious consideration. Whatever, said Mr. C., impedes the intercourse of the extremes with this, the centre of the Republic, weakens the Union. The more enlarged the sphere of commercial circulation, the more extended that of social intercourse; the more strongly are we bound together; the more inseparable are our destinies. Those who understand the human heart best, know how powerfully distance tends to break the sympathies of our nature. Nothing, not even dissimilarity of language, tends more to estrange man from man. Let us then, said Mr. C., bind the Republic together with a perfect system of roads and canals. Let us conquer space. It is thus the most distant parts of the Republic will be brought within a few days travel of the centre; it is thus that a citizen of the West will read the news of Boston still moist from the press. The mail and the press, said he, are the nerves of the body politic. By them the slightest impression made on the most remote parts is communicated to the whole system; and the more perfect the means of transportation, the more rapid and true the vibration. . . .

The Sentinel of Freedom.

Newark Free School.

NOTICE is hereby given, that the FREE SCHOOL, taught by Mr. Alpheus Hews over the Market, is now open for the admission of Scholars. Residents within the Township of Newark wishing to avail themselves of the priviledge of this School, or of the Schools at Camp-Town or Lyons Farms for the year ensuing, are requested to make their applications to Joseph Wilbur, David Hays, James Bruen, John C. Burnet, or William Tuttle. By order of the School Committee.

WM. TUTTLE. *Sect.*

April 24, 1820.

MRS. BROWN

From Stitesville, near Elizabeth-Town. Has removed to this place, and now occupies the house directly opposite the Episcopal Church in Broad-street — where she will teach a class of YOUNG LADIES PAINTING on velvet, in oil, and in water-colours. Also artificial flowers, fancy work, etc. etc. Hours of tuition from 9 to 11 o'clock. Terms one dollar per week. Lessons on the Piano Forte, fifty cents per lesson.

ORIGINAL COMMUNICATION.

President Adams on Manufactures. Extract of a letter from President Adams to the Editor of the Journal, dated December 14, 1819.

"Sir—I have received your polite favour of the 10th, the subject of which, is of great importance.

"I am old enough to remember the war of 1745, and its end—the war of 1755 and its close—the war of 1775 and its termination—the war of 1812 and its pacification. Every one of these has been followed by a general distress, embarassments on Commerce, destruction of manufactures, fall of the price of Products and Lands, similar to those we feel at the present day—and all produced by the same causes. I have wondered that so much experience has not taught us more caution. British merchants and manufacturers, immediately after the peace, disgorged upon us all their stores of merchandise and manufactures—not only without profit, but with a certain loss for a time—with the express purpose of annihilating all our manufactures and ruining all of our manufacturers. The cheapness of the articles lures us into extravagances—and at length produces universal complaint.

"What would be the consequences of the abolition of all restrictive, exclusive, and monopolizing laws if adopted by all the nations of the earth, I pretend not to say: but, while all the nations, with whom we have intercourse, persevere in cherishing such laws, I know not how we can do ourselves justice without introducing, with great prudence and discretion however, some portions of the same system.

"The gentlemen of Philadelphia have published a very important volume upon the subject, which I recommend to your perusal. Other cities are cooperating in the same plan. I heartily wish them all success, so far as this at least—that Congress may take the great subject into their most serious deliberation and decide upon it according to their most mature wisdom.

JOHN ADAMS

Wm. E. Richmond, Esq. Providence.

Latest from Europe.

House of Commons, Aug 21

It is confidently asserted in Paris, that one of the objects of the last audience which Prince Esterhazy, the Austrian ambassador to our court, had with his majesty, was to make known to the king of England, that the 5 years of imprisonment of Bonaparte, agreed on in 1815, having expired, Austria will no longer be a party to his detention, and would no longer send out a commissioner, in which sentiments Russia concurred.

Domestic News.

THE NEW JERSEY CANAL.

A law has been enacted by the legislature of this State, incorporating a company to form a canal between the Raritan and Delaware Rivers. The width and depth of the Canal are to be sufficient for the passage of coasting vessels of ordinary size. The advantages of such a canal, when completed, not only to a considerable portion of the state, but also to the cities of Philadelphia and New York, cannot easily be computed.

It will be 29 miles long, 9 feet deep and 56 feet on the surface of the water, it will be on a dead level from tide water to tide water, requiring but two locks, one at each extremity. It is ascertained that the supplied of water will be abundant; that to complete it will not require more than $800,000—that the transport through it will be immense, not only of goods and articles shipped coastwise, but of other articles of domestic production of the contiguous states of New York, Pennsylvania and of this state; and should a war occur, and our coast be blockaded at any time, the use and profits of the canal must be of inestimable value.

Should a company be formed and complete the canal the benefit resulting to the citizens of this state would be incalculable.

1. Near a million dollars will be laid out on the spot, distributing the means of livlihood and comply to thousands, and affording a market for every species of production and material required for such an operation.

2. The price of lands for 20 miles on each side of the canal will be greatly appreciated and facilities afforded for the transportation of commodities, which are now of little value.

INDIAN MISSION.—The Rev. Dr. *Morse* left Albany a few days since on his way to Buffalo &c. being employed by government, on a mission for investigating the actual conditions of the Indians, in the western and north western parts of the Union—preparatory to a distribution of the funds that have been appropriated by Congress for the civilization of the Indians.—Dr. Morse will proceed from Detroit to Mackinaw from thence across the north western territory, to the falls of St. Anthony, and in this way will visit, all the tribes of Indians that reside in that country. He will then probably descend the Mississippi, and on his return examine the condition of the Tribes in the western States. The intention of government, in this mission we learn, is to obtain an accurate account of the state of all the savages north of the Ohio.

NAVAL WONDER. On the evening of the 15th inst. the beautiful Steamship, Robert Fulton arrived at New York, 17 days from New Orleans, by way of the Havana and Charleston. She stopped two days at the Havana and four at Charleston making her run from New Orleans to New York only eleven days. She brought about 70 passengers who speak in unqualified praise of her accommodations and from the experience they had during their passage, declare all apprehension for her safety in rough weather to be, in their opinion, groundless.

From the Compiler Monarchy and Republicanism, or Great Britain & the United States A Contrast.

A correspondent observes, that from an article in the last *Enquirer*, taken from a London paper, it is computed that the expense of the approaching coronation of his *Britannic Majesty George IV*, will *exceed eight hundred thousand pounds sterling.* This at $4.44 the pound sterling, amounts to the sum of *three millions five hundred and fifty two thousand dollars*, of the currency of the United States.

This sum would pay the *salaries* of the *President of the United States,* for a succession of ONE HUNDRED AND FORTY-TWO YEARS, and leave a balance of two thousand dollars remaining.

New Brunswick.

BREACH OF PROMISE OF MARRIAGE. At the sitting of the Circuit Court in this city last week, Mr. Hartwell, a gentleman of the bar in the adjoining county of Somerset, was arraigned on a charge of breach of promise of marriage to Miss Edgar, of Short Hills, in this county. After a patient and interesting investigation of two days, the cause was submitted to the jury, who, after an absence of two hours, returned with a verdict for the plaintiff of *twelve hundred and fifty dollars* damages! A verdict equally honorable to their feelings as fathers, and to their integrity as citizens. Mr. Hartwell is a man of small property we understand.

The great novelty and delicacy of this case, attracted an unusual assemblage; and the Court house was crowded almost to suffocation. The counsel on both sides managed with much skill and address; but the counsel for the plaintiff, having the popular and right side of the question, gratified the audience with a display of honorable feeling, sarcastic reproach, and vibrating eloquence, seldom equalled. Such a lash of censure, to a man of the least sensibility, must have been like the sting of scorpions.

Natchez.

STEAM BOAT DISASTERS.— Arrived on Monday evening last, the Steamboat Hecla, five days from New Orleans, destined for St. Louis. We learn from a gentleman who came passenger in the Hecla, that a few days since, the Steam boat Volcano bursted her boiler near St. Francisville, while ascending the Mississippi. The engineer and two negroes were instantly killed, and the mate very severely scalded. We also learn that the Steamboat Newport, on her way to Alexandria, on Red River, has been sunk, and a small part of her cargo saved.—We are further informed by a Louisville paper that the Steamboat Perseverance, on her way from Louisville to Cincinnati, took fire near Madison, Indiana, and burnt to the water's edge. The flames spread so rapidly that it was with difficulty the passengers could get ashore; many of them lost their clothing.

Foreign Intelligence.

ENGLAND

From the National Advocate, July 25

Nothing will be more mortifying to the pride of George the fourth, who is inaptly called "a dandy of 60", if the Queen shall succeed with the people in causing herself to be crowned. The ceremony cannot be separately performed; they must be crowned together, although they may ride to Westminster Abbey in separate coaches, or walk under separate canopies. It will not be the most pleasant duty for his Majesty to take the hand of his "vera sposa", to whom he has not spoken for 15 years—to lead her to the velvet cushion—to put himself, the crown on her head, and go through all the respectful, devoted, though after all, ridiculous ceremonies of coronation—and to hear the cries of God Save the Queen, when from the bottom of his heart he wishes her with his satanic majesty. Yet this may all happen. George Rex is obstinately determined she shall not be crowned, while she is obstinately insisting upon her rights. This day week will settle the contest, and in about six weeks we hope to learn who wears the breeches.

Our latest Liverpool paper, states that WALTER SCOTT is confined to his bed by sickness.

We learn that the ship Elizabeth, sent out by the Colonization Society of this city, with people of colour, and all kinds of implements of husbandry, for the purpose of making a settlement in Africa, arrived at Sierra Leone, in the remarkable short passage of 36 days, all well. After waiting there about a week, and the Cyane, her convoy, not arriving, she proceeded down the coast to Sherbro, the place given them by one of the African kings to make their settlement on.—Three days after the Elizabeth left Sierra Leone, the Cayne also arrived at that port, and, after stopping two or three days, followed on.

Don Onis, the late Minister of Spain to the United States, has fallen into disgrace with King Ferdinand even at the very moment when he plumed himself most on the favor of his master. An argument is drawn from this circumstance, that the treaty whereby the Floridas were ceded to the United States and which was altogether the work of Onis, will not receive the sanction of the Court of Madrid. The troops of the United States are, however, in possession of Pensacola and St. Marks, and we fear that the King of Spain, in his present state of imbecility, would find some difficulty in rescuing them from the talons of the republican eagle.

MID-VICTORIAN AMERICA

As illustrated by the PARLOR OF ROOSEVELT HOUSE, *an accurate restoration*

on the original site of the birthplace of Theodore Roosevelt

by the Woman's Roosevelt Memorial Association in New York City

WALL A

WALL B

WALL C

WALL D

F.M.

0 3 6 9 12ⁿ

2' 1'

PLASTER CEILING ROSE SHOWN IN CENTER; SECTION OF CARPET AT RIGHT

Historical Note

W HAT were things like in the United States in the year 1858, the year in which Theodore Roosevelt was born, in the house which we are about to illustrate and discuss?

To ask this question is to be reminded at once that hindsight is sometimes a disadvantage as well as an advantage. Most of us, when we try offhand to place the year 1858 in American history, think inevitably of the Civil War, which then was only three years in the future. The history books deal with 1858 largely in thems of the approaching conflict, focusing their attention on the political cleavage between North and South, which was becoming more and more definite and serious. And it is quite true, of course, that the low rumble of thunder was clearly audible along the horizon. It was in 1858 that Abraham Lincoln, debating with Douglas, quoted, "A house divided against itself cannot stand." But it is doubtful if many Americans seriously feared, in 1858, that there would be any such tragic division in this house as was destined to occur. Ordinary life went on without much regard to the political issues of slavery and states rights, just as to-day ordinary life in most American communities goes on without much regard to the political strife over the New Deal. When we go back to read the contemporary newspapers and magazines, we can hardly help being struck by the extent to which popular attention was fixed upon other events and other issues. Slowly we became aware of the fact that to the men and women of 1858 the time was one of furious national expansion and of rising, if undisciplined and irregular, prosperity; a time of hope rather than a time of fear.

"We are now in the first flush of success," wrote a contemporary chronicler in the Editor's Table of *Harper's Monthly Magazine* in 1858. "Every year new territories are opening, fields of enterprise enlarging; so that novelty has hardly time to thrill the mind with a suddenly-vivid impression before another startling object presses upon its sensitive nerve." Within the space of thirteen years, Texas, California, and the intervening territory had been added to the United States, and the boundaries of Oregon had been definitely settled; gold had been discovered in California and had brought about a mad rush to the Pacific Coast; and the expansionist spirit—the sense that Americans now had almost a whole continent to subdue and exploit, a continent full of unimaginable riches—had brought about a speculative boom. The boom had broken in the panic of 1857—banks closing, businesses collapsing—but already a quick recovery was under way. The North and West had been hard hit, but were regaining confidence; the South had been only slightly affected (a circumstance which was destined to give the Southerners a

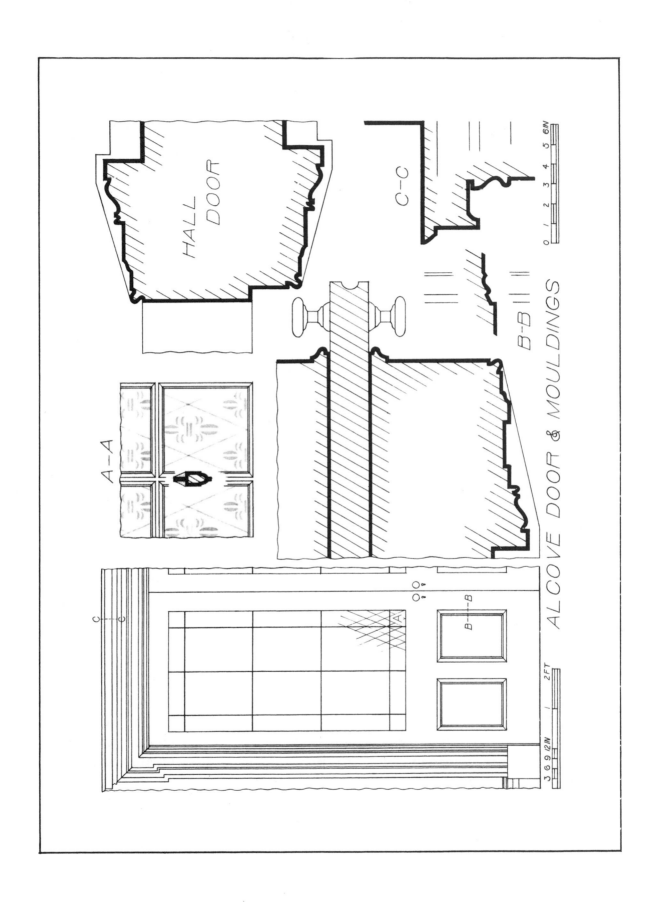

HALL DOOR

A—A

C—C

B—B

B—B

ALCOVE DOOR & MOULDINGS

0 1 2 3 4 5 6 IN

3 6 9 12 IN 1 2 FT

fatal belief in the superior strength of their economic resources). And now in 1858 a new series of events seemed to point the way toward a grand era of expansion, of prosperity, and of progress.

The first experiment of overland mail service with the Pacific Coast was successfully carried out, mail being carried from San Francisco to St. Louis, across mountains and plains, in the bewildering time of twenty-three days and four hours. President Buchanan was now proposing that Congress consider seriously a plan for a transcontinental railroad. Utah, where the Mormons had defied the Federal power, was more peaceful. Gold was discovered near Pike's Peak, in what is now Colorado; would the new gold mines rival those of California? Minnesota was admitted to the Union—a fact which called attention to the rapid development of the territories beyond the Mississippi River. (For twenty years there had been about as many Americans living west of the Alleghanies as east of them; at last the Middle West was becoming the heart of the country.) And—most important of all these events in the eyes of the people of 1858—the Atlantic cable was successfully laid. Over it Queen Victoria and President Buchanan exchanged messages of friendship and of hope; editorial optimists proclaimed that the transatlantic telegraph (as they called it) would unite the hemispheres in closer and ever closer bonds of prosperity and amity.

So much for the country at large. But let us narrow our focus—shutting out the raw sprawling towns of the Middle West and South, the Mississippi steamboats, the plains where covered wagons still crawled westward, the thrilling and lawless mining-camp life of California—and look briefly at the life of the well-to-do in the eastern cities: the sort of life which was lived in the Roosevelts' New York.

The metropolis already had about half a million inhabitants. Social life centered near Fifth Avenue, below Thirty-fourth Street. Work was just being begun on Central Park, so named because it was in the center of Manhattan Island, though it was then on the northern outskirts of the city. A six-story building attracted attention by its unusual height; the church steeples still dominated the skyline. Up in Boston, Amos Lawrence rode his horse to his office daily from Brookline, three miles outside the city (after seven o'clock breakfast in a big house heated throughout by air-tight stoves); Mrs. Lawrence, when she had errands to do in town, took the family carriage, drawn by a pair of gray horses, "a large English coach with C springs, a great brocaded coachman's box, massive lamps heavily mounted with silver." Even the more crowded city of New York was not so closely built as to prevent wealthy citizens from having stables of their own, in yards full of greenery. City boys could easily reach places where they could coast, skate, play baseball and football, swim, sail; and there was always the fascinating pageant of the clipper ships along the waterfront, where the scent of spices hung on the air and everything spoke of the romance of the China trade.

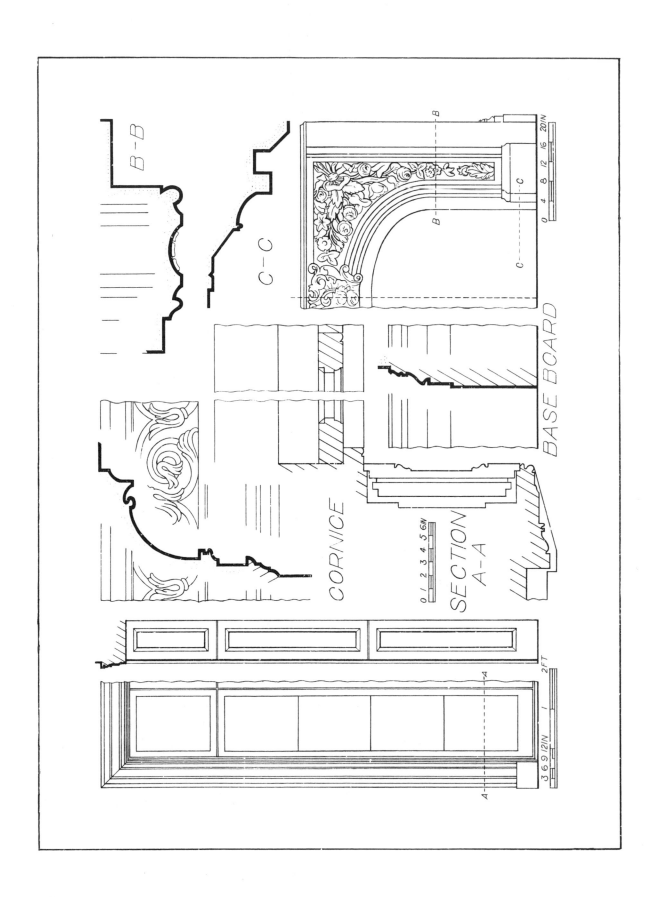

B–B

C–C

CORNICE

BASE BOARD

SECTION A–A

B

B

C

C

0 4 8 12 16 20 IN

0 1 2 3 4 5 6 IN

A

A

3 6 9 12 IN

1

2 FT

"Broadway," Thackeray had written in 1852, "is miles upon miles long, a rush of life such as I have never seen; not so full as the Strand, but so rapid. The houses are always being torn down and built up again, the railroad cars drive slap into the midst of the city. There are barricades and scaffoldings everywhere. I have not been into a house . . . but something new is being done to it . . . or steps are down, or the family is going to move." That had been during the boom days, but even in 1858, after the panic of '57, the sense of movement, of change, of expansion was vivid. What if the cobblestones made the carriages and public omnibuses jounce and lean, and rudimentary methods of sewage disposal made many a tree-lined street unsavory?

Said Thackeray, "The ladies . . . are as lean as greyhounds; they dress prodigiously fine, taking for their models the French actresses, I think, of the Boulevard theatres." (Such dresses! —snug bodices, full sleeves, and huge bell-shaped skirts, some of them three or four yards in circumference; little beribboned bonnets—or, for indoor wear, little beribboned lace caps worn on the back of the head. You should picture these ladies being accompanied abroad by gentlemen in tailed coats, stovepipe hats, and narrow, uncreased trousers.) Wrote Fanny Kemble from Nahant in 1858: "How you would open your eyes and stop your ears if you were here! This enormous house [a new summer hotel] is filled with American women, one prettier than the other, who look like fairies, dress like duchesses or *femmes entretenues*, behave like housemaids, and scream like peacocks."

Behave like housemaids! One is reminded of the comment of an Englishman on an American diplomat of that time in London, that he would soon get over his dyspepsia if he chewed his food half as much as he did his filthy tobacco. But there was much agreeable and comely society along the eastern seaboard in 1858. In Nahant itself —Boston's favorite summer-resort, comparable to Philadelphia's Cape May, or New York's Tarrytown—lived families of distinction and cosmopolitan culture, like the Longfellows, Holmeses, Lodges, Lawrences. Thackeray, who found the West and South ugly and scraggly, thought Boston, New York, and Philadelphia "not so civilized as our London, but more so than Manchester and Liverpool. At Boston," he remarked, "is a very good literate company indeed; it is like Edinburgh for that—a vast amount of toryism and donnishness everywhere. That of New York the simplest and least pretentious; it suffices that a man should keep a fine house, give parties, and have a daughter, to get all the world to him."

The New Yorker of 1858 could go to the opera at the Academy of Music on Fourteenth Street; or go to Laura Keene's theatre and see *Our American Cousin* just beginning its long career, with Sothern as Dundreary and young Joseph Jefferson as Asa Trenchard; or to Wallack's or other theatres, or to Barnum's Museum (Tom Thumb and other attractions). At the fashionable balls he could dance the "soft waltz, wild mazurka, slow schottische," or the lancers, with lovely doe-eyed innocents in evening dresses which barely clung to their shoulders, and rustling, billowing crinolines. In those days, as in every other, the younger generation had its wild element, suggested in a contemporary rhyme about a fast young girl.

> In her own right an heiress—a plum at the least—
> A Plantation down South, and a coal-mine down East

> who

> Smuggled candy in school, smoked cigars, and—oh fie!—
> Read a great many very queer books on the sly.

But entertainment was mostly simple and very decorous: if you read the contemporary letters of young New Yorkers you will find, as likely as not, that the most exciting social event of a winter's week was a sleigh-ride, twenty young people (well chaperoned) driving, all bundled up in a monster sleigh, to somebody's house outside the city to play games.

Storm clouds on the horizon? Civil War approaching? Well, the newspapers and the men of affairs talked much about the bitter disputes over the extension of slavery into the western territories. But to most Americans the clouds still seemed small. America was on its way to a great and dazzling destiny, and meanwhile life could be very pleasant.

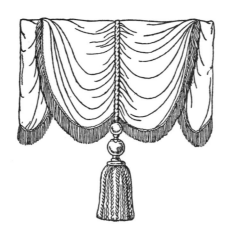

WALL A

COPPER PLATE ENGRAVING

GILDED MANTEL GLASS

COPPER PLATE ENGRAVING
AFTER RAPHAEL'S "LA FORNARINA"

PAIR OF UPHOLSTERED SOFAS
ROSEWOOD

Mid-Victorian America

I N 1847, when the house which contains the present Theodore Roosevelt Memorial* was started, eclecticism in architectural taste was already
beginning to attract popular interest; by 1858, when Theodore
Roosevelt was born, it was universally accepted and generally
triumphant. As early as 1844, the *North American Review* had
carried in its April number a well-written article by the architect
Arthur Gilman supporting eclecticism; under the guise of a review of Shaw's *Rural Architecture* he made a bitter attack on the
classic revival, paid grudging respect to the Gothic, but reserved
his enthusiasm for the Italian Renaissance, and suggested for
America a sort of universal borrowing. Four years later, Robert
Dale Owen's *Hints on Public Architecture*, while written from a rationalist stand-
point, and supporting an architectural ideal reasonable above all else, is in its style
criticism tolerant, almost omnivorous. The day of the classic revival was mani-
festly over.

The house shows the naïve hesitancy that such a period of experiment, of dawning style self-consciousness, produced. Its quiet brownstone façade, with tall windows capped by thin Tudor drip-moulds, is delicately "Gothic"—Gothic of a peculiar local New York type, used often and perhaps invented by James Renwick.
It is a Gothic that is no more trying to copy mediaeval houses than the designers of
the delicate red brick "Greek Revival" houses of Washington Square and Waverly
Place were trying to copy Greek temples—a Gothic which did not disdain cast-
iron balconies and front-stoop railings in which there is not a little of classic feeling. But, once the front door is passed, the Gothic is forgotten and the new free
eclecticism, the then newest fashion, takes its place. Here, as so often happens, it is
in interior work that style changes first appear; and, just as a few years ago "modern" furniture and wall finishes began to show themselves hesitantly in houses
whose exteriors might still be strictly traditional, so in the forties heavy stuffed
furniture, marble mantels with realistic foliage, and heavy plaster mouldings of
distantly "French" type began to appear with growing frequency behind the neat
red brick walls and white doors of Greek Revival houses, or within the dignified
and rectangular "Gothic" of the newer Romantic buildings.

It could not have been otherwise. Not only in America, but all over the Western
world, new forces were at work, changing personal ideals and popular tastes with a
speed almost unprecedented. A world was being opened for exploitation; the industrial development of the fifty preceding years was at last beginning to be understood; its opportunities for wealth were being eagerly seized; as its spawning of

---

* Roosevelt House, 28 East Twentieth Street, New York City, restored by and the property of the Woman's Roosevelt Memorial Association.

slums and rickets and poverty progressed, so also grew fortune after fortune. To a society so conditioned, the aristocratic restraint and refinement of the taste of the early century could have little appeal; something more "solid"—and more showy —was demanded. One has only to look at a lovely colored drawing of a Greek Revival interior by A. J. Davis in the New York Historical Society to realize how inevitable was the change. In that classical and exquisite rendering one sees high clear spaces, a screen of two slim Ionic columns separating what is obviously a front and back parlor, and a few pieces, judiciously placed, of furniture halfway between Empire and Duncan Phyfe. In such an interior one can imagine the ladies of the time, with their lovely gowns, so revealing of their charms, flowing in unbroken curves from breast to hem, moving easily, at home, conversing with men whose long coats, colored vests, and tight trousers still looked back almost as much to the elegancies of the eighteenth century as they looked forward to the wrinkled looseness of the later nineteenth century. Such an atmosphere was all too ethereal for a new industrially based populace; it was not "hearty" enough. There was a fever over the world, a new gold fever; and new success, more rapid and "brilliant" than ever before, demanded showier ways of expressing itself, more solid evidences of its own achievements. Even the most conservative taste could not help following the trend. Indeed religion itself was affected; on February 5, 1846, Philip Hone remarks in his diary, somewhat ironically: "The new church [Grace] . . . is nearly finished. . . . The pews were sold last week, and brought extravagant prices, some $1200 to $1400, with a pew rent of . . . eight per cent, so that the word of God, as it came down to us from fisherman and mechanics, will cost the quality who worship in this splendid temple about 3 dollars every Sunday. . . ."

So, just as the simplicity of Empire dresses gave way to flounces and ruffles—one can trace the development clearly in the fashion magazines of the time, each year, it would seem, between 1820 and 1860 adding another ruffle, another ornament, another foot around the skirt—so the furniture and the interior fittings grew stuffier and more solid, richer and more heavy. It is halfway in this transition that the Roosevelt House was built, at perhaps just the most interesting point of indecision. The ruffles, as it were, are there, but not the exaggerated crinolines of Civil War days; the age of black walnut was still to come.

Any transitional example has elements of both limits of the change. The door trim of this room, for instance, is still in the pure vein of Greek Revival work. Wide and flat, and "croisetted" at the upper corners, it has a delicacy of section and a purity of profile that speak of the fine craftsmanship of earlier decades. The white marble arched fireplace, on the other hand, is of the other—the so-called "Victorian"—type; its realistic vines that fill the spandrels owe nothing to the classic. But it is in the plaster ornament that the greatest break with the past is to be found; its full, round, undercut mouldings, and the foliage in high relief of the

WALL C

GLASS CHANDELIER
Mid 19th Century

CHICKERING PIANO. LOUIS XIV MODEL
ROSEWOOD CASE. 1849
PIANO STOOL
ROSEWOOD. *c.* 1850

MUSIC RACK
ROSEWOOD
1850–1860

UPHOLSTERED BERGÈRE
ROSEWOOD
1850–1860

SIDEBOARD
ROSEWOOD WITH
MARBLE SHELF
c. 1860

E. MELADY

12IN   0   1   2FT

cornice and the ceiling rosette, have nothing of the revival in them—they are prophetic in every curve, despite their still delicate scale, of the lavish, heavy forms that were to be the rule in the Civil War period and were to remain the standard types for ordinary New York City houses for almost thirty years thereafter.

The furnishings of the room have the same transitional character. All represent various types of that French-inspired style we usually lump together as Victorian, but they vary from the delicacy of early Victorian rosewood to the heavy complexity of the mid-Victorian work of later date. It is manifest that not all the furnishing of the room was done at the same time. Much of it evidently dates from the period of 1854, when Theodore Roosevelt's parents came to live in the house; but some is obviously many years later.

The earlier date seems to cover the greater part of the delicate chairs, the sofa (which shows signs of Empire influence), and the lovely, rather classic blue-green and gray carpet, whose interlaced wreaths are closer to the classic revival type than to the realistic and sprawling foliage of later work. The charming wallpaper, reproduced from preserved fragments of the old, is more difficult to date, for similar patterns were used over long periods; yet here, too, the clarity and delicacy of the effect have none of the over-rich heaviness and darkness of most papers of the post-Civil-War era. The carving on the chairs combines the acanthus with realistic foliage; it is all delicately in tune with the generally Louis XV inspiration of the design. The rich Chickering square piano is heavier, but still in the same feeling; one of the best examples of its type, it shows how much easier to design was the old square piano than its recent descendants, the upright and the grand. The table, too, is good early Victorian, and its intricate apron and delicate cabriole legs bring out with special emphasis the Louis XV character that was the precedent for the entire style.

Just why all the fashionable furniture designers of England, France, and America (with a few exceptions) should have turned so unanimously to early eighteenth-century France for inspiration is a difficult question. Without a doubt, the restoration of the monarchy in France after the fall of Napoleon made an impression on English and American culture difficult for us to realize to-day. To many of the "best people" it must have seemed a return to some kind of solid and traditional security, and all the constant political tumult of the years of that monarchy went almost unnoticed. The superficiality of the appeal that Louis XVIII, Charles X, and Louis Philippe had for the French themselves—which led to revolution and the meteoric rise of Napoleon III—seemed less important, probably, than the vague feeling that the troubled and wealthy conservatives, frightened by the popular clamors of '48, had that somehow, at least in Paris, the old conservative ways were again in favor. Even after Napoleon III became emperor, something of the same feeling persisted. Louis Napoleon himself proved adept at riding two horses at the same time—one, the sentimental adoration of the great Napoleon; the other, the idea that his own court was "solid," businesslike, and yet at the same time conservatively "modern." All of this conspired to give French precedent great prestige in the minds of that wealthy minority who made commercial fashion. It was natural enough to find the Restoration kings—or even, in his special position, Napoleon III—using the French Louis XV style as a basis for inspiration; then, due to this French prestige, it became almost world-wide. Yet in none of it was actual copying attempted; the ideals of a new and successful business aristocracy were too different to accept that. It must all be *new*, too; new and obvious.

The history of Victorian furniture design is largely the history of this originally French inspiration as it gradually disintegrated under the impact of growing commercialism, a growing use of machines in furniture manufacture, and a growing demand for ostentation. Delicate hand-carving became both more realistic and coarser, the band saw and the lathe made mere intricacy seem a modern virtue, slim cabriole legs became obese and shapeless, and finally the insistent black of ebony and the heavy gloom of black walnut, in shapes growingly huge and unwieldy, put an end to the last ray of delicacy and restraint. The thirty-five years from 1840 to 1875 saw the whole cycle.

Of these later developments of Victorianism there is at least one example in this room—the so-called whatnot, whose elaborate brackets, tortured outline, white marble top, and mirrored doors express an aesthetic ideal quite different from the delicacy of the chairs and sofa, or the gracefulness of the rococo table. The pierced music rack, too, seems to evoke a feeling somewhat more eloquent of the later than of the earlier ideas, though here dating is more difficult, for such racks were made over a long period of time. Yet even these two pieces, though they show the start of a development that was to culminate in ponderous and contorted black walnut and in shiny black haircloth, are nevertheless themselves still comparatively light and delicate, and through similarity of material and discreet placing take their part in giving the room its total effect of quiet harmony.

And, after all, it is this totality of effect which is important and revealing. Whatever one may think of the minor details of the room—its heavy glass chandelier, its wax fruit under a glass bell, its over-heavy scrolled ormolu curtain hold-backs— the room itself is not unpleasant. Even its "quaintness," its obvious "old-fashioned" character, is less striking than its general atmosphere of quiet warmth, of pleasant colors well blended, of a polished (if a little stiff) formality. It is a room eloquent of an interesting age; an age in which conservative classicism, restrained and quiet, was blending with a new eclecticism, a striving for things new, brilliant, and showy; an age in which the ostentation of commercialism had not yet quite overwhelmed the evidences of older and quieter ideals. For the Victorian period was a restless, an inventive, and even a creative age, seeking new forms to express new ideals and

WALL D

E MELADY

12IN 0 1 2FT

PIER GLASS, GILT

UPHOLSTERED   WAX FRUIT IN GLASS CASE
SIDE CHAIR   MARBLE TOP TABLE
ROSEWOOD   ROSEWOOD. 1850-1860
1850-1860

new techniques; its faults were inherent perhaps in the ideals themselves of un-trammeled and greedy industrialism which forced the changes—but an age crea-tive, nevertheless. Just at its dawn, its virtues of freedom and of novelty were not yet obscured by the disintegration of taste that accompanied the feverish expansion of its full growth. It is this moment—this interesting dawn of a day which was so tragically to belie the promise of its dawning—which here is enshrined and finds its almost perfect expression.

CONTEMPORARY DOCUMENT

EXTRACTS FROM THE DIARY OF PHILIP HONE SHOW THE ACCELERATION OF EVERYDAY LIFE IN AMERICA AS THE MIDDLE OF THE NINETEENTH CENTURY DRAWS NEAR.

1830 One of the locomotive engines on the Liverpool and Manchester Railroad traversed the distance between the two places, thirty-two miles, in thirty-three minutes,— about *fifty-eight miles an hour!*

1832 The boast that our country is the asylum for the oppressed in other parts of the world is very philanthropic and sentimental, but I fear that we shall, before long, derive little comfort from being made the almshouse and place of refuge for the poor of other countries.

1834 The old Yankee character appears to me to be nearly extinct. I have taken pains to bring out some originals among the persons I have met since we left Boston; I have found them generally civil and obliging and disposed to be communicative, but there are no oddities such as we used to meet in former days. The march of refinement and the progress of improvement which has substituted cotton-mills and railroads for mountains and cataracts has made men ashamed of those broad lines of national character which became them so well.

1836 Oh, for a steamboat at such a time!... Wind and sails are nothing now compared to steam and paddles, and we had the mortification of realizing this fact this afternoon, by seeing a large steamer (I am in England now, and must talk as the English talk) puffing and wheezing and smoking rapidly on her course towards the Irish shore, while we were flapping and rolling and making no headway.

1837 There never was a nation on the face of the earth which equalled this in rapid locomotion. The President's message was brought on to this city, by railroad, steamboats, and horsemen, and carried from hence to Boston, which place it reached in the inconceivably short period of twenty-four hours from Washington, a distance of five hundred miles.

1838 I noticed a fact at the dinner table to-day, which proves the increased intercourse between the people of the United States and Europe. Of a party of twenty seated at the table every person has been to Europe, although of the number only two, Mr. Schmidt and Mr. Maitland, were foreigners.

1839 The "Great Western" arrived at New York yesterday [July 22], having sailed from Bristol on the 6th. The movements of this fine vessel have gotten to be as regular as the rising and setting of the sun, or the flux and reflux of the tide.

1839 Times are certainly hard. Money is scarce and provisions dear. Goods won't sell, and customers don't pay. The banks won't discount; stocks are down to nothing, and real estate unavailable. And yet, with all this, the rage for amusement is unabated. Indeed, men seem to reason that, as they cannot last long, a dollar more or less will make very little difference either to themselves or their creditors, as the case may be.

1839 I went this morning by invitation of Monsieur Francois Gouraud to see a collection of the views made by the wonderful process lately discovered in France by Monsieur Daguerre, which is called by his name. . . .

[179]

1840 The good people of Boston are so delighted at the prospect of rivalling New York, that they are in perfect ecstasies at the arrival of the steamship "Britannia", and have made a glorification of my little friend Cunard, the enterprising proprietor of the line, of the most magnificent proportions.

1841 —sailed (I must write sailed until some other word is invented; but how can it be called sailing when no sails are used?)

1842 The author of the "Pickwick Papers" is a small, bright-eyed, intelligent looking young fellow, thirty years of age, somewhat of a dandy in his dress, with "rings and things and fine array," brisk in his manner, and of a lively conversation. If he does not get his little head turned by all this, I shall wonder at it.

1844 The annexation of Texas to the United States—a measure which many of our best and wisest citizens have looked at with most anxious apprehension—seems now likely to take place. . . . A war with Mexico would be the immediate consequence of this measure. . . .

1844 How long will it be before this *liberty* of ours becomes so licentious that we shall be compelled to take refuge in the arms of despotism?

1844 Here is the great question of severance between the North and the South, which is one day to shake this overgrown Republic to its center. The Southern States desire the annexation of Texas to the Union, to strengthen their position geographically and politically by the prospective addition of four or five slaveholding States. We of the North and East say we have already more territory than we know what to do with, and more slavery within our borders than we choose to be answerable for before God and man.

1846 The whole extent of this newly discovered phenomenon was never made so apparent to me as on the day of the meeting of the convention; during the hour of adjournment to dinner a message was sent by the telegraph to Mr. Fillmore, at Buffalo. The answer came immediately that "Mr. Fillmore was not in his office, and could not be found." . . . This was handed to me on my taking the chair, and had travelled four hundred and seventy miles during our short recess of an hour.

1848 Our newly acquired territory of California, having passed from the hands of Spaniards and Indians into those of the enterprising Yankees, who run faster, fly higher, and dig deeper than any people under the sun, has now developed its riches. The region of country watered by the river Sacramento is found to abound in pure gold; the shining tempter of mankind is found in the land and crevices of the rocks, and all the world have become diggers and delvers. The towns are deserted by all but the women; business is neglected; houses stand empty; vessels are laid up for want of hands; the necessaries of life cannot be obtained, and the people are starving, with their pockets full of gold.

1849 The tone of writing and speaking in Europe on the subject of the United States is greatly altered of late. . . . The Yankees may be ignorant of the most approved method of using the knife and fork; but it cannot be denied that they are competent to make a good use of the sword and musket. They eat fast, but they go ahead wonderfully; they use some queer expressions, but in defence of their rights are apt to talk much to the purpose.

Selections from The Diary of Philip Hone.

NEW YORK HERALD.

Selected from Issues in the 1850's.

OVERLAND TO SAN FRANCISCO

Starting of the Great Overland Mail from St. Louis and Memphis.

SPECIAL CORRESPONDENCE OF THE NEW YORK HERALD.
St. Louis.

Today the first overland mail to San Francisco from St. Louis and Memphis, under contract with the Overland Mail Company, started from this city under the direction of Mr. John Butterfield, the president of the company. . . .

Thus is inaugurated under the administration of Mr. Buchahan, a second great event of the age. The first linked two nations together; the second cements a union of the extremes of a nation separated heretofore by time and distance, but now to be united by the facilities of rapid communication; and both tend to bind more closely, those who before were united in the bonds of brotherhood. The importance of the first practical step towards the Pacific Railroad, can hardly be overrated, and I think may safely pronounce it another great event of the age. If the overland mail succeeds, the railroad and telegraph will soon follow its course; the settlements along the line will be built up with rapidity, our vast possessions in New Mexico will be opened up to us and to the world, and instead of a circuitous route to our Pacific possessions, tedious in time of peace, and extremely impracticable in time of war, we shall have an easy, safe and rapid route, where but a few years since nature in her wildest aspects reigned supreme.

It is in pursuance of Mr. Buchanan's policy of developing the resources of the country and studying its best interests, instead of truckling to the political hobbies of the day, that these benefits are to be gained. Under the supervision of his administration, the great unexplored centre of our continent has been thrown open to civilization. It has established a route through Northern Texas from San Antonio to San Diego, a regular mail from St. Joseph to Salt Lake, from Independence to Santa Fe, and now the climax is capped by the successful commencing of this great enterprise. The theory that mountains separate nations, or that there lay between us and our California brethren an impassable obstacle, erected by the hands of God, is thus scattered to the winds.

This is the largest contract for land mail service ever given, and what is a curious coincidence, has to compete with a steam route which starts nearly at the same time. The six o'clock train today took a mail east to go by steamer to California, while the eight o'clock train took a mail west. Which will get there first?

Washington, Dec. 22, 1857.

Major Mix, the acting commissioner of Indian affairs, received this afternoon a visit of ceremony at the Indian Office, from the delegation from the Pawnee tribe. The Major received them very kindly and entered into familiar conversation with them, on the understanding that it was merely an introductory visit and not one of ceremony. He gave them some good advice about civilizing their habits, and recommended them to take their squaws out of the fields and put them into their houses, which particular suggestion, however, did not appear to meet with the usual very emphatic grunt of assent. On parting, the old chief embraced Major Mix, and said, with much feeling, "My grandfather, I have seen you today, and do not feel poorer for it. I think the Great Spirit hears what is said today, and will take particular notice of it. My grandfather, I have a copy of the treaty in my lodge and I will listen to what it says. My grandfather, I see you do not look poor. Look at us; our bodies are almost naked. We are very poor." One of the chiefs made a very touching remark. He said that his wife had died just before he left his country, and his heart pained him that he could not tell her of the honor with which he had been received here.

A Ride in the Steam Carriage.

Many of our readers have doubtless noticed the small steam carriage which has been driven about the streets of New York and vicinity within the last nine months. It is an odd looking machine and has much the appearance of an artillery wagon from its low size and the projecting boiler, which is not unlike a cannon. . . .

The carriage . . . was invented by Mr. Richard Dudgeon, a mechanic of English birth, but who learned his trade in America. He is the inventor of the portable hydraulic jack, which is well known to steamboat men, and also of other minor applications of hydraulic power. He is simply a good locomotive machinist, knows nothing of the history of previous attempts in the making of steam carriages, and is unable to explain wherein his carriage differs from others except that it promises to be successful, while it is certain that all former ones have not been deemed so.

Mr. Dudgeon's carriage weighs 2,700 pounds and may be described as a half or quarter sized locomotive with very large wheels and no smoke pipe. It has no peculiarity in the arrangement of the steam machinery which is a simple tubular boiler with improved valve gear. . . .

Upon invitation of Mr. Dudgeon, one of our reporters took a trip with him in his steam carriage some time since.

Although it met numberless carts on the journey, there was no collision as it could be managed with much greater ease and certainty than a horse and wagon. Its progress of course attracted great attention, everyone stopping on the walk to look at it. The majority evidently regarded it as a good joke and thought it incumbent on him or her to laugh at it in passing. The juveniles, however, were its most ardent admirers, and on the outskirts of the city they fairly swarmed around the (to them) novel vehicle and were clamorous for a ride.

The route taken was up the track of The Second Avenue Railroad to Harlem and back again to Grand Street, a distance that was accomplished in less than two hours, with frequent stoppages, though there was no effort to make the run fast. . . .

The cost of the machine under notice is $1,500. It requires two persons to manage it; a lad, however, is quite as competent as a grown person for this duty.

There is one objection to these carriages—at least, in crowded cities—that will raise a great outcry against them, and that is the alarm it creates among horses. These sensitive animals will manifest their fear at its approach, and serious consequence will some day ensue.

A Paris letter in the 'Indépendance' of Brussels, gives some details of the ladies' dresses at the reception at the French Court on New Year's Eve:—the Empress wore a crimson velvet mantle, embroidered with gold, and her majestly was positively dazling with diamonds. Contrary to the custom observed last year, her Majesty had no one to bear her train. Among the ladies present, the toilettes were specially remarked of Mrs Baring, sister of the Duc de Bassano, who had a dress and court mantle of moire antique of pale green; the Duchesse d'Istrie, a dress shot with silver, edged with red, and a rose colored mantle; Mme. Poujade, niece of the Caimacan of Wallactria, a dress of blue satin, and a mantle of the same material, ornamented with bouquets of flowers and cherries, which produced a charming effect; and the Baroness de Brigode, a white satin dress and mantle of great elegance.

The New Catholic Cathedral.
July 14, 1858.

Archbishop Hughes contemplates erecting a new cathedral on Fifth Avenue, which is designed to be a structure of extraordinary magnificence, the grandest specimen of ecclesiastical architecture on this continent. The cost will probably exceed a million of dollars, and the Archbishop is now engaged, we believe, in an endeavor to raise that amount. It is a very proper and commendable undertaking doubtless; a building of such cost and grandeur as this is intended to be a rival of the cathedrals of the Old World—might well be the glory and pride of the metropolis; but it is very probable that it will never be completed. It will be like the cathedral of Cologne, which was commenced before the Reformation, and is not finished yet.

Religious Intelligence.

More Nice than Wise. — The introduction of a melodeon in the Front Street M. E. Church, in Trenton, N. J., has caused the withdrawal of some twelve persons, who allege themselves conscientiously opposed to having instrumental music in the church.

Re. I. S. Kalloch attended an evening meeting at the Baptist meeting house in Rockland, Me., last Sunday evening, and took part in the proceedings. He got into a sharp discussion with Deacon Wilson, who was a prominent witness in the famous Kalloch trial, and Elder Baker, a Baptist preacher. Mr. Kalloch took offense at some remarks of Elder Baker, which he understood to apply to him. The discussion ended in something very much like a row, which was at length ended by the gas being turned off, leaving the audience in great temporal darkness. This, of course, broke up the meeting.

The Great Prize Fight.

October 22, 1858.

The fight between John Morrissey and John Heenan, the Benicia Boy, came off on Wednesday afternoon at Long Point, Canada, between seventy and eighty miles from Buffalo. Eleven terrific rounds were fought in twenty-two minutes, when Morrissey was declared the victor. A more severe fight for the time it lasted never took place in this country. Morrissey was the favorite at one hundred to sixty. About two thousand persons witnessed the fight, who behaved themselves in the most orderly manner, and everything passed off very quietly. Morrissey was seconded by Kelley, of Australia, and an assistant. The Benicia Boy was seconded by Aaron Jones, an English pugilist, and Johnny Mackey. Persons from all parts of the United States and Canada were present to witness the fight. Heenan had the best of the fight at the commencement, but after the fifth round Morrissey took the lead and kept it. He has improved greatly since his fight with Yankee Sullivan.

The fight is over and the battle won. Another of those brutal exhibitions which disgrace the civilization of the age—a relic of the barbarism of Rome and of the Middle Ages—has taken place, and the victor wearing the laurels of triumph, is the "observed of all observers", and is admired and acknowledged as the champion gladiator of America. Are we at that height of progress in civilization that we claim to be, or are we in a condition that the laws, moral or legal, are powerless to prevent these occasional disgraceful displays of human brutality. In spite of the laws prohibiting prize fighting, two men have been allowed to prepare for a contest which might have resulted in the death of one or the other of the parties engaged, in the very faces of the officers of the law, and almost in the sanctuary of justice. Pretended efforts of the authorities were made to arrest the principals in the affair, but which, in fact, were only a notification for them to select a locality out of their immediate jurisdiction, and which would afford greater facilities for the officers themselves to learn how matters were progressing. The laws of the State do not tolerate prize fighting but a successful prize fighter seems to hold a prominent position among the politically pious and moral of the community.

Since the formation of this match, which was made on the 24th of June last, to the present day, this fight has been the theme of conversation throughout the country, among all classes of men, more particularly among the youth who, in all pursuits of life, from the schoolhouse to the workshop, seemed to have thought of nothing else than the fight for the championship, and everyone had his favorite in the contest. To the bar rooms, it has been a source of great profit, for there it was that the merits of the men were principally discussed, and much of the betting done. Many a disfigured face has been the result of these discussions; many a reputation blemished, and many a long friendship broken by the altercations which it led to. It is over now, and we hope the country may never be again disgraced by the repetition of such another exhibition of human depravity.

As Canada was the place selected for the fight, Buffalo was chosen as the rendezvous where the closing preliminaries were arranged, and from whence the parties proceeded to the spot selected as the battleground, and for several days previous to the 20th that city was fairly overrun with hordes of pugilists from all sections of the country who congregated about the sporting houses of Izzy Lazarus and others, in great numbers, discussing the probabilities of the result of the expected contest, and awaiting impatiently for the battle day.

Washington, Dec. 22, 1857.

In the Senate, today, Mr. Foster presented a petition for the abolition of slavery by the general government by purchase—the compensation plan—which was laid on the table.

Personal Intelligence.

July 9, 1858.

Madame Jenny Lind Goldschmidt, with her husband and two children (son and daughter), arrived in London during the week ending 19th ultimo, with the intention of residing in England for some time. The whole family, including domestics, have taken possession of a neat villa, called "Roehampton Lodge", situated near to the south side of Barnes Common, and about a mile from Putney. The house is in a retired position, and in the immediate vicinity of Putney Common and the picturesque village of Roehampton.

St. Johns, N. F., July 2, 2 P.M.

The telegraph line between this city and the Bay of Bull's Arm, at which point the cable is to be landed, is now in good order. The steamer Porcupine is stationed off the mouth of the Bay, and will remain there until the Niagara arrives, when she will pilot her in and assist in landing the cable. The Niagara is momentarily expected.

The weather this afternoon is dull but not unfavorable for the telegraph fleet.

St. John's, N. F., July 2, 10 P.M.

There is as yet no appearance of the Niagara at the Bay of Bull's Arm. No further dispatch will be sent tonight unless she should be signalled.

Some of the best penmen in Berlin are engaged in making copies in German, English and French, of the marriage contract, between Prince Frederick William of Prussia and the Princess Victoria of England. Copies are also being made in German, Portuguese and French of the marriage contract of the King of Portugal and the Princess Stephanie of Hohenzollern.

Several of the English and French Journals are much exercised at the events which are passing on this side of the ocean. Some of them see an imminent necessity for a standing army in New York to keep down by the Bayonet thousands of starving men; others find in Kansas the germ of a terrible civil war; others, again look upon Brigham Young as the forerunner of a grand social cataclysm that is to engulf us; another set hold that the filibustering spirit prevalent among us is a growing defiance of all law and order, while the whole of them see but one possible result from all these things, which is an early breaking up of the Union. . . . (From an editorial.)

NEWPORT.

Newport, R. I.

The season, such as it is, is about opening but the prospects of the hotel keepers look squally. There will, we fear, be no rush to Newport this summer. It is not that the air is less delicious, the sea fog less regenerating to complexions faded by city winter dissipation; no, the complaint is elsewhere. The "Cant-get-away Club" after the recent financial smash-up, includes even our fashionables, and we can't afford Newport—at least so say many who used to summer here.

MISCELLANEOUS.

LARGE INHERITANCES OF ENGLISHMEN, MARRIED AND DECEASED IN AMERICA.

Wanted, relatives of William Canning; came to the United States in 1841, Mary Cardy, alias Ellicott; came 1830. Evan Davis, John Kelly, late of North River, New York. Robert Loudon came about 1786. . . . Mr. Hay's Heraldry and next of kin Office, 827 Broadway, New York.

INDEX

Index

Index

Index

Thyme, 86.
Tickets, *f*.133.
Tiles, 101.
Tiles, scripture, 102.
Timber, 10, 59.
Timber for fencing, 76.
Timber for firewood, 76.
Timber, foundation, 98.
Tinfoil, *f*.121.
Toaster, 43.
Tobacco, 59, *f*.133, 137, 171.
Tobacco tongs, 43.
Tobacco trade, 125.
Toddy, 131.
Toddy irons, *f*.87.
Tom Thumb, 171.
Tongs, 14, 143.
Tools, 3, 26.
Toryism, 171.
Totoket district, 54.
Toupees, *f*.181.
Tour Through the Whole Island of Great Britain, A, by Daniel Defoe, 127.
Towels, 14.
Tower of London, *f*.106.
Town meetings, 83.
Town records, 21.
Towne, Ithiel, 160.
Toys, 27.
Trade, 59, 130, 153.
Trade, East India, 143.
Trade, foreign, 68.
Trade, import, 68.
Trade, Russian, 138.
Trade, West Indies, 144.
Traffic regulations, 35.
Trambells, 43.
Trammels, 5, 11, 29.
Transatlantic telegraph, 169.
Transportation, 157, 163.
Traps, 37.
Travel, 81.
Trays, 104.
Trees, linden, 160.
Trees, magnolia, 160.
Trees, shade, 8.
Trenchers, wooden, 3.
Trestles, 12, 13.
Trim, 87.
Tristram-Shandy, *f*.120.
Trivet, 43.
Trousers, 174.
Trousers, nankeen, 155.
Trousers, narrow uncreased, 171.
Trousers, striped woolen, *f*.91.
True, Joseph, 148.
Trunk, 14, 43.
Tubs, 5, 14.
Tudor roses, carved, 56.

Tudor drip-moulds, 173.
Tufts, Dr. Simon, 42, 43.
Turf, 5.
Turkey work, 103.
Turkeys, 81.
Turners, 148.
Turnings, bulbous, 72.
Turnings, trumpet, 73.
Tyng, Jonathan, 46.

ULSTER County, New York, 37.
Underbedstead, 43.
Union, 163.
United States frigate "Boston," *f*.151.
Urn, Sheffield, *f*.149.
Ushak carpet, 148.
Utah, 169.
Utensils, iron, 103.

VAIL works, 157.
Valdararaio, 44.
Valence, 12, 29, 103.
Valley of the Hudson, 98.
Van Borsum, Egbert, 98.
Van Tilborg, 102.
Varnish, *f*.121.
Vases, 148.
Vegetables, 6, 86.
Velvet, *f*.76, *f*.77, 102.
Velvet, red Italian, *f*.43.
Veneer, 28, 71.
Veneer, burled walnut, 73.
Veneer, walnut, *frontis.*
Veneered surface, 161.
Venice, 116.
Vermeer, Jan, 102.
Versailles, 58, *f*.132.
Vessels of silver, 44.
Vests, colored, 174.
Vines, realistic, 174.
Violin, bass, 35.
Violins, 35, *f*.61, *f*.107, 123, 131.
Virginia, 59, 123, 135, 136.
Virtues, the, 160.
von Erlach, Fischer, 41.

WAGON, 81.
Wainscot, 70, 90, 116.
Wainscot, shadow-moulded, 26.
Wainscoting, 87.
Wainscotted, 101, 102, 115.
Waists, 14.
Waldo, Samuel, 162.
Walking, 120.
Walks, gravel, 119.
Wallabout Bay, 95.
Wallack's theatre, 171.
Wallpaper, 175.
Wall, brick, 99.

Wall, clay, 139.
Wall, fireplace, 69.
Wall light, ormolu and crystal, *f*.147.
Wall, outside, 99.
Wall, section of, 22.
Walls, 139.
Walls, cream-colored plaster, 162.
Walls, pale-tinted plaster, 159.
Walls, panelled, 103.
Walls, plastered, 11.
Walls, shaped, 159.
Walls, whitewashed, 101.
Waln, Anne W., *f*.161, 162.
Waltz, 123, 171.
Wampum, 98, 105.
War, 163.
War, Civil, 155, 167, 172, *f*.181.
War, Dutch, 18.
War, French and Indian, 63, 68, 137, 141, 143, 153.
War, King Philip's, 85.
War, Napoleonic, 155.
War of 1812, 153.
War, prevalence of, 21.
War, Revolutionary, 63, 65, 136.
War with Mexico, 180.
Wars, Colonial, 63, 85.
Wars, French, 109.
Ware, Isaac, 116.
Ware, Maskell, 162.
Ware's book on architecture, 146.
Warming pan, 14, 43, *f*.87.
Warren, Dr., 83.
Warren, Joseph Alonzo, 12.
Wash bench, 5.
Washington, D. C., 155.
Washington, George, 82, 113, 121, 125, 128, *f*.147.
Washington, Mrs., 125.
Washington Society of Alexandria, 125.
Washington Square, 173.
Washington Street, Boston, Mass., 10.
Watchmaker, *f*.121.
Waterman, Thomas, 75.
Watermen on the River Thames, *f*.47.
Watertown, town of, 83.
Wattles, 139.
Waverly Place, 173.
Wax fruit, 176, *f*.177.
Wayland, town of, 88.
Wayside Inn, 77.
Wearing apparel, 16, *f*.18, 26.
Weaver, 21, *f*.121.
Weather vane, 15.
Weaving, 95.
Wedding, shift, 81.